STUDY GUIDE

to accompany

LIPSEY   RAGAN   COURANT

MACROECONOMICS

NINTH CANADIAN EDITION

STUDY GUIDE

to accompany

LIPSEY RAGAN COURANT

MACROECONOMICS

NINTH CANADIAN EDITION

E. KENNETH GRANT
University of Guelph

WILLIAM J. FURLONG
University of Guelph

RICHARD G. LIPSEY
Simon Fraser University

Addison-Wesley Publishers Limited

Don Mills, Ontario • Reading, Massachusetts • Menlo Park, California
New York • Harlow, England • Amsterdam • Bonn
Sydney • Singapore • Tokyo • Madrid • San Juan
Paris • Seoul • Milan • Mexico City • Taipei

Study Guide to accompany Lipsey/Ragan/Courant MACROECONOMICS, Ninth Canadian Edition

Printed and bound in Canada.

ISBN 0-673-98465-6

A B C D E –MP– 01 00 99 98 97

TO THE STUDENT

The content of this book tests and reinforces the student's understanding of the concepts and analytical techniques stressed in each chapter of *Macroeconomics*, ninth edition, by Professors Lipsey, Ragan, and Courant. Our own teaching experience has led us to believe that students have the most trouble understanding technical information and applying theoretical concepts to particular situations. Consequently, most multiple-choice questions and exercises are technical and numerical in nature. We feel that policy issues and specific applications of theory to real-world examples are primarily the responsibility of the textbook. You will find excellent discussions of issues and policy applications in the body of the text, especially in the Applications sections that appear in each chapter.

Each chapter in this *Study Guide* corresponds to a text chapter and is divided into four basic sections. The *Chapter Overview* provides a brief summary of the important concepts and issues addressed in the chapter. It serves to enable the student to anticipate topics covered in the chapter.

The *Learning Objectives* section provides the student with a list of study goals. Upon completion of a chapter it would prove useful to revisit the list to ensure that an adequate knowledge of all items has been acquired. Our experience is that the items in these lists are the most frequently tested on introductory economics examinations.

The *Multiple-Choice Questions* test your comprehension of definitions, analytical concepts, and numerical techniques. When you answer these, avoid the temptation to leap at the first answer that seems plausible. There is one best answer for each question. You should be able to explain why any other answer is not as satisfactory as the one you have chosen.

In some ways the greatest reinforcement to learning economics comes from doing the questions in the *Exercises* section. Some of our colleagues have indicated that students rarely attempt the questions in this section, since the format of many introductory economics examinations consists primarily of multiple-choice questions. We urge you *not* to make this mistake. These questions often require you to demonstrate numerically and/or graphically the sense of what has been expressed verbally. You may wish to review the mathematical exercises in Chapter 2 before attempting the questions in subsequent chapters. In addition, you are often asked to explain your method of analysis and your results. The ability to solve problems and to communicate and interpret results are important goals in an introductory economics course. We firmly believe that the exercises will enhance your ability to do well on multiple-choice questions! Do not be discouraged if you have difficulties with certain questions. Those marked with an asterisk (*) are quite challenging for the beginner, and a full appreciation of the points involved can be achieved only after you have participated in lectures and have carefully read the text. Unlike other study guides, answers are provided for all questions in this one. However, we caution that our answers are brief. Your instructors often require much fuller explanations on midterm and final examinations.

Acknowledgments

We would like to thank those individuals who provided invaluable assistance in the preparation of this ninth edition of the *Study Guide*: Brian Henderson, Madhu Ranadive, Suzanne Schaan, and Linda Scott of Addison-Wesley for editorial assistance; John Spafford for computerizing all of the artwork; Monique Roch for her computing and research assistance; Mara and Mark Grant for their research and clerical assistance; and Steve Wilkinson for his critical review of the manuscript.

Finally, we dedicate this edition of the *Study Guide* to our respective families: Monique, Dylan, and Liam; and Baiba, Mark, and Mara.

William J. Furlong
E. Kenneth Grant

CONTENTS

PART ONE

THE NATURE OF ECONOMICS

CHAPTER 1

THE ECONOMIC PROBLEM

• • • • • • • • • • • •
CHAPTER OVERVIEW

This introductory chapter discusses the major issues that confront all economies. The resources with which an economy is endowed are scarce (i.e., limited). Choices must be made regarding what is produced, for whom it is produced, how to avoid unemployment, and how to ensure adequate growth over time. Different types of economic systems make these choices through different processes.

Just as resources are scarce for an entire economy, individuals also do not have enough resources to meet all of their their wants and needs. Since we can't satisfy all of our desires, we must choose among competing ends.

Changes in the Canadian economy over the past century demonstrate the importance of rising output per person, or productivity, in allowing a higher standard of living. Productivity growth has slowed in recent decades as the share of output and employment devoted to services such as transportation, product design, marketing, insurance, and finance has increased dramatically. At the same time the revolution in transportation and communications has spurred the globalization of modern economies. In Canada, for example, both exports and imports comprise a large share of output, and services comprise a sizable share of its international trade activity. International investment has always been an important part of Canada's development. Recently, Canada has become a growing source of outward-bound foreign investment.

Any debate over economic policy must distinguish between means and ends. Evaluation of economic policy identifies the objectives and determines if the policy meets these goals. In addition, it examines if there are any adverse side effects and considers alternative means of reaching the same objectives. Trade-offs in policy making are pervasive.

• • • • • • • • • • • •
LEARNING OBJECTIVES

After studying this chapter, you should be able to:

- understand the problem of scarcity and the need for choice;
- illustrate the relationship between scarcity, choice, and opportunity cost with a production possibility boundary;
- explain why growth in a country's productive capacity can be represented by an outward shift in its production possibility boundary and why unemployment of resources can be represented by points inside its production possibility boundary;
- contrast how economic decisions are coordinated and who owns productive resources in traditional, command, and market systems;
- appreciate that people's living standards are affected by the availability of jobs, the productivity of labour in those jobs, and the distribution of income produced by those jobs;
- summarize how the economic structure of the Canadian economy has changed over the past century and what role the growing globalization of the world economy has played in this evolution;
- better appreciate the trade-offs in economic policy making.

1. The fundamental problem of economics is, in short,
(a) too many poor people.
(b) finding jobs for all.
(c) the scarcity of resources relative to wants.
(d) constantly rising prices.
(e) None of the above.

2. Scarcity is a problem that
(a) more efficient production would eliminate.
(b) is nonexistent in wealthy economies.
(c) exists due to finite amounts of resources and unlimited human wants.
(d) arises when productivity growth slows down.
(e) exists in command economies but not market economies.

3. Which of the following is not an example of a factor of production?
(a) A bulldozer.
(b) A mechanic.
(c) A farm hand.
(d) A tractor.
(e) A haircut.

4. If the factors of production available to an economy were unlimited
(a) the opportunity cost of producing more cars would be zero.
(b) the price of cars would be infinitely high.
(c) there would be no unemployment.
(d) scarcity would become the most serious economic problem.
(e) All of the above.

5. Opportunity cost measures the
(a) different opportunities for spending money.
(b) the monetary cost of purchasing a commodity.
(c) alternative means of producing output.
(d) amount of one good forfeited to obtain a unit of another good.
(e) market price of a good.

6. If a compact disc costs $10 and a cassette costs $5, then the opportunity cost of five compact discs is
(a) 50 cassettes.
(b) 10 cassettes.
(c) 5 cassettes.
(d) 2 cassettes.
(e) $25.

7. Assuming the alternative is employment, the opportunity cost of a university education is
(a) tuition costs only.
(b) tuition and book costs only.
(c) the forgone salary only.
(d) tuition costs plus book costs plus the forgone salary.
(e) the direct costs of university such as residence fees and books.

8. If a 12-month membership in a fitness club costs as much as tickets for 24 Montreal Expos baseball games, the opportunity cost of a one-month membership in the fitness club is
(a) 1/2 baseball game.
(b) 1 baseball game.
(c) 2 baseball games.
(d) 12 baseball games.
(e) 24 baseball games.

9. A downward-sloping production possibility boundary that is also a straight line implies
(a) constant opportunity costs.
(b) zero opportunity costs.
(c) only one good is produced.
(d) rising opportunity costs.
(e) None of the above.

Questions 10 to 13 refer to Figure 1-1.

10. If a market economy is operating at point *A*,
(a) resources are fully employed.
(b) there is considerable unemployment.
(c) the central planner values corn more than cars.
(d) car producers are losing money due to low sales.
(e) the opportunity cost of producing cars is zero.

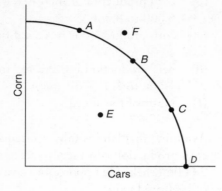

Figure 1-1

11. Point *E* represents a situation that
    (a) is currently unattainable and can be expected to remain so.
    (b) will be attainable only if there is economic growth.
    (c) results from inefficient use of resources or failure to use all available resources.
    (d) has a higher opportunity cost than points on the boundary itself.
    (e) can never occur in a market economy.

12. With currently available resources, point *F* represents a situation that
    (a) results if resources are not fully employed.
    (b) can be achieved if consumers demand fewer cars than at point *C*.
    (c) is currently attainable.
    (d) can be achieved if all resources were allocated to the production of cars.
    (e) None of the above.

13. Assuming the initial situation is point *B*, which one of the following represents a reallocation of resources away from car production to corn production?
    (a) Point *A*.
    (b) Point *C*.
    (c) Point *E*.
    (d) Point *D*.
    (e) Point *F*.

14. Which of the following causes an outward shift in the production possibility boundary?
    (a) A decrease in unemployment.
    (b) A loss in the productive capacity of agricultural acreage caused by a prolonged drought.
    (c) An increase in the productivity of all

factors of production.
    (d) Shifting resources away from the production of corn to cars.
    (e) Any or all of the above.

15. Putting currently unemployed resources to work can be illustrated by
    (a) shifting the production possibility boundary outward.
    (b) a movement along a given production possibility boundary.
    (c) moving from a point on the boundary to a point outside it.
    (d) moving from a point inside the boundary to a point on it.
    (e) moving from a point on the boundary to a point inside it.

Questions 16 through 23 refer to the following production possibilities for combinations of corn and beef using a land tract of a given acreage.

Corn (bushels)	Beef (kilograms)
10,000	0
8,000	900
6,000	1,200
4,000	1,400
2,000	1,475
0	1,500

16. What would be the opportunity cost of producing 400 additional kilograms of beef if the current acreage were producing 8,000 bushels of corn and 500 kilograms of beef?
    (a) 500 bushels of corn.
    (b) 400 kilograms of beef.
    (c) Zero.
    (d) 900 kilograms of beef.
    (e) None of the above.

17. What would be the opportunity cost of producing 2,000 additional bushels of corn if the current acreage were producing 6,000 bushels of corn and 1,200 kilograms of beef?
    (a) 900 kilograms of beef.
    (b) 1,200 kilograms of beef.
    (c) 300 kilograms of beef.
    (d) Zero.
    (e) None of the above.

18. Which of the following combinations represent unattainable production levels with the current acreage?
    (a) 8,000 bushels of corn and 500 kilograms of beef.
    (b) 8,000 bushels of corn and 1,200 kilograms of beef.
    (c) 2,000 bushels of corn and 1,475 kilograms of beef.
    (d) 6,000 bushels of corn and 1,300 kilograms of beef.
    (e) Both (b) and (d).

19. What is the opportunity cost of increasing beef from 1,475 kilograms to 1,500 kilograms?
    (a) 2,000 bushels of corn.
    (b) 50 bushels of corn.
    (c) 25 kilograms of beef.
    (d) 800 bushels of corn.
    (e) None of the above.

20. The opportunity cost of increasing corn production from 4,000 to 6,000 is
    (a) the same as the opportunity cost of increasing corn production from 8,000 to 10,000.
    (b) the same as the opportunity cost of increasing corn production from 2,000 to 4,000.
    (c) approximately equal to 0.1 kilograms of beef per additional bushel of corn.
    (d) 1,200 kilograms of beef.
    (e) None of the above.

21. Which of the following events is likely to lead to an outward shift of the production possibility boundary?
    (a) A reallocation of acreage such that corn production increases from 6,000 bushels to 8,000 bushels while beef production decreases from 1,200 kilograms to 900 kilograms.
    (b) Some of the land is lost due to a flood.
    (c) Twenty of the existing acres are not used for either beef or corn production.
    (d) Corn prices fall relative to beef prices.
    (e) None of the above.

22. The opportunity cost per additional bushel of corn is 3/20 kilograms of beef when
    (a) corn production is increased from 8,000 to 10,000.

    (b) corn production is increased from 6,000 to 8,000.
    (c) corn production is increased from 4,000 to 6,000.
    (d) beef production is decreased from 1,500 to 1,475 kilograms.
    (e) None of the above.

23. Assuming that land is fully utilized and that corn production continually increases by 2,000 bushels, the opportunity cost in terms of beef production
    (a) increases.
    (b) decreases.
    (c) is zero.
    (d) remains constant.
    (e) is undefined.

24. In a command economy, where to produce on the production possibility boundary is determined by
    (a) the preferences of consumers, who spend their income accordingly.
    (b) a central plan established by the government.
    (c) traditional patterns of spending that change little from year to year.
    (d) the preferences of workers, who vote to indicate their preferences.
    (e) relative prices of goods.

25. Decisions on resource allocation are
    (a) necessary only in centrally planned economies.
    (b) made by central planners in traditional economies.
    (c) necessary only in economies that are not industrialized.
    (d) decentralized, but coordinated by the price system, in market economies.
    (e) primarily determined by traditional customs in market economies.

26. A rising standard of living is most likely to occur in an economy
    (a) that does not allow imports.
    (b) that produces goods requiring skilled labour inputs.
    (c) where output per worker is rising.
    (d) that does not produce agricultural goods.
    (e) where the labour-output ratio is rising.

27. The pattern of employment and production in the Canadian economy has changed considerably over the past century. As part of this evolution,
    (a) the relative importance of agriculture has risen, due to a growing demand for food in foreign countries.
    (b) the relative importance of services has risen, due to greater demand by consumers and by firms.
    (c) less jobs were available in the early 1990s than in the early 1900s.
    (d) the trend of labour productivity over the past century has been downward.
    (e) All of the above.

28. Using the *rule of 72*, which one of the following annual productivity rates will double output per worker in 12 years?
    (a) 8.6 percent.
    (b) 6.0 percent.
    (c) 60 percent.
    (d) 16.5 percent.
    (e) 84 percent.

29. Which of the following would be a source of similarity among alternative types of economic systems?
    (a) Ownership of resources (private and public)
    (b) The process for making economic decisions.
    (c) The need to determine what is to be produced and how to produce it.
    (d) The role that tradition plays in determining production and employment.
    (e) Both (a) and (c).

30. Which of the following has *not* been an aspect of the globalization process?
    (a) Developed countries have been able to protect their unskilled labour from international competition.
    (b) Increased international capital flows.
    (c) Corporations, called *transnationals*, now produce in many countries.
    (d) Domestic economies are more reliant on foreign markets.
    (e) Advances in communication networks and systems around the world.

31. Which of the following is a potential source of debate associated with economic policy?
    (a) The effectiveness of alternative means in achieving agreed upon ends.
    (b) Pursuit of different ends.
    (c) Different values placed on alternative ends.
    (d) The opportunity cost of a policy.
    (e) All of the above.

• • • • • • • • • • • • • •

EXERCISES

1. Four key economic problems are identified in Chapter 1:
   (1) What is produced and how? (resource allocation)
   (2) What is consumed and by whom? (distribution)
   (3) How much unemployment and inflation are there? (total employment and the price level)
   (4) How is productive capacity changing? (economic growth)

   After each of the topics listed next, place the appropriate number indicating which type of problem applies. Use each classification only once.
   (a) Rises in oil prices during the 1970s induced a switch to alternative energy sources.
   (b) The standard of living in Canada, measured by real output per capita, has risen steadily over the past century.
   (c) Large harvests cause worldwide lower grain prices, helping consumers but hurting farmers.
   (d) The unemployment rate increased in the early 1990s.

2. A certain economy produces only two consumer goods, X and Y. Only labour is required to produce both goods, and the economy's labour force is fixed at 100 workers. The table below indicates the amount of X and Y that can be produced daily with various quantities of labour.

Number of workers	Daily X production	Number of workers	Daily Y production
0	0	0	0
20	10.0	20	150
40	20.0	40	250
60	25.0	60	325
80	27.5	80	375
100	30.0	100	400

(a)   Draw the production possibility curve for this economy, using the grid provided in Figure 1-2. (*Hint:* The labour force must always be fully employed along the production possibility boundary.)

Figure 1-2

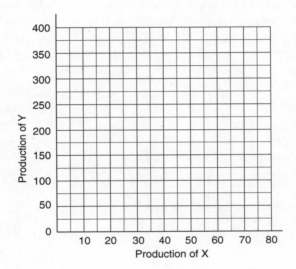

(b)   What is the opportunity cost of producing the first 10 units of good X? What is the opportunity cost of producing the next 10 units of X (i.e., from 10 to 20)? What happens to the opportunity cost of X as its production is continuously increased?

(c)   Suppose that actual production for a given period was 20 units of X and 250 units of Y. What can you infer from this information?

(d)   Suppose that a central planner in this economy were to call for an output combination of $X = 35$ and $Y = 150$. Is this plan attainable? Explain.

(e)   New technology is developed in X production, so that each worker can now produce double the daily amount of X indicated in the schedule. What happens to the production possibility curve? Draw the new curve on the graph. Can the planner's output combination in (d) now be met?

3. Junior gets a weekly allowance of $10. He spends all of his allowance on only two commodities: video games at the arcade and chocolate bars. Assume that the price of a video game is 50 cents and the price of a chocolate bar is $1.

   (a) Plot Junior's weekly consumption possibilities using the grid provided in Figure 1-3.

   Figure 1-3

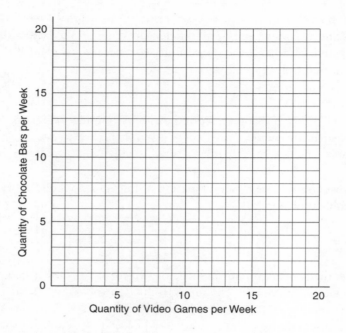

   (b) Can Junior attain the following consumption combinations?
      (i)   15 video games and 2 chocolate bars
      (ii) 4 video games and 8 chocolate bars
      (iii) 7 video games and 7 chocolate bars
   (c) What is the opportunity cost of Junior's first chocolate bar? his second? his third?

   (d) By visual inspection of Junior's consumption possibility boundary, what could you say about his opportunity cost of consuming each of these commodities?

4. Pamela, a first year student at Lakehead University, is considering whether or not to advance her studies by taking summer courses. Her pocket expenses would be: tuition, $1,000; books, $350; and living expenses, $1,500. Her alternative is to work as a lifeguard, which would earn her $3,500 for the summer. What is Pamela's opportunity cost of taking summer courses?

*5. An economy's production possibility boundary is given by the mathematical expression $20 = 4A + B$, where A is the quantity of good A and B is the quantity of good B.

    (a)   If all resources in the economy were allocated to producing good A, what is the maximum level of production for this good? What is the maximum level of production for good B?

    (b)   Suppose that the production of B is increased from 12 to 16 units and that the economy is producing at a point on the production possibility boundary. What is the opportunity cost per unit of good B? What is the opportunity cost per unit of good B if the production of this good was increased from 16 to 20?

    (c)   In what way is this production possibility boundary different from that in exercise 2 in terms of opportunity costs?

    (d)   In what way does the combination of four units of good A and five units of good B represent the problem of scarcity?

*6. Consider the production possibilities for two totally dissimilar goods, such as apples and machine tools. Some resources are suitable for apple production and some for the production of machine tools. However, there is no possibility of shifting resources from one product to another. In this case, what does the production possibility boundary look like? Explain and show graphically.

● ●

ANSWERS

Multiple-Choice Questions

1. (c)	**2.** (c)	**3.** (e)	**4.** (a)	**5.** (d)
6. (b)	**7.** (d)	**8.** (c)	**9.** (a)	**10.** (a)
11. (c)	**12.** (e)	**13.** (a)	**14.** (c)	**15.** (d)
16. (c)	**17.** (c)	**18.** (e)	**19.** (a)	**20.** (c)
21. (e)	**22.** (b)	**23.** (a)	**24.** (b)	**25.** (d)
26. (c)	**27.** (b)	**28.** (b)	**29.** (c)	**30.** (a)
31. (e)				

2. (a)   Figure 1-4

Exercises

    1.   (a) 1 (b) 4 (c) 2 (d) 3

(b) 25 units of good Y (i.e., Y decreases from 400 to 375). 50 units of good Y. The opportunity cost of producing X is increasing—increasing X production by yet another 10 units from 20 to 30 would imply forgoing an additional 325 units of Y.

(c) This production combination lies inside the production possibility boundary, so some workers are unemployed or inefficiently used.

(d) This combination is outside the production possibility boundary and is therefore unattainable with current resources and technology.

(e) The production possibility boundary shifts to the right as graphed in (a). The planner's output combination is now attainable but is inside the new boundary, implying that if it were indeed achieved, the economy would be inefficiently using its resources.

3. (a) **Figure 1-5**

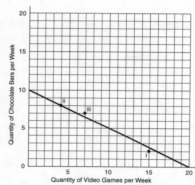

(b) (i) Yes, this combination lies inside his consumption possibility and is therefore affordable with $10.

(ii) Yes, this combination is on his consumption possibility boundary and therefore costs exactly $10.

(iii) No, this combination lies outside his consumption possibility boundary and therefore costs more than a $10 allowance permit.

(c) To purchase the first chocolate bar, Junior must pay $1, which could have been used to purchase two video games. Thus, the opportunity cost of the first chocolate bar is two video games. The opportunity cost of the second and third bars is also two video games each.

(d) Since the consumption possibility boundary is linear (i.e., a straight line), the opportunity cost is constant.

4. $4,850. Living expenses would have to be incurred regardless of her decision.

*5. (a) If all resources were allocated to the production of good A, there is no production of good B. Hence, according to the mathematical expression, the maximum production of good A is five units. If all resources were used to produce good B, then $B = 20$ and the production of good A is zero.

(b) The increase from 12 to 16 units of B requires a loss in production of good A of one (from two to one). An increase in B from 16 to 20 requires a loss in production of good A of one (from one to zero). Therefore, the opportunity cost *per unit* of good B is 0.25 units of A in each case.

(c) The opportunity cost is constant, whereas it was increasing for exercise 2.

(d) According to the equation, four units of A and four units of B are possible. The combination of four units of A and five units of B is not feasible and indicates that more resources are required than are currently available.

*6. When all resources suitable to apple production are employed, the resulting apple output is A' in Figure 1-6. When all resources suitable to machine tool production are employed, the resulting quantity of machine tools is M'. Since there is no possibility of shifting resources between these two outputs, the production possibility boundary is simply the point corresponding to the coordinates (A', M'). Any combination of apples and machine tools either inside or on the dashed lines implies unemployed or inefficiently used resources.

Figure 1-6

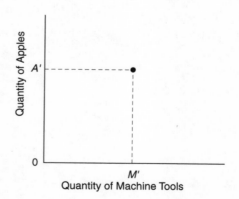

CHAPTER 2

ECONOMICS AS A SOCIAL SCIENCE

CHAPTER OVERVIEW

The previous chapter provided an overview of the types of issues economists consider. This chapter presents important distinctions that economists make and discusses the approaches used to analyse economic questions.

Economists evaluate hypotheses that claim to explain economic behaviour. An important distinction is made between positive statements, which concern what is, was, or will be and normative statements, which are judgments of what should be done. Disagreements over positive, testable statements are appropriately settled by an appeal to the facts. Disagreements over normative statements cannot be settled in this way.

Theories are designed to give meaning to observed sequences of events. A theory typically consists of definitions of variables and assumptions about how things behave. Any theory has certain logical implications that must be true if the theory is true. These are the theory's predictions or hypotheses. Theories are tested by checking their predictions against the evidence. In economics the evidence is most often comprised of data drawn from the real world.

The relationships among variables in economic theories are usually presented in tabular, graphical, or algebraic form. These provide compact summaries of a large number of data observations, and play an important role in economic modelling.

LEARNING OBJECTIVES

After studying this chapter, you should be able to:

- distinguish between positive and normative statements;
- explain how the "law" of large numbers allows successful predictions about group behaviour;
- understand the basic structure of economic theories;
- understand the roles of variables, assumptions, and predictions in developing and testing theories;
- distinguish between endogenous and exogenous variables;
- interpret graphs and equations;
- graph linear relationships between economic variables.

MULTIPLE-CHOICE QUESTIONS

1. Normative statements
   (a) concern an individual's beliefs in what ought to be.
   (b) are based on value judgments.
   (c) cannot be subjected to empirical scrutiny.
   (d) cannot be deduced from positive statements.
   (e) All of the above.

2. "Capital punishment deters crime" is an example of a
   (a) positive statement.
   (b) value judgment.
   (c) normative statement.
   (d) analytic statement.
   (e) untestable statement.

3. "Capital punishment should be reintroduced in Canada" is an example of a
   (a) positive statement.
   (b) normative statement.
   (c) analytic statement.
   (d) testable hypothesis.
   (e) None of the above.

4. Which of the following is the best example of a positive statement?
   (a) Equal distribution of national income is a desirable goal for society.
   (b) Foreign ownership is undesirable for Canada and should therefore be eliminated.
   (c) Although free trade may cause some Canadians to lose their jobs, it will significantly increase the income of the average Canadian.
   (d) Taxes should be lowered.
   (e) Deficit reduction should be the government's priority.

5. Economic predictions are intended to
   (a) forecast the behaviour of each consumer.
   (b) forecast the behaviour of groups of individuals.
   (c) test normative statements.
   (d) anticipate the irrational behaviour of certain odd individuals.

   (e) Both (b) and (c) are correct.

6. The "law" of large numbers basically says that
   (a) the greater the number of observations, the greater the sum of each variable.
   (b) measuring error increases with the number of observations.
   (c) a few observations are just as accurate as a large number of observations.
   (d) erratic behaviour by individuals tends to offset itself in a large group.
   (e) the greater the number of observations, the greater is the potential for prediction errors.

7. In measuring the area of a room, the "law" of large numbers implies that
   (a) more people will make small errors than large ones.
   (b) roughly the same number of people will understate the area as overstate it.
   (c) the average error of all individuals is approximately zero.
   (d) the more people taking the measurement, the smaller is the average error.
   (e) All of the above.

8. With respect to agriculture, weather is an example of
   (a) an exogenous factor of production.
   (b) an endogenous input.
   (c) a dependent variable.
   (d) an induced input variable.
   (e) a positive statement.

9. If the assumptions imposed in an economic theory are unrealistic, then the theory
   (a) will always be refuted by the evidence.
   (b) is incorrect and should be rejected.
   (c) will not predict well and should be rejected.
   (d) will require more complex statistical techniques for testing.
   (e) may nonetheless predict better than any alternative theory.

10. The role of assumptions in theory is to
   (a) represent the world accurately.
   (b) abstract from reality.
   (c) avoid simplifications of the real world.
   (d) ensure that the theory considers all features of reality, no matter how minor.
   (e) None of the above.

11. If annual per capita consumption expenditure decreases as average annual income decreases, these two variables are then said to be
   (a) negatively related.
   (b) positively related.
   (c) randomly related.
   (d) independent of each other.
   (e) None of the above.

12. Which of the following statements about economic theories is most appropriate?
   (a) The most reliable test of a theory is the realism of its assumptions.
   (b) The best kind of theory is worded so that it can pass any test to which it is applied.
   (c) The most important thing about the scientific approach is that it uses mathematics and diagrams.
   (d) We expect our theories to hold only with some margin of error.
   (e) Economic theories are based upon normative statements, and can therefore never be refuted.

13. A theory may contain all but which of the following?
   (a) Predictions about behaviour that are deduced from the assumptions.
   (b) A set of assumptions defining the conditions under which the theory is operative.
   (c) Hypotheses about how the world behaves.
   (d) A normative statement expressed as a functional relation.
   (e) Hypothesized relationships among variables.

14. A scientific prediction is a conditional statement because it
   (a) takes the form "if that occurs, then this will result."
   (b) is conditional on being correct.
   (c) is impossible to test.
   (d) is true in theory but not in practice.
   (e) is derived from normative statements.

15. The term "economic model" may refer to
   (a) an application of a general theory in a specific context.
   (b) a specific quantitative formulation of a theory.
   (c) a particular theory or subset of theories in economics.
   (d) an illustrative abstraction of some real world phenomenon.
   (e) All of the above.

16. Economic hypotheses are generally accepted only when
   (a) the evidence indicates that they are true with a high degree of probability.
   (b) they have been proved beyond a reasonable doubt.
   (c) they have been established with certainty.
   (d) the evidence supports the hypotheses in all cases.
   (e) Both (c) and (d) are correct.

Appendix Questions

The following multiple-choice questions are based on the material in the appendix to this chapter. Read the appendix before answering these questions.

17. The slope of a straight line is
   (a) always positive.
   (b) calculated by dividing the variable measured on the horizontal axis by that measured on the vertical axis.
   (c) zero.
   (d) constant.
   (e) increasing or decreasing, depending upon whether the slope is positive or negative, respectively.

18. The relationship between two variables on a scatter diagram
    (a) may be obscured by the movement of another variable.
    (b) cannot be significant because of errors of observation.
    (c) will show a wavelike pattern if the variables are related to time.
    (d) will usually be a straight line.
    (e) All of the above.

19. Suppose that a scatter diagram indicates that imports are, on average, positively related to national income over time. If in one year imports fall when national income increases, the observation
    (a) disproves the positive relationship between the two variables.
    (b) suggests that other factors also influence the quantity of imports.
    (c) proves a negative relationship between the two variables.
    (d) suggests that a measurement error has necessarily been made.
    (e) suggests that the two variables are independent of each other.

20. In statistical testing of a theory, choosing a random sample of observations is important because
    (a) it increases the chance that the sample will be representative of the entire group.
    (b) it allows the calculation of the likelihood that the sample is unrepresentative of the whole group.
    (c) economic theories cannot be tested using scientific methods.
    (d) Both (a) and (b).
    (e) None of the above are correct.

21. The statement that the quantity produced of a commodity and its price are positively related is
    (a) an assumption economists usually make.
    (b) a testable hypothesis.
    (c) a normative statement.
    (d) not testable as currently worded.
    (e) a value judgment.

22. Which of the following equations is consistent with the hypothesis that federal income tax payments (T) are positively related to family income (Y) and negatively related to family size (F)?
    (a) $T = -733 + 0.19Y + 344F$.
    (b) $T = -733 - 0.19Y - 344F$.
    (c) $T = -733 + 0.19Y - 344F$.
    (d) $T = +733 - 0.19Y + 344F$.
    (e) None of the above.

23. Suppose that regression analysis estimates the following relationship between imports (IM) and national income (Y): $IM = 100 + 0.15Y$. This means that
    (a) imports are negatively related to national income.
    (b) when national income is zero, imports are zero.
    (c) imports are 15 percent of national income.
    (d) imports are 15 times greater than national income.
    (e) other things remaining constant, for every increase of $1 in national income, imports will rise by 15 cents.

Questions 24 to 26 refer to Figure 2-1.

Figure 2-1

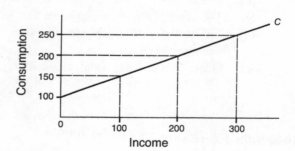

24. In the graph above, the slope of the line showing the relationship between consumption and income is
    (a) −2.
    (b) 0.5.
    (c) 2.
    (d) 2.5.
    (e) 150.

25. According to the graph above, when an individual has no income, consumption is
- (a) –200.
- (b) –100.
- (c) 0.
- (d) 100.
- (e) None of the above.

26. The line showing the relationship between consumption (C) and income (Y) can be represented mathematically as
- (a) $C = 0.5Y$.
- (b) $C = 2Y$.
- (c) $C = 100 + 0.5Y$.
- (d) $C = 100 + 2Y$.
- (e) $C = -100 + Y$.

• • • • • • • • • • • • • •

EXERCISES

1. After each phrase, write P or N to indicate whether a positive or a normative statement is being described.
- (a) A statement of fact that is actually wrong. _____
- (b) A value judgment. _____
- (c) A prediction that an event will happen. _____
- (d) A statement about what the author thinks ought to be. _____
- (e) A statement that can be tested by evidence. _____
- (f) A value judgment based on evidence known to be correct. _____
- (g) A hurricane forecast. _____

2. You are to distinguish between cause and effect in the following statements. Are the italicized variables endogenous (N) or exogenous (X)? You might also regard this as a distinction between independent or autonomous variables (i.e., exogenous) and dependent or induced variables (i.e., endogenous).
- (a) *Market price and equilibrium quantity* of a commodity are determined by demand and supply. _____
- (b) The number of sailboats sold annually is a function of *national income.* _____
- (c) The *condition of forest ecosystems* can be affected by regional air pollutants. _____
- (d) The quantity of housing services purchased is determined by the *relative price of housing, income, and housing characteristics.* _____
- (e) Other things being equal, *consumer expenditures* are negatively related to interest rates. _____

Appendix Exercises

The following exercises are based on the material in the appendix to this chapter. Read the appendix before attempting these exercises.

3. Suppose the relationship between saving (S) and income (Y) is represented by the following equation: $S = -100 + 0.10Y$. What is the amount of S for each of the indicated values of Y? Plot the relationship on the graph in Figure 2-2.

Figure 2-2

Y	S
0	___
500	___
1,000	___
1,500	___
2,000	___

(graph with vertical axis labeled S: 300, 300, 100, 0, -100 and horizontal axis labeled Y: 0, 1,000, 2,000)

4. Suppose that an economist hypothesizes that the annual quantity demanded of a specific manufacturer's personal computers (Q^D) is determined by the price of the computer (P) and the average income of consumers (Y). The specific functional relationship among these three variables is hypothesized to be the expression $Q^D = 1Y - 4P$.

    (a) Which of these variables are endogenous and which are exogenous?

    (b) What does the negative sign before the term $4P$ imply about the relationship between Q^D and P? What does the implicit positive sign before the term $1Y$ imply about the relationship between income and quantity demanded?

    (c) Suppose for the moment that average income equals $8,000. Write a simplified expression for the demand relationship.

    (d) Assuming that $Y = 8,000$, calculate the values of Q^D when $P = 0$, $P = \$500$, $P = \$1,000$, and $P = \$2,000$.

    (e) Plot the relationship between P and Q^D (assuming $Y = \$8,000$) on the graph in Figure 2-3. Indicate the intercept values on both axes.

Figure 2-3

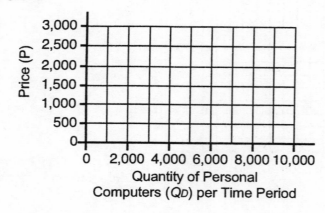

(f) Assuming that $Y = \$8,000$, calculate the change in the quantity demanded when the price increases from \$1,000 to \$2,000. Do the same for a price increase from \$500 to \$2,000. Call the change in the quantity demanded ΔQ^D and the change in the price ΔP. Determine the ratio $\Delta Q^D / \Delta P$. Is this ratio constant?

(g) Now suppose that evidence indicates that in subsequent time periods, the average income of consumers changes to \$9,000 per month. Plot the new relationship between P and Q^D. What are the intercept values and the slope?

5. The following exercise demonstrates how to obtain a solution to a system of equations diagrammatically. Suppose two variables are related by the following equations:

$$(1)\ N_1 = 5 + 0.5X$$
$$(2)\ N_2 = 55 - 0.5X$$

(a) Complete the table using the N_1 column for equation (1) and the N_2 column for equation 2.

X	N_1	N_2	N_3
10	_____	_____	_____
20	_____	_____	_____
30	_____	_____	_____
40	_____	_____	_____
50	_____	_____	_____
60	_____	_____	_____

(b) Plot the relationships between X and N_1 and N_2 in the graph provided below.

Figure 2-4

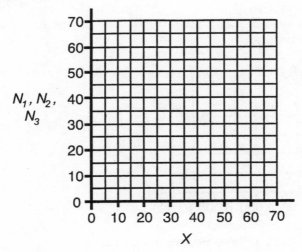

(i) The linear curve relating variables X and N_1 has a (positive/negative) _____ slope of _____.

(ii) The linear curve relating variables X and N_2 has a (positive/negative) _____ slope of _____.

(c)   These equations are said to be solved when $N_1 = N_2$—call this the solution value N. When does $N_1 = N_2$, and what are the corresponding values of N and X?

(d)   Assume that the constant term in equation 1 increases from 5 to 25. Complete column N_3 in (a), and plot the new relationship on the graph in (b). The curve in equation (1) has shifted _____. The slope is _____.

(e)   What is the new solution to this system of equations?

6.   The following exercise reviews the procedure for solving a system of simultaneous equations by algebraic methods. This approach is extremely useful in both micro and macro chapters of this Study Guide. It is an alternative to diagrammatic solutions that were reviewed above in question 5.

Consider two equations describing the relationships between two variables x and y

$$x_1 = a + by, \qquad (1)$$
$$x_2 = c - dy. \qquad (2)$$

where a, b, c, and d are positive constants. The objective is to find values of x and y for which both equations are satisfied. First, note that there are two equations and three unknowns—the unknowns are the solution values to x_1, x_2, and y. Thus, if a unique solution exists, there is a missing equation. The missing equation to this system simply states that in the solution:

$$x_1 = x_2 \qquad (3)$$

The solution procedure requires elimination of unknowns and equations by means of substitution. Each substitution must reduce the system by both an unknown and an equation, until all that remains is a single unknown in a single equation.

(a)   Eliminate equation (1) and x_1 from the system. Count the remaining equations and unknowns.

(b)   Now eliminate equation (2) and x_2 from the system. Count the remaining equations and unknowns.

(c)   Solve for the solution value of y.

(d)   Use the solution value of y to obtain solution values for x_1 and x_2.

(e)   Often the constants in equations (1) and (2) are numerical. For example, suppose a=200, b=2, c=400, and d=3. Repeat questions (a) to (d) to solve for the numerical values of x and y.

ANSWERS
Multiple-Choice Questions

1. (e)	**2.** (a)	**3.** (b)	**4.** (c)	**5.** (b)
6. (d)	**7.** (e)	**8.** (a)	**9.** (e)	**10.** (b)
11. (b)	**12.** (d)	**13.** (d)	**14.** (a)	**15.** (e)
16. (a)	**17.** (d)	**18.** (a)	**19.** (b)	**20.** (d)
21. (b)	**22.** (c)	**23.** (e)	**24.** (b)	**25.** (d)
26. (c)				

Exercises

1. (a) P (b) N (c) P (d) N (e) P (f) N (g) P

2. (a) N (b) X (c) N (d) X (e) N

3. S = -$100; -$50; 0; $50; $100

4. (a) Q^D and P are determined in the market for personal computers; they are endogenous variables. Average income, which is determined in many other markets, is not influenced to any significant extent by the computer market; it is exogenous to the market for computers.

(b) Q^D and P are negatively related; as P increases, Q^D falls. Q^D and Y are positively related; as Y increases, Q^D increases.

(c) The equation becomes $Q^D = 8,000 - 4P$.

(d) Q^D = 8,000; 6,000; 4,000; 0.

(e) The intercept on the P axis is 2,000, and the intercept on the Q^D axis is 8,000. Your plotting should also indicate that the demand curve is a straight line that slopes downward with a slope of $-\frac{1}{4}$.

(f) The change in quantity demanded is $-4,000$ when P increases from 1,000 to 2,000. When P increases from 500 to 2,000, quantity demanded falls by 6,000. In both cases the ratio $\Delta Q^D/\Delta P$ is equal to -4 (i.e., the inverse of the slope).

(g) The intercept on the P axis is $2,250 and the intercept on the Q^D axis is 9,000. The slope remains $-\frac{1}{4}$.

5. (a)

X	N_1	N_2	N_3
10	10	50	30
20	15	45	35
30	20	40	40
40	25	35	45
50	30	30	50
60	35	25	55

(b) Figure 2-5

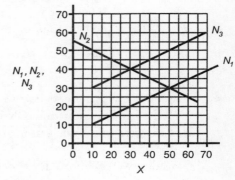

(i) positive; $+\frac{1}{2}$

(ii) negative; $-\frac{1}{2}$

(c) $N_1 = N_2$ when the two curves intersect. $N = 30$ and $X = 50$ solves this system of equations.

(d) leftward (or equivalently, upward); unchanged at $+\frac{1}{2}$.

(e) $N = 40$ and $X = 30$.

6. (a) Substitute equation (1) into equation (3) for x_1. This yields
$$a + by = x_2. \qquad (3')$$
There are two remaining equations, (2) and (3′), and two remaining unknowns, x_2 and y.

(b) Substitute equation (2) into (3′) for x_2. This yields
$$a + by = c - dy. \qquad (3'')$$
There is only one equation remaining (3′) and only one unknown y.

(c) Rearranging terms in (3″) yields: $by + dy = c - a$, or equivalently, $(b + d)y = c - a$. Division by $(b + d)$ yields $y^* = (c - a) / (b + d)$, which is the solution value for y.

(d) Substitute y^* into equation (1), which yields
$$x_1{}^* = a + b(c - a)/(b + d)$$
which simplifies to $x_1 = (ad + bc)/(b + d)$. In view of equation (3), this is also the solution value to $x_2{}^*$.

(e) $x_1 = x_2 = x = 280$ and $y = 40$.

CHAPTER 3
AN OVERVIEW OF THE MARKET ECONOMY

CHAPTER OVERVIEW

Economists focus on three sets of decision-making agents in a market economy: households (consumers), firms, and the government. Consumers are assumed to have the objective of maximizing their satisfaction or well-being, while firms' decisions are made with the goal of maximizing their profits. Government may have multiple objectives.

Microeconomics and macroeconomics differ in the level of aggregation. They study different aspects of a single economic system, and both are needed for a complete understanding of the whole.

Microeconomics deals with the determination of prices and quantities. Market prices and profits provide the signals for allocating resources to a particular product or industry. A rise (fall) in a commodity's price usually implies that a larger (smaller) output is more profitable. If profits in a particular industry rise, resources will shift into that industry; losses will cause firms to leave that industry.

The macroeconomic interactions between households and firms through markets is best illustrated in a circular flow diagram that traces the real and money flows between producers and consumers. In producing goods and services, firms must pay workers, natural resource owners, and lenders. Those who receive such payments spend their income on goods and services produced by firms. Leakages of income (taxes, savings, and imports) and injections of spending (investment, government expenditure, and exports) must balance at the equilibrium level of output.

LEARNING OBJECTIVES

After studying this chapter, you should be able to:

- understand how modern economies are based on the specialization and division of labour;
- explain how three kinds of economic decision makers—households, firms, and government—interact in a market economy;
- explain the distinction between market and nonmarket sectors and between the private and public sectors;
- begin using economic reasoning to explain how the price system coordinates decentralized decision making in determining resource allocation;
- explain the complementary relationship between microeconomics and macroeconomics;
- illustrate the circular flow of income and expenditures;
- understand the distinction between injections and leakages in the circular flow of income.

MULTIPLE-CHOICE QUESTIONS

1. In economics, the term "market economy" refers to
   (a) institutions such as the Toronto Stock Exchange.
   (b) a place where buyers and sellers gather on Saturday mornings.
   (c) a society where individuals specialize in productive activities and enter voluntary trades.
   (d) a society where most economic decisions are made by marketing analysts.
   (e) an economy in which advertising is central to the marketing of goods and services.

2. In a barter economy, individuals
   (a) haggle over the price of each and every commodity.
   (b) trade goods directly for other goods.
   (c) use money to lubricate the flow of trades.
   (d) must each be a "jack of all trades."
   (e) All of the above.

3. The introduction of production lines where individuals specialize in performing specific tasks is known as
   (a) the division of labour.
   (b) the specialization of labour.
   (c) the market economy.
   (d) the advent of labour as a factor of production.
   (e) lean production.

4. In a market economy, the allocation of resources is determined by
   (a) the government and its marketing boards.
   (b) the various stock exchanges in the country.
   (c) a central planning agency.
   (d) the millions of independent decisions made by individual consumers and firms.
   (e) the sobering discussions at the annual convention of the Canadian Economics Association.

5. The "invisible hand"
   (a) can only be seen by economists.
   (b) refers to excessive government taxation.
   (c) refers to a market economy's price system.
   (d) refers to the central planning agency of a command economy.
   (e) refers to hidden taxes.

6. Economic theory assumes that households
   (a) make consistent decisions as though each were comprised of a single individual.
   (b) seek to maximize profits.
   (c) are the principal buyers of the factors of production.
   (d) are comprised of a single individual.
   (e) are the sole buyers of goods and services in a market economy.

7. One reason for not assuming that governments behave in a consistent manner is that
   (a) different public officials have different objectives.
   (b) governments have become too big.
   (c) too many irresponsible policies have been introduced.
   (d) by offering higher salaries, the private sector has attracted most of the smart university graduates.
   (e) governments make too many separate decisions.

8. A central assumption in economic theory regarding firms is that they
   (a) are each owned by a single individual.
   (b) must be incorporated.
   (c) seek to maximize profits.
   (d) must all be making profits.
   (e) are the principal owners of the factors of production.

9. An example of a nonmarket activity is
   (a) volunteer coaching for Little League baseball.
   (b) government provision of weather reports.
   (c) police protection.
   (d) Big Sisters.
   (e) All of the above.

10. The distinction between the private sector and the public sector depends on whether the
   (a) product is sold or given away.
   (b) company is listed on a stock exchange.
   (c) organization is owned by individuals or the state.
   (d) financial statements of the organization are available for public scrutiny.
   (e) None of the above.

11. If households increase their desire to purchase fresh pasta, more resources will ultimately be allocated to the production of fresh pasta because
   (a) firms do not want dissatisfied consumers.
   (b) fresh pasta has good nutritional content.
   (c) the price of fresh pasta will be driven up and thereby permit profits to be made.
   (d) consumer organizations will inform pasta manufacturers of the change in demand.
   (e) regulatory agencies will inform pasta manufacturers of the change in demand.

12. If a hailstorm destroys a significant proportion of the Niagara Peninsula's peach crop, the average household in Ontario will desire to purchase fewer peaches because
   (a) of empathy for peach producers.
   (b) of altruistic concern that all households get their fair share of peaches.
   (c) the shortage will drive the price of peaches up.
   (d) peach purchases will be rationed by supermarkets.
   (e) the provincial government will ration consumption.

13. Macroeconomics is concerned with aggregate flows within the entire economy, whereas microeconomics might study how
   (a) price is determined in a single market.
   (b) resources are allocated across markets.
   (c) total employment in the automobile industry changes in response to government policies.
   (d) free trade affects production levels in the Canadian textile industry.
   (e) All of the above.

14. Macroeconomics involves the study of each of the following except
   (a) total employment in the economy.
   (b) aggregate demand.
   (c) changes in the overall price level.
   (d) the national level of employment.
   (e) national consumption of oil.

15. Which of the following is a leakage from the circular flow of income?
   (a) Household savings.
   (b) Consumption expenditure.
   (c) Investment in plant and equipment.
   (d) National defence expenditure.
   (e) Export sales.

16. The two major types of markets in the circular flow of income are
   (a) public markets and private markets.
   (b) product markets and factor markets.
   (c) free markets and controlled markets.
   (d) markets for goods and markets for services.
   (e) regulated markets and "laissez faire" markets.

17. The circular flow of income refers to
   (a) the flow of goods and services from sellers to buyers.
   (b) the flow of money in and out of the banking system.
   (c) the flow of money incomes from buyers to sellers.
   (d) Both (a) and (c) are correct.
   (e) Both (b) and (c) are correct.

18. Which of the following is an injection into the circular flow of income?
   (a) Government expenditure on highway construction.
   (b) Government expenditures on recycling programs.
   (c) Exports of goods produced in Canada.
   (d) Investment expenditures on plant and equipment by firms.
   (e) All of the above are correct.

Questions 19 and 20 refer to the following data:

Purchases of goods and services by Canadian households	800
Savings	100
Government purchases	200
Investment	150
Imports	75
Taxes	225
Exports	50

19. According to the above data, total injections are
    - (a) 1000.
    - (b) 1050.
    - (c) 350.
    - (d) 125.
    - (e) 400.

20. According to the above, total leakages equal
    - (a) 400.
    - (b) 300.
    - (c) 125.
    - (d) 225.
    - (e) 50.

21. The price system in a free market economy works in *all but which* of the following ways?
    - (a) Price is a determinant of a firm's profits and therefore encourages or discourages production.
    - (b) Prices signal to consumers how much they must sacrifice to obtain a commodity.
    - (c) Prices indicate relative scarcities and costs of production.
    - (d) Prices allocate resources equally among sectors of the economy.
    - (e) Prices are a means of coordinating individual, decentralized decisions.

22. Which of the following is *not* one of the reasons that transition from command economy to market economy has proved to be lengthy and difficult for republics of the former Soviet Union?
    - (a) Many agents believed that the government may reverse reforms.
    - (b) The government allowed too many firms to go bankrupt.
    - (c) Institutions that protect and enforce commercial law had to be developed.
    - (d) It took time to retool factories from production of military and industrial goods to production of consumer goods.
    - (e) The process of privatization has proved to be complicated, involving both political and economic debates.

• • • • • • • • • • • • • •

EXERCISES

1. Indicate whether or not the following events would occur in a market economy with a shift in interest from snowmobiling to skiing. Explain each answer.
   - (a) Initially, a shortage of ski equipment and a surplus of snowmobiles will develop.

   - (b) Prices of snowmobiles will be increased to maintain profit levels.

   - (c) Profits of ski equipment producers and retailers will rise; profits of snowmobile producers and dealers will tend to fall.

   - (d) Central authorities will shift resources from production of snowmobiles to production of skis.

(e) Production of skis will be expanded.

(f) Resources will shift from production of snowmobiles to production of skis.

(g) Resources particularly suited to producing snowmobiles will earn more, obtaining a greater relative share of national income.

2. Indicate whether the following economic transactions are attributable (in Canada) to the market economy (M) or the nonmarket economy (NM) and to the private sector (PR) or the public sector (PU).
   (a) Provision of national defence. _____
   (b) Home repairs done by the homeowner. _____
   (c) The sale of fresh produce at the local farmers' market. _____
   (d) A government-operated toll bridge. _____
   (e) Tenants' rent payments to the landlord. _____
   (f) Albertan beef sales to the Soviet Union. _____
   (g) Municipal all-volunteer fire brigade. _____

3. Classify the following transactions in the circular flow of income. Specifically, identify each as a household consumption expenditure, factor payment, injection, or leakage.
   (a) Government buys office equipment. _____
   (b) Households purchase automobiles. _____
   (c) Government receives business tax payments. _____
   (d) Firms borrow from banks for investment purposes. _____
   (e) Firms pay their workers. _____
   (f) Households deposit money with banks. _____
   (g) Governments purchase goods from firms. _____
   (h) Firms retain some profits and deposit these in banks. _____
   (i) Households pay butlers and maids. _____
   (j) Households pay income taxes. _____

4. (a) Through a biological quirk, the avocado, regardless of when or where the tree is planted, yields crops that are far greater in odd years of harvest than in even years. Under a market system, we would predict that the potential gluts in good crop years would result in _____ prices and that the potential shortages in poor crop years would lead to _____ prices.
   (b) In the period 1965 to 1977, the prices of avocados tended to increase more rapidly than the general price level. We would predict that this increase would result in _____ land and other resources being dedicated to avocado production.
   (c) In fact, avocado production more than doubled. The reasonable inference is that consumer demand had substantially _____.
   (d) Relative prices of avocados dropped significantly in 1978 and 1979 as compared with the previous poor and good crop years. What could this signal mean to growers and potential growers?

ANSWERS

Multiple-Choice Questions

1. (c)	**2.** (b)	**3.** (a)	**4.** (d)	**5.** (c)
6. (a)	**7.** (a)	**8.** (c)	**9.** (e)	**10.** (c)
11. (c)	**12.** (c)	**13.** (e)	**14.** (e)	**15.** (a)
16. (b)	**17.** (d)	**18.** (e)	**19.** (e)	**20.** (a)
21. (d)	**22.** (b)			

Exercises

1.
   (a) Likely to occur if shift takes place rapidly.
   (b) No, lower prices are likely.
   (c) Likely to occur.
   (d) No, changing prices and profits will signal the shift automatically.
   (e) Likely to occur as profits rise.
   (f) Likely to occur as profits rise in skis and fall in snowmobiles.
   (g) No, exactly the opposite will occur.

2.
   (a) NM, PU.   (b) NM, PR.
   (c) M, PR.   (d) M, PU.
   (e) M, PR.   (f) M, PR.
   (g) NM, PU.

3.
   (a) Injection.   (b) Consumption.
   (c) Leakage.   (d) Injection.
   (e) Factor payment. (f) Leakage.
   (g) Injection.   (h) Leakage.
   (i) Factor payment.   (j) Leakage.

4.
   (a) Lower; higher.
   (b) More.
   (c) Increased (increased popularity in salads, in Mexican food, and greater familiarity with an unusual fruit could be reasons).
   (d) To be wary of expanding output further; present and prospective profits have almost certainly been reduced.

PART TWO

AN INTRODUCTION TO DEMAND AND SUPPLY

CHAPTER 4

DEMAND, SUPPLY, AND PRICE

• • • • • • • • • • • • •

CHAPTER OVERVIEW

This chapter introduces the economic model of demand and supply. This model describes how the actions of buyers and sellers determine the equilibrium price and quantity exchanged in markets for goods and services.

A downward-sloping demand curve shows the relationship between price and quantity demanded. From a buyer's perspective, the lower the (relative) price of a product, the more attractive it is to purchase. A supply curve shows the relationship between price and quantity supplied. From a seller's perspective, higher relative prices for a product make it more attractive to sell. If quantity supplied does not equal quantity demanded, we expect the price to change until the plans of buyers and sellers are satisfied at the equilibrium price.

Using the method of comparative statics, the effects of a shift in either demand or supply can be determined. The equilibrium price and quantity exchanged respond to changes in the determinants of demand (income, tastes, population, and prices of substitutes or complements) or supply (prices of inputs, technology, and the number of firms). These responses are called the "laws" of demand and supply.

• • • • • • • • • • • • •

LEARNING OBJECTIVES

After studying this chapter, you should be able to:

- ■ understand the concepts of quantity demanded, quantity supplied, and quantity exchanged;
- ■ explain how demand (supply) schedules and demand (supply) curves show the relationship between quantity demanded (supplied) and price;
- ■ indicate what factors are most relevant in determining the demand (supply) for a good;
- ■ understand what causes a movement along a demand or supply curve and what causes a shift in the curve;
- ■ solve for the equilibrium price and quantity exchanged;
- ■ use comparative static analysis to show how equilibrium price and quantity exchanged are affected by demand and supply shifts.

MULTIPLE-CHOICE QUESTIONS

1. The term "quantity demanded" refers to the
   (a) amount of a good that consumers are willing to purchase at some price during some given time period.
   (b) amount of some good that consumers would purchase if they only had the income to afford it.
   (c) amount of a good that is actually purchased during a given time period.
   (d) minimum amount of a good that consumers require and demand for survival.
   (e) amount of a good that consumers are willing to purchase regardless of price.

2. An increase in quantity demanded refers to
   (a) rightward shifts in the demand curve only.
   (b) a movement up along a demand curve.
   (c) a greater willingness to purchase at each price.
   (d) an increase in actual purchases.
   (e) a movement down along a demand curve.

3. The demand curve and the demand schedule
   (a) each reflect the relationship between quantity demanded and price, *ceteris paribus*.
   (b) are both incomplete in that neither can incorporate the impact of changes in income or tastes.
   (c) are constructed on the assumption that price is held constant.
   (d) illustrate that in economic analysis, only two variables are taken into account at any one time.
   (e) characterize the relationship between price and actual purchases.

4. When the Multiple Listing Service (MLS) reports that in the month of April at an average selling price of $250,000, total sales of homes in Toronto were 2,000, they are referring to
   (a) quantity demanded.
   (b) quantity supplied.
   (c) equilibrium quantity.

   (d) actual purchases, which may or may not equal quantity demanded or quantity supplied.
   (e) Both (a) and (c) are correct.

5. A decrease in the price of VCRs will result in
   (a) an increase in demand for VCRs.
   (b) a decrease in supply of VCRs.
   (c) an increase in the quantity demanded of VCRs.
   (d) a movement up along the demand curve for VCRs.
   (e) a rightward shift in the demand curve for VCRs.

6. An increase in demand means that
   (a) consumers actually buy more of the good.
   (b) at each price, consumers desire a greater quantity.
   (c) consumers' tastes have necessarily changed.
   (d) price has decreased.
   (e) All of the above are correct.

7. A decrease in the price of compact disc (CD) players will induce
   (a) a leftward shift in the demand curve for record turntables (a substitute).
   (b) an increase in demand for vinyl records.
   (c) a rightward shift in the demand curve for CDs (a complement).
   (d) a rise in demand for CD players.
   (e) Both (a) and (c) are correct.

8. If goods *A* and *B* are complements, an increase in the price of good *A* will lead to
   (a) an increase in the price of good *B*.
   (b) a decrease in the quantity demanded of good *B*.
   (c) a decrease in demand for good *B*.
   (d) no change in demand for good *B* because *A* and *B* are not substitutes.
   (e) a rightward shift in the demand for good *B*.

9. Increased public awareness of the adverse health effects of smoking
   (a) is a noneconomic event that cannot be incorporated into the demand and supply model.
   (b) is characterized as a change in tastes that leads to a leftward shift in the demand curve for cigarettes.
   (c) will lead to an eventual increase in the price of cigarettes due to shifts in the demand curve for cigarettes.
   (d) induces a decrease in the supply of cigarettes.
   (e) decreases the quantity demanded of cigarettes.

10. A change in demand could be caused by *all but which* one of the following?
    (a) A decrease in average income.
    (b) An increase in the price of a substitute good.
    (c) A decrease in the cost of producing the good.
    (d) An increase in population.
    (e) A government program that redistributes income.

11. An increase in the supply of broccoli could be caused by *all but which* of the following?
    (a) An decrease in the price of broccoli.
    (b) A decrease in the price of labour employed in harvesting broccoli.
    (c) An improvement in pesticides, which would decrease the variability in broccoli output.
    (d) A change in the number of producers.
    (e) An improvement in harvesting technology.

12. A movement along a supply curve could be caused by
    (a) an improvement in technology.
    (b) a change in the prices of inputs.
    (c) a shift in the demand curve.
    (d) a change in the number of producers.
    (e) a decrease in production costs.

13. Excess demand exists whenever
    (a) price exceeds the equilibrium price.

(b) quantity supplied is greater than quantity demanded.
(c) the equilibrium price is above the existing price.
(d) there is downward pressure on price.
(e) there is surplus production.

Questions 14 and 15 refer to the following diagram.

Figure 4-1

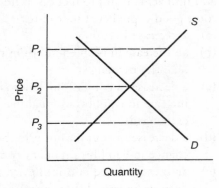

14. At a price of P_1,
    (a) there is upward pressure on price.
    (b) demand will rise to restore equilibrium.
    (c) quantity supplied is greater than quantity demanded.
    (d) the market has reached an equilibrium price.
    (e) a shortage exists.

15. When price equals P_3,
    (a) quantity exchanged equals quantity demanded.
    (b) there is excess supply.
    (c) there is a tendency for price to rise.
    (d) the market is in equilibrium.
    (e) a surplus exists.

16. The "laws of demand and supply" are
    (a) federal statutes and are therefore enforced by the RCMP.
    (b) enshrined in the Canadian Constitution.
    (c) irrefutable propositions concerning economic behaviour.
    (d) basic assumptions in economic theory.
    (e) predictions of economic behaviour that have tended to withstand much, but not all, empirical testing.

17. An increase in both equilibrium price and quantity exchanged is consistent with
    (a) an increase in supply.
    (b) a decrease in supply.
    (c) a decrease in quantity supplied.
    (d) an increase in demand.
    (e) a decrease in demand.

18. Assuming a downward-sloping demand curve, an improvement in production technology for some good is predicted to lead to
    (a) a decrease in supply.
    (b) an increase in both equilibrium price and quantity exchanged.
    (c) a decrease in equilibrium price and an increase in equilibrium quantity exchanged.
    (d) a decrease in equilibrium price but no change in equilibrium quantity exchanged.
    (e) an increase in equilibrium price and a decrease in equilibrium quantity exchanged.

19. Should polyester leisure suits become fashionable, economic theory predicts
    (a) a decrease in the price of these suits but an increase in the quantity exchanged.
    (b) an increase in both equilibrium price and quantity.
    (c) a shift in the supply curve to the right.
    (d) an increase in equilibrium price and a decrease in equilibrium quantity.
    (e) a leftward shift of the demand curve.

20. Simultaneous increases in both demand and supply are predicted to result in
    (a) increases in both equilibrium price and quantity.
    (b) a higher equilibrium price but a smaller equilibrium quantity.
    (c) a lower equilibrium price but a larger equilibrium quantity.
    (d) a larger equilibrium quantity but no predictable change in price.
    (e) a higher price, but no predictable change in equilibrium quantity.

21. A decrease in input prices as well as a simultaneous decrease in the price of a good that is substitutable in consumption will lead to
    (a) a lower equilibrium price and a larger equilibrium quantity.
    (b) a lower equilibrium price but no change in equilibrium quantity.
    (c) a lower equilibrium price and an uncertain change in quantity.
    (d) a lower equilibrium price and a smaller equilibrium quantity.
    (e) an unpredictable change in both price and quantity.

22. Which of the following is *not* a potential cause of an increase in the price of housing?
    (a) Construction workers' wages increase with no offsetting increase in productivity.
    (b) Cheaper methods of prefabricating homes are developed.
    (c) An increase in population.
    (d) An increase in consumer incomes.
    (e) The price of land (an input) increases.

23. Comparative statics
    (a) is the analysis of market equilibria under different sets of conditions.
    (b) is the analysis of demand without reference to time.
    (c) refers to constant equilibrium prices and quantities.
    (d) describes the path by which equilibrium price changes.
    (e) refers to disequilibrium prices and quantities.

24. Today the price of strawberries is 60 cents a litre, and raspberries are priced at 75 cents a litre. Yesterday strawberries were 80 cents and raspberries $1. Thus, for these two goods,
    (a) the relative price of raspberries has fallen.
    (b) the relative price of strawberries has fallen by 20 cents.
    (c) the relative prices of both goods have fallen.
    (d) relative prices have not changed.
    (e) the relative price of strawberries has risen.

25. In price theory, which of the following represents a relative price increase for strawberries, assuming that the average price level rises by 10 percent?
(a) An increase in price from $1.00 to $1.05 per litre.
(b) An increase in price from $1.00 to $1.10 per litre.
(c) An increase in price from $1.00 to $1.15 per litre.
(d) Both (a) and (c) are correct.
(e) All of the above are correct.

• • • • • • • • • • • • • •

EXERCISES

1. The demand and supply schedules for high-top, athletic pump shoes sold in the local mall (in pairs per month) are hypothesized to be as follows:

(1) Price	(2) Quantity demanded	(3) Quantity supplied	(4) Excess demand (+) Excess supply (−)
$120	40_____	130	_____
110	50_____	110	_____
100	60_____	90	_____
90	70_____	70	_____
80	80_____	50	_____
70	90_____	30	_____
60	100_____	10	_____

(a) Using the grid provided in Figure 4-2, plot the demand and supply curves (approximately). Indicate the equilibrium levels of price and quantity.

Figure 4-2

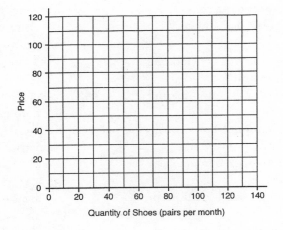

Quantity of Shoes (pairs per month)

(b) Fill in column 4 for values of excess demand and excess supply. What is the value of excess demand (supply) at equilibrium?
(c) Suppose there is a change in teenage fashion such that a substitute shoe, Doc Martens, becomes trendy. As a result, the quantity demanded of high-top, athletic pump shoes at the local mall decreases by 30 units per month at each and every price. Fill in the new quantity demanded in column (2) in the above schedule, and draw the new demand curve on the grid.

(d) Supposing that price initially remains at the level you reported in answer (b), explain the pressures that are exerted upon price by this change in tastes.

(e) After price has adjusted to the new equilibrium, what are the equilibrium price and quantity?

2. Read the description of certain events in the markets for selected commodities. Predict the economic impact of these events by drawing the appropriate shifts in the diagrams provided in Figure 4-3. Also, use + and − to indicate whether there will be an increase or decrease in demand (*D*), supply (*S*), equilibrium price (*P*), and equilibrium quantity (*Q*). If there is no change, use *0*. If the change cannot be deduced with the information provided, use *U* for uncertain.

Market	Event	Figure 4-3	D	S	P	Q
(a) Canadian wine	Early frost destroys a large percentage of the grape crop in British Columbia		__	__	__	__
(b) Wood-burning stoves	The price of heating oil and natural gas triples		__	__	__	__
(c) Videocassette recorders (VCRs)	Technological advances reduce the costs of producing VCRs		__	__	__	__
(d) Gold	Vast gold deposits are discovered in northern Ontario		__	__	__	__
(e) Fast foods	The public shows greater concern over high sodium and cholesterol; also, there is an increase in the minimum wage		__	__	__	__
(f) Bicycles	There is increasing concern about physical fitness; also, the price of gasoline rises		__	__	__	__
(g) Beer	Population of drinking age increases; also, brewery unions negotiate a large increase in renumeration		__	__	__	__

3. Suppose that student demand for on-campus concert tickets is as follows:

Price	Quantity demanded
$6	8,000
8	5,000
10	2,500
12	1,500
14	1,000

Concert pricing policy is set by the Executive of the Students' Association, which has decided that all seats will sell at the same price regardless of location or popularity of the performer (clearly, there are no economics majors on the Executive). Also, the only concert hall available on campus has a seating capacity of 5,000.

(a) If the Executive sets a price of $10 per seat, is there an excess demand or supply of concert tickets?

(b) What price would fill the concert hall without creating a shortage of seats?

(c) Suppose the above demand schedule refers to an "average" concert, and when a particularly popular performer is booked the quantity of tickets demanded at each price doubles. What would be the equilibrium ticket price for a popular performer?

(d) Do you think ticket scalping would be more profitable if the Executive set price equal to, above, or below equilibrium? Explain.

4. The purpose of this question is to encourage you to obtain the market equilibrium by algebraically solving a system of simultaneous equations. You may refer to Chapter 2 of this Study Guide before attempting this exercise.

The demand and supply of widgets are given by

$$Q^D = 30 - 1.0P, \text{ and}$$

$$Q^S = 1.0P, \text{ respectively.}$$

(a) Plot the demand and supply curves on the grid in Figure 4-4, and label them D and S, respectively.

Figure 4-4

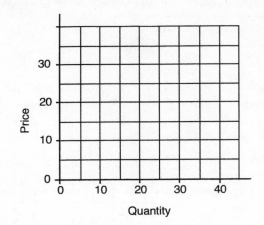

(b) Determine the equilibrium price and the equilibrium quantity. Do this using two methods. First interpret the diagram. Then impose the equilibrium condition that

$$Q^D = Q^S$$

and solve algebraically.

(c) Now suppose that the demand curve changes to

$$Q^D = 30 - 1.5P$$

but the supply curve is unchanged. Plot the new demand curve and label it D′. Before price adjustments from your answer in (b), is there excess demand or excess supply in the market? How much?

(d) Once price responds to market pressures created by the change in demand, what will be the new levels of equilibrium price and quantity?

5. The following question demonstrates how changes in exogenous variables impact upon market equilibrium.

The quantity demanded of gadgets (Q^D) depends on the price of gadgets (P) and average household income (Y) according to the following relationship:

$$Q^D = 30 - 10P + 0.001Y$$

The quantity of gadgets supplied (Q^S) is positively related to the price of gadgets and negatively related to W, the price of some input (e.g., labour) according to

$$Q^S = 5 + 5P - 2W$$

(a) Assume initially that $Y = \$40,000$ and $W = \$5$. Substitute these values into the equations to obtain the demand and supply curves.

(b) Now use the equilibrium condition $Q^D = Q^S$ to solve the demand and supply curves simultaneously for the equilibrium price.

(c) Finally, substitute the equilibrium price into either the demand or supply curve to obtain the equilibrium quantity.

(d) Use the grid in Figure 4-5 to graph the demand and supply curves for gadgets in (a), and label them D_o and S_o, respectively. Confirm that your answers in (b) and (c) are correct.

Figure 4-5

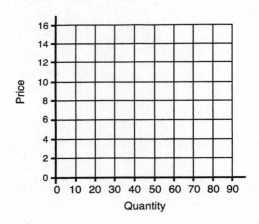

(e) Suppose that average household income increases to $55,000 but W remains constant. What are the new levels of equilibrium price and quantity? Plot the new demand curve, label it D_l, and confirm your answer.

(f) Now assume that the input price W increases to $12.50. Using the demand curve you derived in (e), determine the new levels of equilibrium price and quantity. Plot the new supply curve, label it S_l, and again confirm your answer.

6. What shifts in demand or supply (or both) best explain the following statements? For each statement, determine if the sentence is referring to a change in demand, a change in quantity demanded, a change in supply, or a change in quantity supplied.

(a) Oil prices rise as OPEC members agree to new restrictions on output.

(b) Prices of personal computers fall despite a substantial increase in the number sold.

(c) Apartment rental prices rise as student enrolment swells.

(d) Lower air fares spark the busiest-ever air travel over a holiday period.

(e) Increases in the prices of Christmas trees spur tree planting on land previously used by dairy farmers.

*7. The diagram in Figure 4-6 illustrates a hypothetical market for farm machinery in Canada.

Figure 4-6

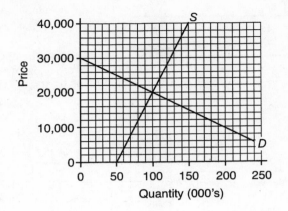

The federal government has decided that output in this industry should increase by 50 percent. Since current industry output is 100,000 units, it therefore plans to purchase 50,000 units of farm machinery *regardless of price*. The government intends to give away these units to less developed countries as part of Canada's foreign aid.

(a) Draw the new demand curve for farm machinery that takes into account government demand. What are the new levels of equilibrium price and quantity?

(b) By how much does industry output increase in percentage terms? Why does this increase fall short of the government's target of 50 percent?

(c) How many units would the government have to purchase in order to satisfy its objective of increasing industry output to 150,000 units? What is the associated quantity demanded by the private sector (i.e., by nongovernment consumers in Canada)?

● ● ● ● ● ● ● ● ● ● ● ● ● ●

ANSWERS
Multiple-Choice Questions

1. (a)	**2.** (e)	**3.** (a)	**4.** (d)	**5.** (c)
6. (b)	**7.** (e)	**8.** (c)	**9.** (b)	**10.** (c)
11. (a)	**12.** (c)	**13.** (c)	**14.** (c)	**15.** (c)
16. (e)	**17.** (d)	**18.** (c)	**19.** (b)	**20.** (d)
21. (c)	**22.** (b)	**23.** (a)	**24.** (d)	**25.** (c)

Exercises

1. (a) **Figure 4-7**

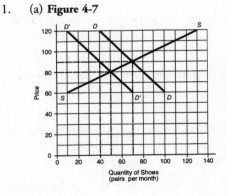

Equilibrium price and quantity are $90 and 70 pairs per month, respectively.

(b)

Price	Excess demand (+) or excess supply (-)
$120	−90
110	−60
100	−30
90	0
80	+30
70	+60
60	+90

There is no excess demand or supply.

(c) See above diagram.

(d) With the change in tastes (i.e., along D') quantity demanded at the original price of $90 is now 40 units per month while quantity supplied remains at 70 units. Thus, 30 units remain unsold each month; this accumulating inventory exerts downward pressure on price.

(e) The new equilibrium obtains at a price of $80 and quantity of 50 units per month.

2.

	D	S	P	Q
(a)	0	−	+	−
(b)	+	0	+	+
(c)	0	+	−	+
(d)	0	+	−	+
(e)	−	−	U	−
(f)	+	0	+	+
(g)	+	−	+	U

3. (a) Excess supply of 2,500 seats.

(b) At $8, quantity demanded and quantity supplied each equal 5,000 seats.

(c) Since quantity demanded doubles at every price, 5,000 tickets would be demanded if price were $10.

(d) Scalpers would do better if price were set below equilibrium which creates excess demand. For example, at a price of $6, the quantity demanded for an "average" concert is 8,000 but only 5,000 are sold. Thus, scalpers who are fortunate to purchase at $6 have a better chance of finding a buyer who is willing to pay more than $6.

4. (a) **Figure 4-8**

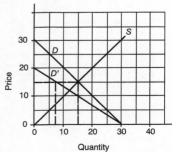

(b) $Q^D = Q^S$ is equivalent to: $30 − 1.0P = 1.0P$, which solves for $P = 15. Now substitute the equilibrium price into the equation for either Q^D or Q^S, and obtain the equilibrium quantity $Q = 15$. (e.g., $Q^S = 1.0(15) = 15$).

(c) When price is $15, $Q^S = 15$ and $Q^D = 7.5$; thus, there is excess supply of 7.5 units.

(d) The new equilibrium obtains at the intersection of D' and S where $P = 12 (i.e., $30 − 1.5P = 1.0P$) and $Q = 12$.

5. (a) Q^D = $30 − 10P + 0.001(40,000)$
     = $70 − 10P$.
     Q^S = $5 + 5P − 2(5) = −5 + 5P$.

(b) For equilibrium, $Q^D = Q^S$, so that:
$70 − 10P = −5 + 5P$, which solves for the equilibrium price of $5.

(c) Substituting this value into either Q^D or Q^S, one obtains the equilibrium quantity of 20 units.

(d) **Figure 4-9**

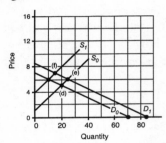

(e) Now $Q^D = 85 − 10P$. Setting $Q^D = Q^S$, or $85 − 10P = −5 + 5P$, yields $P = 6 and $Q = 25$.

(f) Now $Q^S = −20 + 5P$ and $Q^D = 85 − 10P$, so that $Q^D = Q^S$ solves for $P = 7 and $Q = 15$.

6. (a) The supply curve for oil shifts to the left, resulting in a higher equilibrium price.

(b) The supply curve for computers shifts to the right, resulting in a lower equilibrium price and a greater quantity exchanged. (Although demand may have also shifted to the right, the effect of the supply shift dominates, resulting in a lower price.)

(c) The demand for apartments increased (i.e., demand curve shifts to the right), resulting in higher rents.

(d) Increase in quantity demanded. Lower air fares induce a movement down along the demand curve.

(e) Increase in quantity supplied. The higher price results in a movement up along the supply curve.

*7. (a) **Figure 4-10**

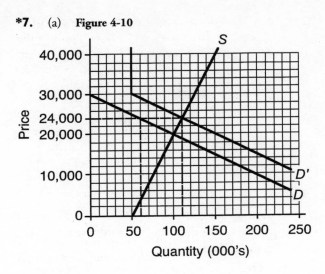

The equilibrium price is $24,000, and the equilibrium quantity is 110,000 units.

(b) Industry output increases from 100,000 to 110,000 units, or by 10 percent. The additional demand of 50,000 units created by the government exerts upward pressure on the price of farm machinery and thereby decreases the quantity demanded by the private or non-government sector of the economy. These private-sector consumers reduce their purchases from 100,000 to 60,000 units.

(c) The government would have to purchase all 150,000 units, which would be supplied only when the price reached $40,000. The quantity demanded by the private sector is reduced to zero when the price reaches $30,000.

CHAPTER 5
· · · · · · · · · · · · · ·
ELASTICITY

· · · · · · · · · · · · · ·
CHAPTER OVERVIEW

The previous chapter showed how supply and demand determine the equilibrium price and quantity exchanged in a market. This chapter characterizes demand and supply in one particularly important way: the magnitude of its responsiveness to changes in price (or other determinants of demand and supply).

A price elasticity is the percentage change in quantity for a given percentage change in price. When the percentage change in quantity demanded exceeds the percentage change in price (in absolute terms), demand is said to be elastic (as opposed to inelastic when the reverse holds, or unit elastic when the two percentage changes are of equal magnitude). If we know the price elasticity of demand for a product, we can predict the percentage change in quantity demanded that will result from a given percentage price change. The magnitude of a product's elasticity allows us to predict whether an increase in its price will result in an increase or a decrease in revenue from sales of the good.

Similar elasticity concepts are relevant when consumer income or the price of another good changes. These are called the income elasticity and cross-price elasticity, respectively. The sign of the income elasticity indicates whether the good is normal or inferior, while that of the cross-price elasticity indicates whether the goods are substitutes or complements.

The distinction between long-run demand and supply elasticities from their short-run counterparts has important implications for the market response to exogenous changes. Also, the distribution of the burden of a sales tax between consumers and producers critically depends upon the relative magnitudes of the elasticities of demand and supply.

· · · · · · · · · · · · · ·
LEARNING OBJECTIVES

After studying this chapter, you should be able to:

- understand elasticity of demand and elasticity of supply and how they are measured;
- explain the significance of elastic and inelastic demand and supply;
- identify what factors determine whether demand or supply is elastic or inelastic;
- understand the relationship between elasticity of demand and total expenditure (total revenue);
- explain the meanings of income and cross elasticities of demand;
- appreciate the distinction between arc and point elasticity;
- be comfortable with alternative ways of writing the same formula for elasticity.

MULTIPLE-CHOICE QUESTIONS

1. The price elasticity of demand refers to a measure that shows the
   - (a) responsiveness of quantity demanded of a good to changes in its price.
   - (b) variation in prices due to a change in demand.
   - (c) size of price changes caused by a shift in demand.
   - (d) degree of substitutability across commodities.
   - (e) magnitude of the shifts in a demand curve.

2. The price elasticity of demand is measured by the
   - (a) change in quantity demanded divided by the change in price.
   - (b) change in price divided by the change in quantity demanded.
   - (c) slope of the demand curve.
   - (d) percentage change in quantity demanded divided by the percentage change in price.
   - (e) average quantity demanded divided by the average price.

3. If the price elasticity of demand for a good is 2 and price increases by 2 percent, the quantity demanded
   - (a) decreases by 4 percent.
   - (b) decreases by 1 percent.
   - (c) decreases by 2 percent.
   - (d) does not change.
   - (e) is indeterminable with data provided.

4. If the percentage change in price is greater than the percentage change in quantity demanded, demand
   - (a) is elastic.
   - (b) is inelastic.
   - (c) is unit-elastic.
   - (d) shifts outward to the left.
   - (e) shifts to the right.

Questions 5 through 8 refer to the four diagrams in Figure 5-1.

Figure 5-1

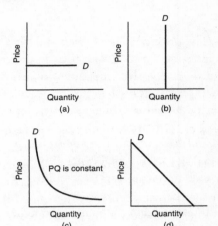

5. The demand curve with an elasticity of zero is
   - (a) a
   - (b) b.
   - (c) c.
   - (d) d.
   - (e) None of the above.

6. The demand curve with an elasticity of unity is
   - (a) a.
   - (b) b.
   - (c) c.
   - (d) d.
   - (e) None of the above.

7. The demand curve with an elasticity of infinity is
   - (a) a.
   - (b) b.
   - (c) c.
   - (d) d.
   - (e) None of the above.

8. The demand curve with an elasticity that is variable is
   - (a) a.
   - (b) b.
   - (c) c.
   - (d) d.
   - (e) Both (c) and (d).

9. An increase in the price of a good and a decrease in total expenditure on this good are associated with
   (a) inferior goods.
   (b) substitute goods.
   (c) normal goods.
   (d) elastic demand.
   (e) inelastic demand.

10. The price elasticity of demand for snowmobiles is estimated to be 1.2; thus an increase in price
    (a) always decreases quantity demanded by 12 percent.
    (b) always decreases quantity demanded by 1.2 percent.
    (c) increases total expenditure.
    (d) decreases total expenditure.
    (e) decreases total expenditure by 1.2 percent.

11. If the demand for some commodity has an elasticity of unity, a decrease in price
    (a) causes a 1 percent decrease in quantity demanded.
    (b) induces no change in quantity demanded.
    (c) results in no change in total expenditure.
    (d) is matched by a unit increase in quantity demanded.
    (e) Both (a) and (c) are correct.

12. The price elasticity of demand for a good will be greater
    (a) the less available are suitable substitutes for this good.
    (b) the longer the time period considered.
    (c) for a group of related goods as opposed to an element of that group.
    (d) the greater is income.
    (e) All of the above are correct.

13. If a 10 percent increase in the price of ski lift tickets causes a 5 percent decrease in total revenue of lift operations, then demand is
    (a) elastic.
    (b) inelastic.
    (c) perfectly inelastic.
    (d) normal.
    (e) inferior.

Questions 14 to 16 refer to the following schedule. (Use average prices and quantities in your calculations.)

Price per unit	Quantity offered for sale
$10	400
8	350
6	300
4	200
2	50

14. As price increases from $4 to $6, the elasticity of supply is
    (a) 1.0.
    (b) 50.
    (c) 0.5.
    (d) 5.0.
    (e) 2.0.

15. As price rises from $6 to $10 per unit, the supply response is
    (a) elastic.
    (b) of unit elasticity.
    (c) of zero elasticity.
    (d) inelastic.
    (e) infinitely elastic.

16. The supply curve implied by the schedule is
    (a) elastic for all price ranges.
    (b) inelastic for all price ranges.
    (c) of zero elasticity for all price ranges.
    (d) of variable elasticity, depending on the initial price chosen.
    (e) of constant elasticity.

17. Which of the following pairs of commodities is likely to have a cross-elasticity of demand that is positive?
    (a) Hockey sticks and pucks.
    (b) Bread and cheese.
    (c) Cassettes and compact discs.
    (d) Perfume and garden hoses.
    (e) Hamburgers and French fries.

18. Margarine and butter are predicted to have
(a) the same income elasticities of demand.
(b) very low price elasticities of demand.
(c) negative cross-elasticities of demand with respect to each other.
(d) positive cross-elasticities of demand with respect to each other.
(e) elastic demands with respect to price.

19. Inferior commodities have
(a) zero income elasticities of demand.
(b) negative cross-elasticities of demand.
(c) negative elasticities of supply.
(d) highly elastic demands.
(e) negative income elasticities of demand.

20. Which of the following goods is more likely to have an income elasticity of demand that is less than one?
(a) Hamburger meat.
(b) Microwave ovens.
(c) Perfume.
(d) Winter vacations.
(e) Sailboats.

21. Which of the following commodities is more likely to have an elastic demand?
(a) Toothpicks.
(b) Cigarettes.
(c) Heart pacemakers.
(d) Broccoli.
(e) Vegetables.

22. A perfectly inelastic demand curve means that
(a) a percentage decrease in price exactly increases quantity demanded by the same percentage.
(b) an increase in price reduces quantity demanded.
(c) the price elasticity of demand is infinity.
(d) any change in price is perfectly matched by a change in quantity demanded.
(e) quantity demanded does not change in response to any price change.

23. A decrease in income by 10 percent leads to a decrease in quantity demanded by 5 percent; the income elasticity of demand is therefore
(a) −0.5.
(b) 2.0.

(c) 0.5.
(d) 50.0.
(e) 15.0.

24. A commodity is classified as a normal good if
(a) a decrease in consumer income results in a decrease in demand.
(b) it is consumed by a majority of the population.
(c) its price and quantity demanded are negatively related, *ceteris paribus*.
(d) an increase in its price leads to an increase in quantity supplied.
(e) a decrease in consumer income results in an increase in demand.

25. Suppose that the short-run demand for a good is relatively more inelastic than its long-run demand. A given rightward shift in the supply curve will lead to
(a) a smaller decrease in price in the long run than in the short run.
(b) a smaller increase in quantity in the long run than in the short run.
(c) a larger decrease in price in the long run than in the short run.
(d) a smaller decrease in both price and quantity in the long run than in the short run.
(e) larger decreases in both price and quantity in the long run than in the short run.

26. If an individual allocates $200 as monthly expenditure on compact discs and decides to spend no more and no less regardless of price, this individual's demand for compact discs is
(a) perfectly inelastic.
(b) perfectly elastic.
(c) of unit elasticity.
(d) less than one but greater than zero.
(e) of zero elasticity.

27. A shift in demand would not affect price when supply is
(a) perfectly inelastic.
(b) perfectly elastic.
(c) of unit elasticity.
(d) a straight line through the origin.
(e) of zero elasticity.

28. Since the Goods and Services Tax (GST) is added to the price a consumer must pay for a commodity, the
(a) entire burden of the tax is borne by consumers.
(b) consumer price increases by the amount of the tax.
(c) seller price is unaffected.
(d) burden is borne by producers who must collect the tax.
(e) distribution of the burden depends upon the elasticities of demand and supply.

29. Consumers bear a greater share of the burden of the tax, the more
(a) inelastic is supply.
(b) elastic is supply.
(c) inelastic is demand.
(d) elastic is demand.
(e) Both (b) and (c) are correct.

Appendix Questions

The following questions are based upon material in the appendix to this chapter. Use Figure 5-2 to answer questions 30 to 33.

Figure 5-2

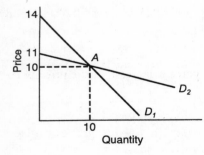

30. The point elasticity of D_1 at point A is (*Hint:* Multiply the ratio of price to quantity at point A by the reciprocal of the slope)
(a) 0.1.
(b) 2.5.
(c) 1.0.
(d) 10.0.
(e) 4.0.

31. The point elasticity of demand for D_2 at point A is
(a) 0.1
(b) 2.5
(c) 1.0
(d) 10.0
(e) 4.0

32. At a price of $10, demand curve D_1
(a) has the same elasticity as any other point along D_1.
(b) is more elastic than at any other price below $10.
(c) is more elastic than D_2.
(d) is inelastic.
(e) None of the above.

33. Starting from point A, a 10 percent reduction in price along D_1 will result in an increase in quantity demanded of
(a) 25 percent.
(b) 100 percent.
(c) 10 percent
(d) 1 percent.
(e) 2.5 percent.

EXERCISES

1. In each of the following scenarios, categorize the price elasticity of demand as elastic, inelastic, or unit-elastic. Where calculations are required, use average price and quantity. Note that categorization may not always be possible with the information provided.

(a) The price of personal computers falls from $2,750 to $2,250, and the quantity demanded increases from 40,000 units to 60,000 units.

(b) Canada Post increases the price of a stamp from 48 cents to 50 cents, but its total revenue remains the same.

(c) The price of matchbooks doubles from 1 cent to 2 cents, but the quantity purchased does not change.

(d) An increase in the demand for blue jeans causes the price to increase from $45 to $55 and the amount purchased to increase from 1 million to 1.1 million.

(e) A sudden decline in the supply of avocados leads to an increase in price by 10 percent and a concomitant reduction in quantity demanded by 20,000 units from the original level of 90,000 units.

(f) A 5 percent decrease in the price of gasoline results in a decrease in total revenue of 5 percent.

(g) A 10 percent increase in consumer income results in a 15 percent increase in the price of snowboards as well as a 15 percent increase in purchases.

2. Two alternative demand curves are depicted in the upper panels of Figure 5-3.

Figure 5-3

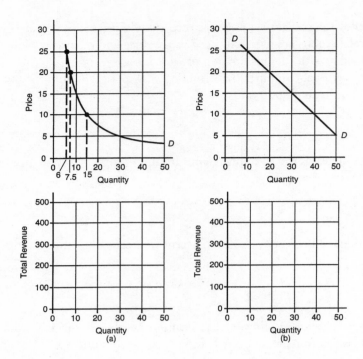

(a) Calculate the total revenue associated with each demand curve at the following prices: $25, $20, $15, $10, and $5. Graph the respective total revenue curves in the grids provided in the lower panels of Figure 5-3.

(b) By inspection of these total revenue curves, what can you say about the price elasticity of demand along each of the demand curves?

3. Fill in the following table:

	Price elasticity	Change in price	Change in total revenue
(a)	2.0	up	_____
(b)	1.0	down	_____
(c)	___	up	none
(d)	0.0	down	_____
(e)	0.6	_____	up

4. Calculate the numerical values of price elasticity along the demand curve in Figure 5-4. Use the four price-quantity segments indicated by the dots on the demand curve.

Figure 5-4

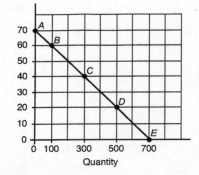

(a) Confirm that elasticity declines as price decreases.

(b) What is the elasticity of demand when the price falls from $40 to $30? What is happening to total revenue as the price falls further?

*5. Suppose that you are hired as a consultant for the Guelph Transportation Commission. Its statisticians inform you that at the current fare of $1.30, the system carries 20,000 riders per day. They also indicate that for each $0.05 increase (decrease) in the fare, ridership decreases (increases) by 1,000 passengers.

(a) What is the arc price elasticity of demand at the current fare? (*Hint:* Consider a change in fare from 5 cents below the current fare to 5 cents above.)

(b) To consider raising total revenue for the transit system, the Guelph Transportation Commission has hired you to determine by how much it should increase the fare. What do you advise? Why?

(c) What fare will maximize total revenue for the transit system? What is the associated ridership?

6. The Honourable Mr. D. Runken, MP from the riding of Temperance, Ontario, has introduced a private member's bill in Parliament that will increase taxes on all alchoholic beverages. He has argued this represents good social policy because it will reduce consumption of liquor, thereby increasing the amount of income families of alchoholics would have available to spend on items such as food and health care. Comment on Mr. Runken's reasoning using the concept of elasticity.

7. (a) If the price of wheat falls 10 percent and farmers produce 15 percent less, what is the elasticity of supply for wheat?

(b) Suppose the government's goal is to raise wheat production by 30 percent to help fight famine. Based upon the elasticity calculated above, by what percentage must price increase to reach this goal?

(c) If the price of wheat falls by 5 percent, by what percentage will wheat production decline, given the elasticity you calculated above?

*8. The table provides data on income and demand for goods x and y.

Period	Income	P_x	Q^D_x	P_y	Q^D_y
(1)	$10,000	$25	10	$10	42
(2)	10,000	28	9	10	40
(3)	10,000	28	8	15	35
(4)	11,000	28	9	15	36
(5)	11,500	34	7	20	32

(a) Why should no elasticities be calculated between periods 4 and 5?

(b) Calculate the following elasticities, selecting appropriate periods and using arc formulas:
price elasticity for x _____, based upon periods _____ and _____;
price elasticity for y _____, based upon periods _____ and _____;
income elasticity for x _____, based upon periods _____ and _____;
income elasticity for y _____, based upon periods _____ and _____;
cross-elasticity of demand for y with respect to the price of x _____, based upon periods _____ and
_____;
cross-elasticity of demand for x with respect to the price of y _____, based upon the periods _____
and _____.

9. (a) Given the supply curves in Figure 5-5, demonstrate that the elasticity of supply equals 1 along S_1 but
falls as price increases along S_2. (Compute arc elasticities between the points indicated.)

Figure 5-5

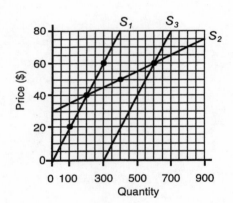

(b) How is the result for S_1 related to the fact that this supply curve passes through the origin?

(c) What does a supply curve such as S_3 imply when price equals zero?

10. The six diagrams in Figure 5-6 represent different combinations of elasticities of demand and supply at the equilibrium price P_E. Indicate which diagrams correspond to each of the following statements. (η_d refers to elasticity of demand, and η_s refers to elasticity of supply).

(a) η_d is greater than one and η_s is unity   _____

(b) η_d is unity and η_s is infinity   _____

(c) η_d is unity and η_s is unity   _____

(d) η_d is greater than one and η_s is zero   _____

(e) η_d is zero and η_s is unity   _____

(f) η_d is infinity and η_s is unity   _____

Figure 5-6

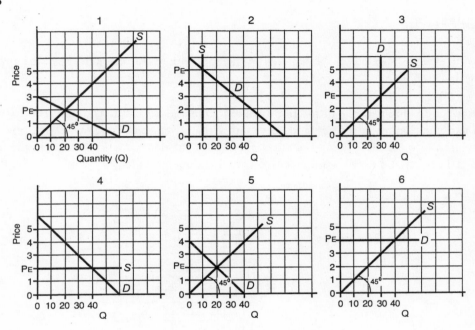

11. The following diagrams depict the demand and supply curves for the beer and orange juice markets in Ontario. Suppose a sales tax of $t per litre is imposed in both of these markets.

Figure 5-7

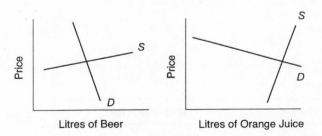

(a) Shift the appropriate curve to show the impact of the tax in each market. Label the new consumer price and seller price in the beer market P_{cb} and P_{sb}, respectively. In the market for orange juice, label them P_{cj} and P_{sj}, respectively.

(b) In which market is most of the burden of the tax borne by consumers? How would you characterize the elasticities of demand and supply in this market?

(c)   In which market is most of the tax borne by producers? How would you characterize the elasticities of demand and supply in this market?

(d)   In which market is the difference between the consumer price and the seller price greater?

Appendix Exercise

The following exercise is based on the material in the appendix to this chapter. Read the appendix before attempting this exercise.

12.   The appendix discusses the distinction between *point* and *arc* elasticity. Point elasticity measures elasticity at a particular point on the demand curve rather than over an interval (arc elasticity). This exercise requires you to calculate point and arc elasticities for the demand curve drawn in the following diagram. (Note: The demand curve is linear with a constant slope of $\Delta P/\Delta Q = -\frac{1}{2}$ or equivalently, $\Delta Q/\Delta P = -2$.)

Figure 5-8

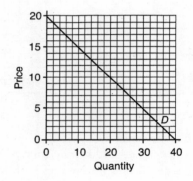

(a)   Calculate the point elasticity of demand at a price of $10.

(b)   Calculate the arc elasticity of demand for the following price changes (calculations should be to two decimal places).

Price change	Arc elasticity
$18 to $10	_____
$14 to $10	_____
$12 to $10	_____
$11 to $10	_____

(c)   What happens to the difference between arc elasticity and point elasticity as the price change gets smaller? When is arc elasticity likely to be a good approximation of point elasticity?

ANSWERS
Multiple-Choice Questions

1. (a)	**2.** (d)	**3.** (a)	**4.** (b)	**5.** (b)
6. (c)	**7.** (a)	**8.** (d)	**9.** (d)	**10.** (d)
11. (c)	**12.** (b)	**13.** (a)	**14.** (a)	**15.** (d)
16. (d)	**17.** (c)	**18.** (d)	**19.** (e)	**20.** (a)
21. (d)	**22.** (e)	**23.** (c)	**24.** (a)	**25.** (a)
26. (c)	**27.** (b)	**28.** (e)	**29.** (e)	**30.** (c)
31. (d)	**32.** (b)	**33.** (a)		

Exercises

1. (a) η = 2.0 = (20,000/500 $\times$ (2,500/50,000); elastic demand.
    (b) Elasticity of unity.
    (c) Perfectly inelastic demand.
    (d) η cannot be determined because the demand curve has shifted.
    (e) η = 2.5 = ((20,000/80,000) $\times$ 100) percent $\div$ 10 percent; elastic demand.
    (f) Perfectly inelastic demand.
    (g) η cannot be determined because the demand curve shifts.

2. (a) **Figure 5-9**

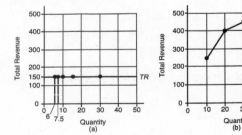

    (b) Panel (a): Since total revenue does not change along the demand curve, the price elasticity of demand is equal to unity at every point along this demand curve.
    Panel (b): Since total revenue increases as price falls from $25 to $20 to $15, demand is elastic over this range. Total revenue is at its maximum value of $450 when price equals $15; this corresponds to unit elasticity. For

further price decreases from $15 to $10 to $5, total revenue decreases, and hence, demand is inelastic along this portion of the demand curve.

3. (a) down; (b) none; (c) 1; (d) down; (e) up.

4. (a) The following measures express elasticity as: $(\Delta Q/\Delta P)(P_A/Q_A)$, where Q_A and P_A are the average quantity and price, respectively.
    A-B, η =(100/10)(65/50)=13.0;
    B-C, η =(200/20)(50/200)=2.5;
    C-D, η = (200/20)(30/400) = 0.75;
    D-E, η =(200/20)(10/600) = 0.167.
    (b) $\eta = (\Delta Q/\Delta P)(P_A/Q_A) = (100/10)(35/350) =$ 1.0. Over this interval, total revenue is constant. With further declines in price, total revenue will decline as we move into the inelastic portion of the demand curve.

*5. (a) Calculate arc elasticity from $1.25 to $1.35 so that the average price corresponds to the current fare of $1.30.

$$\eta = \frac{2,000}{0.10} \times \frac{1.30}{20,000} = 1.3$$

    (b) Since demand is elastic, any increase in price only serves to decrease total revenue. Thus, you should recommend that the price be decreased in order to increase total revenue.
    (c) Try successively lower fares until total revenue begins to decrease. The maximum total revenue is found to be $26,450, which will be obtained at a fare of $1.15 and a ridership of 23,000 passengers per day.

6. The Honourable Mr. D. Runken assumes a downward sloping demand curve for alcohol—as price increases, its consumption will fall. However, he also assumes that total expenditure on alcohol also decreases. This would only be correct if demand were elastic; in the case of alcohol, demand is more likely to be inelastic so that total expediture on alcohol would increase in response to higher taxes. The impact of this bill would be the exact opposite of what the MP intended.

7. (a) $\eta_s = 15/10 = 1.5$.

(b) The neceassary price change is 20 percent. It is obtained by dividing the output increase of 30 percent by the elasticity of 1.5. Since $\eta_s = \%\Delta Q / \%\Delta P$, it follows that $\%\Delta P = \%\Delta Q / \eta_s$.

(c) The fall in output is 7.5, which is calculated by multiplying the price decrease of 5 percent by the elasticity of 1.5.

*8. (a) Elasticity measures are calculated under the *ceteris paribus* assumption that other factors affecting demand are unchanged. Between periods 4 and 5, not only has income changed, but so have the prices of x and y.

(b) periods (1) to (2), price elasticity for
$$x = -\frac{9-10}{28-25} \times \frac{(28+25)/2}{(9+10)/2} = 0.93$$
periods (2) to (3), price elasticity for
$$y = -\frac{35-40}{15-10} \times \frac{(15+10)/2}{(35+40)/2} = 0.33$$
periods (3) to (4), income elasticity for
$$x = \frac{9-8}{11,000-10,000} \times \frac{(11,000+10,000)/2}{(9+8)/2} = 1.24$$
periods (3) to (4), income elasticity for
$$y = \frac{36-35}{11,000-10,000} \times \frac{(11,000+10,000)/2}{(36+5)/2} = 0.30$$
periods (1) to (2), cross-elasticity of demand for y with respect to the price of
$$x = \frac{40-42}{28-25} \times \frac{(28+25)/2}{(40+42)/2} = -0.43$$
periods (2) to (3), cross-elasticity of demand for x with respect to the price of
$$y = \frac{8-9}{15-10} \times \frac{(15+10)/2}{(8+9)/2} = 0.29$$

9. (a) Starting from the origin for S_1, the elasticities of supply are: $(100/20)(10/50) = (100/20)(30/50) = (100/20)(50/250) = 1.0$. For S_2 when price rises from 40 to 50, the price elasticity of supply is: $(200/10)(45/300) = 3.0$, but when price rises from 50 to 60, the elasticity is $(200/10)(55/500) = 2.2$.

(b) Because S_1 passes through the origin, P and Q always change in the same proportion, which gives an elasticity value of 1.

(c) S_3 implies that firms are willing to supply the good (300 units) even when the price they receive is zero.

10. (a) 1 and 6.   (b) 4.
(c) 5.   (d) 2.
(e) 3.   (f) 6.

11. (a) **Figure 5-10**

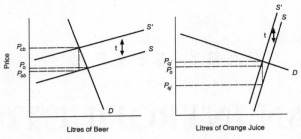

(b) The tax on beer is borne primarily by consumers. The relative slopes of the demand and supply curves in these markets suggest that the demand for beer is relatively inelastic, while its supply is relatively elastic.

(c) The tax on orange juice is borne primarily by producers. Demand in this market is relatively elastic, while supply is inelastic.

(d) The difference between consumer and seller prices are the same in each market. Specifically, the vertical distance by which each supply curve shifts is $t in each market.

12. (a) Point elasticity $= -1.00 = (-2 \ (10/20)$, or 1.00 neglecting the negative sign.

(b)

Price change	Arc elasticity
$18 to $10	2.33
$14 to $10	1.50
$12 to $10	1.22
$11 to $10	1.11

(c) As the change in price gets smaller, the values of arc elasticity and point elasticity converge. Thus, arc elasticity serves as a good approximation of point elasticity for small changes in price.

PART SEVEN

....

AN INTRODUCTION TO MACROECONOMICS

. . . .

CHAPTER 21

WHAT MACROECONOMICS IS ALL ABOUT

. . . .
CHAPTER OVERVIEW

Macroeconomics examines the behaviour of such broad aggregates and averages as the price level, national income (output), potential national income (output), the output or GDP gap, employment, unemployment, the exchange rate, and the balance of payments.

One central concept is the value of total output of the economy, which is often measured as gross domestic product (GDP). Comparing actual GDP to potential GDP indicates the economy's position of the business cycle and the social loss from unemployment and under-utilized resources. Long-term economic growth is reflected by an increasing GDP, which allows the standard of living to increase.

The average price level is measured by a price index, which measures the cost of a set of goods in one year relative to their cost in a "base" year. Extension 21.3 discusses how a consumer price index is constructed. The inflation rate measures the rate of change of the price level. Unexpected changes in inflation redistribute purchasing power within an economy. The expected rate of inflation is an important determinant of the nominal interest rate.

The exchange rate is the number of Canadian dollars needed to purchase one unit of foreign currency. A rise in the exchange rate is a reduction in the external value of the Canadian dollar. The balance of payments is a record of all international transactions made by Canadian firms, households, and governments.

. . . .
LEARNING OBJECTIVES

After studying this chapter, you should be able to:

■ distinguish how macroeconomics deals with the operation of the economy as a whole rather than the behaviour of individual markets;

■ explain the importance of key macroeconomic concepts such as gross domestic product, unemployment, inflation, economic growth, interest rates, the exchange rate, and the balance of payments;

■ recognize the issues that arise in measuring and interpreting these macroeconomic variables, especially the need to correct for inflation to express variables in *real* terms;

■ learn how to calculate an inflation rate from price index information;

■ understand the consequences of unanticipated and anticipated inflation on the purchasing power of various decision makers;

■ summarize long-term trends and short-term fluctuations in these macro variables over the past half century in Canada.

MULTIPLE-CHOICE QUESTIONS

1. Which of the following is not a macroeconomic issue?
   (a) Changes in the unemployment rate.
   (b) A fall in the Consumer Price Index.
   (c) Historical trends in the growth of real per capita national income.
   (d) Short-term fluctuations in national income around its long-run trend.
   (e) The change in the price of VCR machines relative to the price of movie theatre tickets.

2. Changes in real gross domestic product (GDP) reflect only changes in output, whereas changes in nominal GDP reflect
   (a) only price changes.
   (b) only changes in potential output.
   (c) changes in neither output nor price.
   (d) changes in both price and output.
   (e) only changes in real purchasing power.

3. If real potential GDP is 893 billion and current real GDP is 890 billion, then
   (a) there is an inflationary gap of 3 billion.
   (b) high-employment income levels have been surpassed.
   (c) there is a recessionary gap of 3 billion.
   (d) the GDP gap is positive.
   (e) Both (a) and (d).

4. In the long run, real national income grows when
   (a) there are persistent inflationary pressures on the economy.
   (b) the same amount of output can be produced by higher uses of resources.
   (c) the resource base, including population, increases.
   (d) output per capita decreases.
   (e) Both (b) and (c).

5. If employment in Canada is 12 million and unemployment is 1 million, the unemployment rate is
   (a) 13 million   (b) 7.7 percent.
   (c) 8.3 percent.   (d) 9.1 percent.
   (e) None of the above.

6. Full employment or high employment in Canada
   (a) implies that the measured unemployment rate is zero.
   (b) occurs when the NAIRU is zero.
   (c) occurs when the output gap is positive.
   (d) has not been achieved in the past 50 years.
   (e) occurs when the only existing unemployment is structural and frictional.

7. An example of frictional unemployment is when
   (a) carpenters are laid off because of a decline in housing starts.
   (b) Montreal textile workers lose jobs due to a loss in Canadian export shares of textile products in world markets.
   (c) unemployed textile workers are refused jobs since they do not have knowledge of computer software packages required by firms in another industry.
   (d) a teenager quits a job at K Mart in order to find a better-paying job at one of the three large department stores in the same city.
   (e) flight crews lose jobs when the airline industry restructures.

8. Actual GDP may exceed potential GDP for a short period of time when
   (a) the unemployment rate is high.
   (b) factors of production are employed at levels that are above normal utilization levels.
   (c) nominal GDP is less than real GDP.
   (d) there is a recessionary gap.
   (e) None of the above.

9. An economy that currently has a negative GDP gap
   (a) suffers a loss in output and economic well-being.
   (b) experiences less severe social problems because individuals are able to enjoy more leisure time.
   (c) has reached the peak stage of the business cycle.
   (d) will have rapidly rising prices.
   (e) Both (c) and (d).

10. If a particular index number in 1989 is 149 and the base year is 1986, then the index shows an increase of
    (a) 4.9 percent between 1986 and 1989.
    (b) 149 percent between 1986 and 1989.
    (c) 49 percent between 1986 and 1989.
    (d) .49 percent between 1986 and 1989.
    (e) An indeterminable percent, since the value of the index in 1986 is unknown.

11. The *Canadian Economic Observer* reported that the CPI increased from 129.6 to 130.0 between January and February 1993. Hence, the monthly inflation rate was
    (a) 0.3 percent.   (b) 0.4 percent.
    (c) 29.6 percent.   (d) 30.0 percent.
    (e) None of the above.

12. According to the information in question 11, the CPI between January and February 1993 was growing at an approximate annual rate of
    (a) 0.3 percent.   (b) 0.4 percent.
    (c) 3.6 percent.   (d) 4.8 percent.
    (e) None of the above.

13. The *Canadian Economic Observer* reported that the CPI increased from 132.1 to 134.4 from January 1995 to January 1996. The rate of inflation during that one-year period was
    (a) 2.3 percent.   (b) 1.7 percent.
    (c) 32.1 percent.   (d) 34.4 percent.
    (e) None of the above.

14. Suppose that a family's income grew from $38,000 to $38,500 from January 1995 to January 1996. Along with your answer to question 13, we can conclude that this family experienced
    (a) an increase in both nominal and real income.
    (b) a decrease in both nominal and real income.
    (c) a decrease in nominal income but an increase in real income.
    (d) a decrease in real income but an increase in nominal income.
    (e) an increase in nominal income but no change in real income.

15. Suppose that a price index was 160 last month and rose by 2 percent during the current month. The price index for the current month is
    (a) 162.0.   (b) 163.2.
    (c) 160.02.   (d) 198.4.
    (e) 192.

16. Unforeseen inflation is likely to
    (a) benefit creditors.
    (b) benefit pensioners whose monthly pension payments are fixed in nominal terms.
    (c) benefit landlords who, because of rent controls, cannot raise nominal rents during the lease period.
    (d) benefit those who have large balances in chequing accounts.
    (e) firms who have negotiated wage freezes in a new contract period.

17. Assume that prices over the year increase by 4 percent. Who of the following will experience a decrease in purchasing power?
    (a) A creditor who negotiated an annual contract at a nominal rate of interest of 6 percent and who wanted a 2 percent real rate of return.
    (b) A firm that is committed to increasing its wages by 5 percent over the year but whose prices are likely to increase only by the overall rate of inflation.
    (c) A person whose pension is totally indexed for price inflation.
    (d) A landlord who successfully negotiates a 7 percent increase in rent over the year.
    (e) An entrepreneur who makes a 5 percent annual rate of return on her wealth portfolio.

18. Inflation is likely to have no effects on purchasing power if
    (a) all decision makers know the inflation rate over the life of any contract.
    (b) all private financial obligations are stated in real terms.
    (c) all individuals are able to adjust quickly and easily to any inflation.
    (d) all tax liabilities are based on real incomes.
    (e) All of the above.

19. If inflation is expected to be 5 percent in the coming year and the annual nominal interest is 8 percent, then the real rate of interest is
(a) 13 percent. (b) 3 percent.
(c) –3 percent. (d) 40 percent.
(e) 0.4 percent.

20. Harry insists on an annual real rate of return of 4 percent. What nominal interest rate should he charge his brother, Bill, if he expects an annual inflation rate of 2.5 percent?
(a) 6.5 percent. (b) 2.5 percent.
(c) 1.5 percent. (d) 4 percent.
(e) less than 2.5 percent; after all, Bill is his brother.

21. If real national income grows 2 percent annually while population grows 3 percent annually, per capita real income is growing on annual basis at
(a) 6 percent. (b) 5 percent.
(c) 1 percent. (d) –1 percent.
(e) 50 percent.

22. The assumption that productivity and the labour force are constant in the short run means that any increase in real GDP will be accompanied by
(a) an increase in employment and a decrease in the unemployment rate.
(b) an increase in both employment and the unemployment rate.
(c) an increase in potential real GDP.
(d) a decrease in employment and the unemployment rate.
(e) a decrease in employment and an increase in the unemployment rate.

23. The *Canadian Economic Observer* reported that between 1989 and 1992, one German mark increased from 63.1 Canadian cents to 77.6 Canadian cents. Hence, from a Canadian perspective,
(a) the external value of the dollar increased.
(b) the exchange rate (the dollar price of marks) increased.
(c) the external value of the dollar decreased.
(d) Canadians could buy more marks per dollar in 1992 than in 1989.
(e) Both (b) and (c).

24. Between 1989 and 1990, the Japanese yen fell from .0086 Canadian dollars to .0081 Canadian dollars. It follows that
(a) the external value of the Canadian dollar rose from 116.3 yen to 123.5 yen.
(b) the external value of the Canadian dollar fell from 123.5 yen to 116.3 yen.
(c) it was more expensive for Canadians to buy yen in 1989 than in 1990.
(d) it was more expensive for the Japanese to buy Canadian dollars in 1989 than in 1990.
(e) None of the above.

25. If the value of a country's merchandise imports exceeded the value of its merchandise exports by $50 million, it follows that
(a) it has a $50 million deficit on its trade account.
(b) the country must also have a positive output gap of $50 million.
(c) its balance of payments must necessarily be in a deficit position of $50 million.
(d) Both (a) and (c).
(e) it has a $50 million surplus on its trade account.

• • • • • • • • • • • • •

EXERCISES

1. An economy produces four different goods and services within the current year. The level of production and the price per unit of each are listed here.

Item	Production level	Price per unit
Steel	500,000 tonnes	$100 per tonne
Wheat	15,000 tonnes	8 per tonne
Haircuts	6,000	9 each
Television sets	10,000 sets	500 per set

(a) Calculate the value of the economy's nominal national income in the current year.

55 174 000

(b) In the next year nominal national income is measured at $55,725,740. Express this value as an index of last year's value.

$$\frac{CURRENT}{BASE} \times 100 = \frac{55.725.740}{55174\,000} \times 100 = 101$$

(c) What is the percentage increase in nominal national income (compared with the base year)? Do this calculation two ways.

DIVIDE $\frac{CURRENT}{BASE}$ *= % change and PI 101*

implies 1% ↑

2. Here are some historical data for Canadian national income measured in terms of gross domestic product (GDP). The first column refers to current dollar (nominal) GDP, the second displays constant dollar (real) GDP, and the third refers to real potential GDP. All values are in billions. Real GDP uses 1981 prices (1981 = 100).

Year	Current GDP	Real GDP	Real potential GDP
1980	309.9	343.4	348.7
1981	356.0	356.0	362.7
1982	374.4	344.5	372.6
1983	405.7	355.5	376.0
1984	444.7	377.9	385.9
1985	478.0	395.9	398.6
1986	504.6	408.1	411.8
1987	550.3	426.4	426.6
1988	601.5	447.8	446.1
1989	648.5	460.6	464.1

(a) Express the 1985 constant dollar value of GDP as an index (to one decimal place) of the 1981 constant dollar value of GDP. Do the same for the 1980 constant dollar value of GDP as an index in terms of 1981.

$\frac{395.9}{356.0} \times 100 = 111.21$ / $\frac{343.4}{356.00} \times 100 = 96.46$

(b) What is the value of the output gap in 1984? In 1988? Were resources fully employed in these two years?

-385.9 + 377.9 = -8.0 → 1984 No
-447.8 - 446.1 = 1.7 → 1988 Yes

(c) What phase of the business cycle is represented by the 1981-1982 period?

RECESSION - INFLATION GAP -↑ 80-81-82 ⇒ RECESSION Trough

(d) What was the percentage increase in current dollar GDP between 1981 and 1985? What was the percentage increase in constant dollar (real) GDP in the same period? What does the difference in the two percentages represent (approximately)?

%34 - %11.2 - 23% in Total output - Prices increase

3. You are given the following price indexes for various years. The base year (year 1) has an index of 100.

Year	Price index	Annual inflation rate (percent)
7	118.1	n.a.
8	121.9	3.2
9	125.1	2.6
10	126.5	1.1

(a) Calculate the annual inflation rate (to one decimal place) for years 8 and 9, and fill in the blanks in the third column.

(b) What was the inflation rate over the period from the base year through year 9?

26.5

(c) Calculate (to one decimal place) the price index for year 1.

4. The following table provides information about the Canadian economy for a seven-year period.

Year	Real GDP 1986 prices	Labour force (billions)	Unemployment (thousands) Unemployed	Employed	Rate (percent)	Population (millions)
1985	489.4	12,532	1311	11,221	10.461	25.2
1986	505.7	12,746	1,215	11531	9.532	25.3
1987	526.7	13,011	1150	11861	8.839	25.6
1988	553.0	13,275	1,031	12244	7.77	25.9
1989	565.8	13,503	1,018	10,597	7.539	26.2
1990	563.1	13681	1,109	12,572	8.106	26.6
1991	553.5	13,757	1,417	12,340	10.30	27.0

(a) Fill in the missing values in the table.

(b) Calculate the percentage change in real GDP between 1987 and 1988. Compare this value with the percentage change in employment in this period. Do the same analysis for the two-year period 1990-91.

a) 5%   b) -1%   c) -2%   d) 2.2%

(c) Does there appear to be a positive or negative relationship between real GDP and employment for these two periods?

negative

(d) Between 1989 and 1990 the unemployment rate increased while employment increased. How is this possible?

Increase Labour Force

(e) Calculate the value of real per capita GDP for 1985 and 1991.

'85 = 19.4   '91 = 20.5

5. The exchange rate is another important macroeconomic variable discussed in Chapter 21. The information here is intended to provide practice interpreting exchange rate changes. The values are actual figures for the Canadian dollar relative to both the German mark and the Japanese yen.

Year	Exchange Rate Dollars per mark	Dollars per yen	External Value of the Dollar Marks per dollar	Yen per dollar
1991	$0.924	$0.01418	_____	_____
1992	0.934	0.01427	_____	_____
1993	1.001	_____	_____	64.267
1994	_____	0.01625	1.003	_____

(a) Fill in the missing entries.

(b) Over the period 1991-92, the external value of the dollar with respect to the German mark (increased, decreased) and the external value of the dollar with respect to the yen (increased, decreased). Over the period 1992-93, the external value of the dollar with respect to the mark and the yen (decreased, increased).

(c) Suppose that you paid 100 marks for a one-year asset at the end of 1991 (at an exchange rate of $0.924). How many dollars did you require to buy this asset?

(d) If the German asset had an annual nominal interest rate of 6 percent, how many marks would you have received at the end of 1992? How many Canadian dollars would you have received when you converted the marks into dollars at the end of 1992? What would be your rate of return over the year as a percentage of the dollar amount you invested?

(e) Suppose that at the end of 1993 you purchased (at an exchange rate of 1.001) a one-year asset worth 10,000 marks, which promised a nominal interest rate of 6 percent. What would be your rate of return at the end of 1994 as a percentage of the dollar amount you invested at the end of 1993?

6. This problem deals with the real interest rate on five-year conventional mortgages in Canada. Suppose that the lender, a financial institution, wishes to have a 4 percent real rate of return on an annual basis. Consider the following data. The nominal interest rates are stated for five-year conventional mortgages beginning in 1975, 1980, and 1985.

Year	Nominal annual interest rate on new five-year mortgages	Annual average inflation rate Expected	Actual	Period
1975	11.4	_____	8.9	1975-1979
1980	14.3	_____	8.7	1980-1984
1985	12.2	_____	4.3	1985-1989

(a) Calculate the institution's expected annual rate of inflation when it set the five-year mortgage rate in 1975. Do the same for the two other five-year periods, and complete the entries in the table.

(b) By comparing the actual annual inflation rate with the nominal interest rate, in what five-year periods did the financial institution make more than its 4 percent real rate of interest on five-year mortgages?

(c) If borrowers shared the same expectations of inflation rates with the financial institution, in what five-year periods did borrowers unexpectedly pay less than a 4 percent real rate of interest?

7. Canadian international trade in goods and services is shown below (in millions of dollars).

Year	Exports	Imports	Net exports
1992	181,190	187,256	_____
1993	209,369	212,534	_____
1994	249,373	243,756	_____

(a) Calculate net exports in each of the three years.
(b) Which year(s) did Canada have a trade surplus?

8. This exercise features the construction of a Consumer Price Index, which is explained in Extension 21.3. Suppose that the government's data collection agency has estimated the prices of six broad groups of consumer expenditure as well as the *average* proportions of consumers' income that is spent on these expenditure groups as follows:

	Prices (base year)	Prices (next year)	Proportion of income consumers spend (on average)
Shelter	$3,000	$3,300	30%
Food	2,500	2,500	25
Transportation	5,000	5,000	15
Clothing	100	110	10
Entertainment	60	60	10
Other	300	330	10

(a) Compute the average price level in the base year and in the next year. (Assume that the proportions do not change.)

(b) The price index for the base year, by definition, is 100. Compute the price index for the next year.

(c) You may have noticed that the price of shelter, clothing, and other goods increased by 10 percent each. Does your answer to (b) indicate a 10 percent increase in the price index from the base year? Why or why not?

(d) Suppose that a group of households in this country consumes the products listed in the table in the following proportions: shelter, 40 percent; food, 30 percent; transportation, 5 percent; clothing, 15 percent; entertainment, 0 percent; other, 10 percent. Does the increase in the overall price index in (b) underestimate or overestimate the cost of living increase for this particular group of households?

•••••••••••••

ANSWERS
Multiple-Choice Questions

1.	(e)	**2.**	(d)	**3.**	(c)	**4.**	(c)	**5.**	(b)
6.	(e)	**7.**	(d)	**8.**	(b)	**9.**	(a)	**10.**	(c)
11.	(a)	**12.**	(c)	**13.**	(b)	**14.**	(d)	**15.**	(b)
16.	(e)	**17.**	(b)	**18.**	(e)	**19.**	(b)	**20.**	(a)
21.	(d)	**22.**	(a)	**23.**	(e)	**24.**	(a)	**25.**	(a)

Exercises

1. (a) $55,174,000. (Calculate price times quantity for each item and add the products of the four equations together.)
   (b) 101. (55,725,740 divided by 55,174,000 × 100.)
   (c) 1 percent. This can be obtained two ways. First, divide the change in income (551,740) by 55,174,000 and multiply by 100 percent. Alternatively, the index value for the next year indicates that the nominal value of output has increased by 1 percent.

2. (a) For 1985: 111.2 (395.9 divided by 356.0 × 100). For 1980: 96.5 (343.4 divided by 356.0 × 100).
   (b) The output gap is defined as actual real GDP minus real potential GDP. Hence there was a negative output gap of –8 (377.9 – 385.9) in 1984 and a positive output gap of +1.7 in 1988. There was unused productive capacity (less than full employment) in 1984, whereas resources in 1988 were fully employed, although their utilization rate was greater than the normal rate of utilization.
   (c) Between the two years, real GDP fell and the output gap increased (compare –6.7 with –8.1). This period represented a recessionary phase or a slump. The trough occurred sometime in 1982.
   (d) Current dollar GDP increased by 34.3 percent; constant (real) dollar GDP increased by 11.2 percent. The difference between these

represents approximately the percentage increase in prices of all final goods and services over this period.

3. (a) Year 8: 3.2 percent (3.8 divided by 118.1 × 100 percent).
      Year 9: 2.6 percent (3.2 divided by 121.9 × 100 percent).
   (b) 25.1 percent.
   (c) 126.5 (125.1 × 1.011).

4. (a) Labour force: 1990: 13,681 (1,109 + 12,572). Unemployed: 1985: 1,311 (12,532 – 11,221); 1987: 1,150 (13,011 × .08839). Employed: 1986: 11,531 (12,746 –1,215); 1987: 11,861 (13,011 – 1,150); 1988: 12,244 (13,275 – 1,031). Unemployment rate: 1988: 7.766 (1031/13,275 × 100%); 1991: 10.300 (1,417/13,757 × 100%).
   (b) 1987-88; real GDP increased by 4.99 percent while employment increased by 3.23 percent. 1990-91; real GDP decreased by 1.70 percent while employment decreased by 1.85 percent.
   (c) Positive relationship; they changed in the same direction.
   (d) The labour force increased more in percentage terms than did employment. That is, more of those who entered the labour force became unemployed than employed.
   (e) 1985: $19,421; 1991: $20,500.

5. (a) Marks per dollar: 1991: 1.082; 1992: 1.071; 1993: 0.999.
      Yen per dollar: 1991: 70.52; 1992: 70.08; 1994: 61.54.
      Dollars per yen: 1993: 00156.
      Dollars per mark: 1994: 0.997.
   (b) Decreased, decreased; decreased.
   (c) $92.40.
   (d) 106 marks (100 × 1.06); $99.00 (106 × .934); 7.14 percent [($6.60/$92.40) × 100%].
   (e) To obtain 10,000 marks in 1993, you paid $10,010. At the end of 1994 you receive

10,600 marks, which converted into Canadian currency is $10,568. Your return is 5.6 percent.

6. (a) Expected inflation: 1975: 7.4 percent (11.4 – 4.0); 1980: 10.3 percent; 1985: 8.2 percent.
   (b) Mortgages in 1980 yielded annually over five years 5.6 percent in real terms (14.3 – 8.7), and mortgages in 1985 garnered a 7.9 percent real rate of return per annum.
   (c) Mortgages extended over the 1975-79 period; the actual, real rate of interest was 2.5 percent (11.4 – 8.9).

7. (a) Net exports are defined as exports minus imports. Net exports were –6,066 in 1992; –3,165 in 1993; +5,617 in 1994.
   (b) There was a trade surplus in 1994, trade deficits in 1992 and 1993.

8. (a) Base year: $(3,000 \times 0.3) + (2,500 \times 0.25) + (5,000 \times 0.15) + (100 \times 0.1) + (60 \times 0.1) + (300 \times 0.1) = 2,321$.
   Next year: $(3,300 \times 0.3) + (2,500 \times 0.25) + (5,000 \times 0.15) + (110 \times 0.1) + (60 \times 0.1) + (330 \times 0.1) = 2,415$.
   (b) Index = $(2,415/2,321) \times 100 = 104.0$.
   (c) No; prices increased by approximately 4 percent. Shelter, clothing, and other goods are only 50 percent of total expenditures.
   (d) The price increase from the base year for this group of households (using their fixed weights) is 5.5 percent. Hence, the overall price increase reflected by the overall price index underestimates the cost of living increase of this group.

CHAPTER 22
....

THE MEASUREMENT OF NATIONAL INCOME AND PRODUCT

....

CHAPTER OVERVIEW

Each firm's contribution to total output is equal to its value added. The sum of all the values added produced in an economy is the economy's total output, which is called gross domestic product (GDP).

GDP can be calculated from the expenditure side, from the income side, or as the sum of values added in the economy. The expenditure side gives the total value of expenditures required to purchase the nation's output, and the income side gives the total value of income claims generated by the production of that output. By standard accounting conventions, these three aggregations define the same total.

Several concepts related to GDP are discussed, including gross national product and personal disposable income. Nominal GDP is distinguished from real GDP. Real measures of national income are calculated to reflect changes in real quantities. Nominal measures of GDP are calculated to reflect changes in both prices and quantities. Appropriate comparisons of nominal and real measures yield implicit or GDP deflators.

GDP must be interpreted with its limitations in mind. GDP excludes illegal, unreported, and nonmarket activities and economic "bads." Hence, GDP does not measure everything that contributes to (or detracts from) human welfare.

....

LEARNING OBJECTIVES

After studying this chapter, you should be able to:

- recognize how summing the value added at each stage of production gives the value of final goods sold (the gross domestic product);
- understand how the value of final output also can be calculated by summing expenditures for currently produced final goods or from the income generated in their production;
- distinguish the four broad categories of final expenditures (consumption, investment, government expenditure, and net exports) and the reasons for treating them separately;
- explain how income received by various factors of production enters the national income accounts;
- understand how to calculate real GDP using implicit deflators;
- summarize major criticisms of national income as a measure of economic welfare, particularly when omitted items are important.

MULTIPLE-CHOICE QUESTIONS

1. Value added in production is equal to
    (a) total value of output excluding the value of intermediate goods.
    (b) profits of all firms.
    (c) total value of output including intermediate goods.
    (d) the total costs in producing final outputs.
    (e) Both (a) and (d).

2. Estimating final output (GDP) by adding the sales of all firms
    (a) will overstate total output because it counts the output of intermediate goods more than once.
    (b) will understate the total value of national output.
    (c) is a measure of income accruing to Canadian residents.
    (d) provides the same value as net national income.
    (e) is the best measure of economic activity.

3. Suppose that a firm sells its output for $40,000, that it pays $22,000 in wages, $10,000 for materials purchased from other firms, and $3,000 to bankers, and that it declares profits of $5,000. The firm's value added is
    (a) $18,000.   (b) $40,000.
    (c) $30,000.   (d) $35,000.
    (e) $22,000.

4. Which of the following would *not* be included in measures of the consumption component of aggregate expenditure?
    (a) Expenditures for new houses.
    (b) Expenditures for durable goods, such as new automobiles.
    (c) Expenditures for services.
    (d) Expenditures for nondurable goods.
    (e) Expenditures on rental accommodations by households.

5. Suppose that the steel industry has a total output of $63.8 billion and purchases $49.0 billion in intermediate inputs. Hence, the value added in billions of the steel industry in that period is

    (a) $112.8.   (b) –$14.8.
    (c) $63.8.   (d) $14.8.
    (e) $49.0.

6. Which of the following would *not* be included in the measures of the investment component of aggregate expenditure?
    (a) Sally Smith buys Canadian Airlines International shares.
    (b) An accounting firm buys three personal computers.
    (c) General Motors (Canada) increases its inventory holdings of parts produced in Brantford, Ontario.
    (d) A construction company builds 20 new homes in Kelowna, British Columbia.
    (e) An oil company expands its refinery facilities in Calgary, Alberta.

7. Which of the following would *not* be included in measures of the government expenditure component of aggregate expenditure?
    (a) Salaries of civil servants whose responsibilities include the collection of the Goods and Service Tax (GST).
    (b) The city of Moncton's purchase of forms from a Mississauga, Ontario, printing company.
    (c) Canada pension payments to residents of Sherbrooke, Quebec.
    (d) Expenditures for new naval minesweepers built in Nova Scotia.
    (e) The government of Newfoundland pays a New York engineering consulting company.

8. Gross domestic product
    (a) is equal to net national product minus depreciation.
    (b) excludes indirect taxes but includes capital consumption allowances.
    (c) must equal gross national product since both include capital consumption allowances.
    (d) includes replacement investment, which is measured by the level of capital consumption allowances.
    (e) is equal to GNP plus capital consumption allowances.

9. GDP from the income side of the national accounts
   (a) usually results in a higher value for total national income than results from the expenditure side of the national accounts.
   (b) usually results in a lower value for total national income than the two other approaches since owner–occupier rents are excluded from the income side.
   (c) includes the value of indirect business taxes.
   (d) includes investment expenditure.
   (e) excludes depreciation.

10. National income can be correctly measured in *all but which* of the following ways?
    (a) By the market value of final goods and services produced.
    (b) By adding all money transactions in the economy, including purchases of financial assets.
    (c) By the market value of expenditures made to purchase final output.
    (d) By the value of payments made to factors of production that have been used to produce final goods and services.
    (e) Both (b) and (d).

11. Disposable personal income is
    (a) always the same as personal income.
    (b) income that is used only for consumption.
    (c) personal income remaining after net income taxes.
    (d) exclusive of transfer payments such as unemployment insurance payments.
    (e) personal income minus capital consumption allowances.

12. Which of the following would *not* be included in the measurement of GDP from the income side of the national accounts?
    (a) Consumption expenditures.
    (b) Depreciation or capital consumption allowances.
    (c) Indirect business taxes net of subsidies.
    (d) Wages and salaries.
    (e) Profits.

13. In a particular year an economy's GDP is $401 billion, net payments to foreigners are $46 billion, and indirect taxes less subsidies are $5 billion. The value of the economy's GNP is
   (a) $447 billion.   (b) $355 billion.
   (c) $350 billion.   (d) $360 billion.
   (e) $452 billion.

14. If nominal GDP is $150 and real GDP is $125, the value of the implicit deflator is
    (a) 120.   (b) 0.83.
    (c) 1.2.   (d) 83.
    (e) 125.

15. If an economy's annual nominal GDP increases by 11 percent and prices increase on an annual basis by 9 percent, then real GDP
    (a) increases by approximately 18.3 percent.
    (b) increases by 1.8 percent.
    (c) decreases by approximately 1.8 percent.
    (d) decreases by $2/9 \times 100$ percent.
    (e) remains constant.

16. If nominal GDP rises from $400 billion to $408 billion and the implicit GDP deflator rises from 125 to 127,
    (a) real GDP has risen from 3.2 billion to 3.21 billion.
    (b) real GDP has risen from 500 billion to 518 billion.
    (c) real GDP is unchanged.
    (d) everyone is necessarily better off since nominal GDP has increased.
    (e) real GDP has risen from 320 billion to 321 billion.

17. If do-it-yourself homeowners stopped building their backyard decks and instead hired self-employed university students, then national income would
    (a) be reduced as now measured.
    (b) be unaffected if the students reported their earnings.
    (c) increase if the students reported their earnings.
    (d) be unaffected since the students are not wage earners.
    (e) include only the costs of materials, but not wages.

18. The implicit deflator
    (a) can be used only on the expenditure side of the national accounts.
    (b) is GDP at base-period prices divided by GDP at current prices times 100.
    (c) is the index used to measure the prices of goods and services purchased by households.
    (d) is GDP at current prices divided by GDP at base-period prices times 100.
    (e) is both (b) and (c).

19. GDP understates the total production of goods and services for *all but which* of the following reasons?
    (a) No allowances are included for the imputed rents of owner–occupied homes.
    (b) Illegal activities are not included in the GDP estimate.
    (c) Legal production in the "underground economy" is not reported for income tax purposes.
    (d) Nonmarketed household services such as gardening and cleaning performed by family members are not included.
    (e) Both (c) and (d).

20. If the implicit deflator increased from 120 in year 7 to 126 in year 8, then prices of final goods and services
    (a) increased 20 percent on average from the base year to year 7.
    (b) increased 5 percent on average between years 7 and 8.
    (c) increased by 6 percent since the index increased by 6 points.
    (d) Both (a) and (b).
    (e) None of the above.

21. Measured from the expenditure side, GDP equals
    (a) $C_a + I_a + G_a + (X_a - IM_a)$.
    (b) $C_a + I_a + G_a - T_a + (X_a - IM_a)$.
    (c) $C_a + I_a + G_a - X_a + IM_a$.
    (d) GNP minus depreciation.
    (e) None of the above.

22. Company *XYZ* receives $50 million from a new issue of stock. It uses $30 million of the proceeds to build a new factory and uses the other $20 million to pay back loans from various banks. This transaction increases measured

GDP in millions of dollars by
    (a) 50.   (b) 30.
    (c) 20.   (d) 100.
    (e) 80.

23. Which of the following statements is correct since the mid-1970s in Canada?
    (a) GDP per capita increased.
    (b) The labour force per capita grew.
    (c) There was a slowdown in productivity growth accompanied by a marked increase in both the number of workers and hours of work relative to the population.
    (d) All of the above.
    (e) None of the above.

24. As a measure of human economic welfare, GDP may be inadequate because it
    (a) overemphasizes the inequality of the distribution of income.
    (b) overstates the value of nonmarket work, such as home do-it-yourself activities.
    (c) focuses on production, not income.
    (d) ignores the influence of government transfer programs on household spending.
    (e) ignores the way current production methods may reduce the quality of life.

For questions 25 to 34, identify the items in the statements according to the following code: *C* = consumption; *I* = investment; *G* = government spending on goods and services; *NX* = net exports (*X* – *IM*); and *N* = not a component of aggregate spending.

25. The Bank of Nova Scotia expands its computer facilities in its Toronto head office.
    (a) *C*.   (b) *I*.
    (c) *G*.   (d) *NX*.
    (e) *N*.

26. As part of her duties, the sales manager of a Canadian-based company stays at the Savoy Hotel in London, England.
    (a) *C*.   (b) *I*.
    (c) *G*.   (d) *NX*.
    (e) *N*.

27. China buys beef cattle from Alberta beef cattle breeders.
    (a) *C*.   (b) *I*.
    (c) *G*.   (d) *NX*.
    (e) *N*.

28. Canadians purchase $5 billion in newly constructed homes.
(a) *C.*   (b) *I.*
(c) *G.*   (d) *NX.*
(e) *N.*

29. Montreal Stock Exchange sales in January are $2 billion.
(a) *C.*   (b) *I.*
(c) *G.*   (d) *NX.*
(e) *N.*

30. Nova Scotians take holidays in Prince Edward Island.
(a) *C.*   (b) *I.*
(c) *G.*   (d) *NX.*
(e) *N.*

31. The government of New Brunswick pays for the services of a Vancouver consulting company.

(a) *C.*   (b) *I.*
(c) *G.*   (d) *NX.*
(e) *N.*

32. Sue buys a used motorcycle from her friend Chuck.
(a) *C.*   (b) *I.*
(c) *G.*   (d) *NX.*
(e) *N.*

33. General Motors (Canada) increases its inventory holdings of glass windshields.
(a) *C.*   (b) *I.*
(c) *G.*   (d) *NX.*
(e) *N.*

34. The city of Cornerbrook issues welfare cheques to some of its needy residents.
(a) *C.*   (b) *I.*
(c) *G.*   (d) *NX.*
(e) *N.*

• • • • • • • • • • • • •

EXERCISES

1. The value of a product in its final form is the sum of the value added by each of the various firms throughout the production process. Using the information provided here, calculate the value of one loaf of bread that is ultimately sold to a household. In doing so, calculate the value added at each stage of production. (This example demonstrates that the value-added approach avoids multiple counting.)

Stage of production	Selling price to the next stage	Value added
1. Farmer (production of wheat)	$0.30	$ _____
2. Milling company (flour)	0.55	$ _____
3. Bakery (production of wholesale bread)	0.90	$ _____
4. Retailer (sale to household)	1.00	$ _____
Total	2.75	

2. You are given the following information about the Canadian economy over the five-year period 1987-1991. All GDP values are in billions of dollars, the population figures are in millions, and all indices have a base year of 1986 (1986=100).

Year	Current dollar GDP	Real deflator	Implicit GDP	Population	Index of output per person employed
1987	551.6	104.7	_____	25.6	101.9
1988	605.9	_____	553.0	25.9	103.1
1989	649.9	114.8	566.1	26.2	102.4
1990	_____	118.6	563.1	26.6	101.7
1991	674.4	121.8	_____	27.0	102.3

Source: *Economic Reference Tables*, Department of Finance, August 1992.

(a) Fill in the missing entries in the table.

(b) Current dollar GDP increased by 9.84 percent between 1987 and 1988. Calculate the percentage increases in constant dollar (real) income and in the implicit deflator. Why doesn't the sum of the two percentages equal the percentage increase in nominal GDP?

(c) Calculate the growth rate in real GDP per capita for 1987-1988 and 1990-1991. Which of the two periods is likely to represent a recessionary phase of the economy?

(d) Calculate the growth rate in "productivity" as measured by output per person employed for 1987-1988 and 1988-1989.

3. This exercise focuses on nominal and real output and the implicit deflator. Assume that there are only two industries in an economy. Output and unit price for each industry are shown for three years. Year 1 is the base year.

Year	Quantity of industry A (tonnes)	Quantity of industry B (metres)	Price in industry A (per tonne)	Price in industry B (per metre)
1	4,000	20,000	$20	$5
2	6,000	21,000	22	4
3	6,000	18,000	24	6

(a) Calculate the nominal value of output in industry A in each of the three years. Do the same for industry B. Find national output in nominal terms for each of the three years by adding the two output values for A and B.

(b) Recalling that year 1 is the base year, calculate the real value of output in industry A for each of the three years. Do the same for industry B. What is the value of real output in the economy for each of the three years? (Use base year prices.)

(c) Calculate the value of the implicit deflator for each of the three years.

4. Suppose that the total output of the metal container industry was $11,522 million and $7,938 million in intermediate inputs were purchased to produce that amount in 1987.
   (a) Calculate the value added in the metal container industry in 1987.

   (b) Indicate which of the following items represent value added in the metal container industry:
      — payment for independent auditors to examine business accounts
      — wages of production workers who make cans
      — profits of metal container companies
      — payments for aluminum used in producing cans
      — interest paid to banks by metal container companies

5. There are two other methods of measuring GDP—from the income side and from the expenditure side. This problem deals with the calculation of gross domestic product using these two approaches. Select only the appropriate items. (Figures are in billions of dollars.)

Government purchases of goods and services	$ 58.5
Indirect taxes less subsidies	29.0
Personal income taxes	41.5
Wages and employee compensation (including personal income taxes)	165.5
Interest on the public debt	15.5
Consumption expenditure	168.4
Exports	90.9
Capital consumption allowance	33.5
Imports	93.3
Gross investment	67.2
Net interest income	19.0
Statistical discrepancy (expenditure side)	+ 0.2
Corporate profits before taxes	36.5
Rental income plus net farm income plus net income of unincorporated business	8.6
Statistical discrepancy (income side)	–0.2

Calculate the following values.
(a) GDP from the income side. _____
(b) GDP from the expenditure side. _____
(c) Assuming that net payments to foreigners had been $8 billion, calculate the value of GNP. _____

6. This exercise focuses on other measures of national income. You are given the following national income measures for an economy in a particular year. (Figures are in billions of dollars.)

Gross domestic product at market prices	$285
Capital consumption allowances (depreciation)	32
Retained earnings	12
Government transfers to households	30
Personal income taxes	42
Indirect taxes less subsidies	30
Consumer expenditure	168
Business taxes	12
Net foreign investment income received	5

(a) Calculate the value for personal disposable income.

(b) Define personal saving as personal disposable income minus consumption expenditure. What is its magnitude?

7. Which of the following transactions (or events) will be recorded in the GDP accounts in that year? Explain.

(a) Jim, who normally earns $20 per hour, volunteers 100 hours of his time to assist a local politician in the 1996 B.C. provincial election.

(b) The federal government sends three Canadian warships to the Persian Gulf area during the Iraq–Kuwait crisis in August 1990.

(c) Drug smugglers, using funds from the drug trade, purchase a new hotel in Vancouver.

(d) A self-employed carpenter buys $1,000 worth of nails and lumber to build a fence for one of his customers. He charges the customer $1,800 but doesn't report the $800 of wages or profits to the tax authorities.

(e) Pollution of the Toronto beachfront forces the City of Toronto to lay off three lifeguards.

(f) All welfare recipients in St. John's are hired as municipal workers.

(g) Publicly supported abortion clinics are closed when the Supreme Court rules that abortions are illegal under the Criminal Code.

8. Figures for the GDP and GNP 1990 values are reported below for five countries (in billions of units of their home currency).

Country	GDP	GNP	Currency
Canada	661.2	636.9	dollar
United States	5,392.2	5,441.0	dollar
Switzerland	314.0	327.6	franc
France	6,492.0	6,468.7	franc
Japan	425,735.0	428,667.0	yen

Source: *National Accounts, Main Aggregates*, OECD, Paris, 1992 and 1993.

(a) Explain what the difference between GDP and GNP implies about net payments of factor income in each country to the rest of the world.

(b) Calculate the Canadian dollar value (in billions) of France's nominal GDP at an exchange rate of .215 Canadian dollars per franc.

(c) Which countries are net creditors on a world-wide basis?

• • • • • • • • • • • • • •

ANSWERS
Multiple-Choice Questions

1. (a)	2. (a)	3. (c)	4. (a)	5. (d)
6. (a)	7. (c)	8. (d)	9. (c)	10. (b)
11. (c)	12. (a)	13. (b)	14. (a)	15. (b)
16. (e)	17. (c)	18. (d)	19. (a)	20. (d)
21. (a)	22. (b)	23. (d)	24. (e)	25. (b)
26. (d)	27. (d)	28. (b)	29. (e)	30. (a)
31. (c)	32. (e)	33. (b)	34. (e)	

EXERCISES

1. (a) The market value of one loaf of bread is $1.00. This is found by the sum of the value added (0.30 from the first stage plus 0.25 from the second stage plus 0.35 from the third stage plus 0.10 from the fourth stage). Thus, the sum of the valued added at each stage equals the value of the final product. Notice that the total $2.75 counts the contribution of the farmer four times.

2. (a) GDP in constant dollars: 1987: 526.8 (551.6 ÷ 1.047); 1991: 553.7.

Implicit deflator: 1988: 109.6 [(605.9 ÷ 553.0) × 100).

GDP in current dollars: 1990: 667.8 (563.1 × 1.186).

(b) Real GDP increased by 4.97 percent while the prices increased by 4.68 percent. The increase in nominal GDP is equal to the product of the two (1.0497)(1.0468) rather than the sum of the two percentages. See footnote #6 in the textbook chapter.

(c) The growth rate in real GDP per capita for 1987-1988 is calculated by first determining real GDP per capita for each of the years. In 1987 per capita real GDP is $20,578 (526.8 billion ÷ 25.6 million) and in 1988 it is $21,351, and hence the percentage increase is 3.76 percent. The percentage change in real per capita GDP between 1990 and 1991 is –3.13 percent (–662 ÷ 21,169 × 100%). The period 1990-1991 was considered a recessionary period.

(d) The percentage changes in productivity in 1987-1988 and 1988-1989 were 1.2 percent and –0.7 percent, respectively.

3. (a)

	Nominal value of output		
Year	In A	In B	In economy
1	80,000	100,000	180,000
2	132,000	84,000	216,000
3	144,000	108,000	252,000

(b) Industry A: real value:
in year 1 = 4,000 × 20 = 80,000.
in year 2 = 6,000 × 20 = 120,000.
in year 3 = 6,000 × 20 = 120,000.
Industry B, real value:
in year 1 = 20,000 × 5 = 100,000.
in year 2 = 21,000 × 5 = 105,000.
in year 3 = 18,000 × 5 = 90,000.
Real output in economy:
in year 1 = 80,000 + 100,000 = 180,000.
in year 2 = 120,000 + 105,000 = 225,000.
in year 3 = 120,000 + 90,000 = 210,000.

(c) Year 1: 180,000 ÷ 180,000 × 100 = 100.0.
Year 2: 216,000 ÷ 225,000 × 100 = 96.0.
Year 3: 252,000 ÷ 210,000 × 100 = 120.0.

4. (a) $3,584 = $11,522 – $7,938.
(b) Items that represent value added are wages of production workers, profits of metal container companies, and interest paid by metal container companies. Payments for aluminum or independent auditors are intermediate inputs.

5. (a) 29.0 + 165.5 + 33.5 + 19.0 + 36.5 + 8.6 – 0.2 = 291.9.
(b) 58.5 + 168.4 + 67.2 + 90.9 – 93.3 + 0.2 = 291.9.
(c) 291.9 – 8.0 = 283.9.

6. (a) Personal disposable income = GDP + net foreign investment income – capital consumption allowance – indirect taxes less subsidies – retained earnings – business taxes + government transfers – personal income taxes; 285 + 5 – 32 – 30 – 12 – 12 + 30 – 42 = 192.
(b) Personal saving = personal disposable income minus consumption expenditure; in this case, $S = 192 – 168 = 24$.

7. (a) This is an example of a nonmarketed activity and therefore would not be included in GDP accounts. If the politician had paid Jim $2,000 for his 100 hours of work, then Jim's income would have been included in the GDP accounts.
(b) This is a straightforward example of a government expenditure that would be recorded in the GDP accounts.
(c) Even though the funds used to purchase the hotel are from illegal activities, the actual purchase would be recorded in the investment component of the GDP accounts.
(d) The $1,000 purchase of nails and lumber would be recorded in the GDP accounts. The carpenter's value added ($800) is not included since the carpenter did not report his income. The $800 represents an "underground" economy transaction.
(e) Although pollution costs are not recorded in the GDP accounts, the effects of pollution on market activity can appear in the GDP accounts. In this case, three lifeguards lost their jobs, and hence the income approach will indicate a decline in overall income (assuming that they were unemployed for a period of time after their dismissal).
(f) The income paid to welfare recipients is not included in the measure of GDP. However, if all were hired as municipal workers, their salaries would be included in the government expenditure component of aggregate expenditures.
(g) Abortion clinics, if financed by some level of government, would be included in the expenditure approach in measuring GDP. However, all other things being equal, their closure would decrease government expenditure. The purchases of abortion services from illegal, private clinics would presumably not be recorded in the GDP accounts.

8. (a) GNP is greater than GDP for the United States, Switzerland, and Japan, while GNP is less than GDP for Canada and France. Clearly, Canada and France made net payments to the rest of the world. The other three countries received net payments from the rest of the world.
(b) 1,395.8 billion Canadian dollars (6,492 × .215).
(c) Japan, Switzerland, and the United States.

PART EIGHT

NATIONAL INCOME AND FISCAL POLICY

CHAPTER 23
• • • • • • • • • • • • • • •

NATIONAL INCOME AND AGGREGATE EXPENDITURE I: CONSUMPTION AND INVESTMENT

• • • • • • • • • • • • • •
CHAPTER OVERVIEW

The previous chapter explained how actual national output and actual components of income are measured. The next four chapters discuss how equilibrium national income is determined. This chapter imposes three simplifying conditions: the price level is fixed and the economy has no government or foreign trade. We focus on two sources of desired demand: consumption and investment. Desired consumption is an increasing function of disposable income. If consumption is known, saving is known, too, since disposable income must be consumed or saved. Desired investment is treated as an *autonomous* expenditure, determined by variables other than the level of national income.

A key relationship in this chapter is the consumption function: the relationship between disposable income and consumption. The constant term in the consumption function is autonomous expenditure and the part of consumption that responds to income is called *induced* expenditure. The responsiveness of a change in consumption to a change in disposable income is measured by the marginal propensity to consume (*MPC*).

Desired consumption and investment together determine aggregate desired expenditure (*AE*) in the economy. Equilibrium national income is defined as that level of national income where desired aggregate expenditure equals actual national income. If desired and actual income are not equal, production will adjust in order to create eventually an equilibrium situation. An alternative condition for national income equilibrium is where desired saving equals desired investment.

Changes in equilibrium occur from changes in autonomous expenditure. The multiplier analysis indicates the quantitative change in equilibrium income from given changes in autonomous expenditure.

• • • • • • • • • • • • • •
LEARNING OBJECTIVES

After studying this chapter, you should be able to:

■ list the principal determinants of desired consumption and investment;

■ explain how the Keynesian consumption function expresses the relationship between desired consumption and current disposable income;

■ derive the aggregate expenditure function, and distinguish between shifts in it and movements along it;

■ demonstrate equilibrium and disequilibrium situations in the *AE* analysis;

■ define the marginal propensity to spend on domestically produced goods and use it to determine the simple national income multiplier;

■ determine the multiplier effect of a change in autonomous expenditure on national income when prices are fixed.

MULTIPLE-CHOICE QUESTIONS

Questions 1 through 6 refer to Figure 23-1.

Figure 23-1

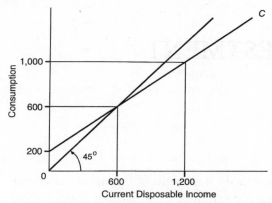

1. The Keynesian consumption function shown above assumes that an individual's desired consumption expenditures are
   (a) in part induced by increases in disposable income.
   (b) in part determined autonomously by factors other than income.
   (c) a function of disposable income in the current year rather than over a lifetime.
   (d) a declining proportion of disposable income.
   (e) All of the above.

2. The marginal propensity to consume (*MPC*) out of disposable income according to Figure 23-1 is
   (a) 200.   (b) 100.
   (c) 2/3.   (d) 1/3.
   (e) 5/6.

3. As disposable income rises from 600 to 1,200, the average propensity to consume
   (a) rises from 1/3 to 1.
   (b) falls from 1 to 5/6.
   (c) remains constant at 2/3.
   (d) remains constant at 1.
   (e) falls from 1 to 1/3.

4. If the individual has no current disposable income,
   (a) consumption must be zero.

   (b) dissaving is 200.
   (c) the average propensity to consume is 1.
   (d) consumption cannot be predicted.
   (e) saving is 200.

5. When disposable income is equal to 600,
   (a) aggregate saving is zero.
   (b) the average propensity to consume is unity.
   (c) the "break-even" level of disposable income is attained.
   (d) desired consumption is equal to actual consumption.
   (e) All of the above.

6. When disposable income is equal to 1,200,
   (a) the marginal propensity to consume is 5/6.
   (b) there is saving of 200.
   (c) there is dissaving of 200.
   (d) desired consumption expenditures exceed actual consumption by 200.
   (e) Both (c) and (d).

7. An *MPC* of less than 1 means that an increase in current disposable income would cause desired consumption expenditures to
   (a) rise by less than the full increase in disposable income.
   (b) fall slightly because the increase in income will increase saving.
   (c) rise such that the average propensity to consume increases as disposable income increases.
   (d) rise by the full increase in disposable income.
   (e) None of the above.

8. An increase in the marginal propensity to consume will
   (a) increase the value of the simple multiplier.
   (b) increase the slope of the consumption function.
   (c) decrease the slope of the saving function.
   (d) decrease the value of the marginal propensity to save.
   (e) All of the above.

9. If the marginal propensity to save out of disposable income is 0.25, then the marginal propensity to consume is
   (a) 0.25.   (b) 4.0.
   (c) 0.75.   (d) 1.0.
   (e) 0.1875.

10. An increase in households' real wealth is predicted to
    (a) shift the consumption function downward.
    (b) shift the saving function upward.
    (c) increase the marginal propensity to consume out of disposable income.
    (d) shift the consumption function upward.
    (e) Both (c) and (d).

11. Desired investment is most likely to rise when
    (a) real interest rates rise.
    (b) sales remain constant.
    (c) expectations of future profits become more optimistic.
    (d) All of the above.
    (e) None of the above.

12. A reduction in real interest rates
    (a) normally reduces the mortgage payments a home buyer must make.
    (b) reduces the incentive for businesses to hold inventories.
    (c) increases the financing costs to firms that must borrow funds.
    (d) will cause the investment function to shift down.
    (e) None of the above.

13. An aggregate expenditure function shows that as national income rises
    (a) employment rises.
    (b) desired expenditures on currently produced goods fall.
    (c) prices rise.
    (d) interest rates must also rise.
    (e) None of the above.

14. The aggregate expenditure function is a relationship between
    (a) actual real expenditure and real national income.
    (b) desired real expenditure and nominal national income.

(c) desired real expenditure and real national income.
(d) real disposable income and saving.
(e) actual nominal expenditure and nominal national income.

15. In a macroeconomic model that includes consumption and investment, equilibrium real national income is attained when
    (a) actual real output is equal to desired real aggregate expenditure.
    (b) the aggregate expenditure function intersects the 45° line.
    (c) the average propensity of desired spending is unity.
    (d) there is no unintended inventory accumulation or reduction.
    (e) All of the above.

16. At a level of national income where aggregate desired expenditure falls short of total output, there will be a tendency for
    (a) national income to rise.
    (b) national income to fall.
    (c) inventories to unexpectedly decrease.
    (d) prices to rise.
    (e) None of the above.

17. When the marginal propensity to spend is 5/6, then
    (a) the marginal propensity not to spend is 1/6.
    (b) the value of the simple multiplier is 6.
    (c) the slope of the *AE* function is 5/6.
    (d) All of the above.
    (e) None of the above.

18. The *simple* multiplier measures
    (a) the extent to which real national income will change in response to a change in autonomous expenditure at a constant price level.
    (b) the rise in desired expenditure caused by a change in real national income.
    (c) the marginal propensity to spend.
    (d) the extent to which national income will change in response to a change in autonomous expenditure at varying price levels.
    (e) the ratio of the change in desired consumption to a change in the marginal propensity to spend.

19. If expenditure in the economy did not depend on the level of real national income, the value of the simple multiplier would be
(a) zero.   (b) unity.
(c) infinite or undefined.
(d) −1.
(e) positive fraction.

20. Assuming constant prices and a marginal propensity to spend of 0.75, an increase in autonomous investment of $1 million should increase equilibrium real national income by
(a) $1 million.   (b) $4 million.
(c) $250,000.   (d) $750,000.
(e) $1.75 million.

Questions 21 through 30 refer to the Figure 23-2. Assume that aggregate expenditure consists only of consumption and investment and that the price level remains constant.

Figure 23-2

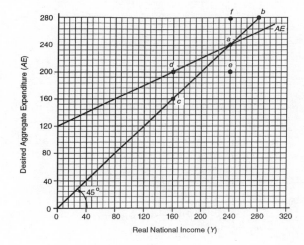

21. According to the graph, the level of desired *autonomous* expenditure is
(a) 120.   (b) 280.
(c) 240.   (d) at point c.
(e) Cannot be determined.

22. When real national income (Y) is 160,
(a) desired aggregate expenditure equals 160.
(b) desired aggregate expenditure is less than 160.

(c) equilibrium national income is attained.
(d) saving is zero.
(e) None of the above.

23. When real national income (*Y*) is 280,
(a) there will be a tendency for national income to fall.
(b) inventories are unexpectedly decreasing.
(c) the average propensity to spend is unity.
(d) there is dissaving of about 20.
(e) None of the above.

24. According to the aggregate expenditure curve labelled *AE*, the current equilibrium level of real national income is
(a) 320.   (b) 240.
(c) 120.   (d) 280.
(e) 160.

25. The *AE* curve has a slope of
(a) 0.5.   (b) 0.6.
(c) 2.0.   (d) 1.0.
(e) 0.4.

26. The value of the simple multiplier is therefore
(a) 2.0.   (b) 0.5.
(c) 2.5.   (d) 0.
(e) 1.67.

27. The value of the marginal propensity not to spend is
(a) 0.5.   (b) 0.4.
(c) 1.0.   (d) 0.
(e) 0.6.

28. Suppose that investment expenditure decreased by 40 at *all* levels of real national income. The aggregate expenditure curve would
(a) shift upward by 40 and intersect the 45° line at point *b*.
(b) shift downward by 40, but its slope would also decrease.
(c) shift downward by 40, have a slope of 0.5, and intersect the 45° line at point *c*.
(d) not shift, but adjustment would involve at movement from point *a* to point *d*.
(e) not shift, but adjustment would involve at movement from point *a* to point *b*.

29. According to the new *AE* curve associated with question 28, if output remains temporarily at 240, desired expenditure is
   (a) 240 (at point *a*), and hence inventories remain unchanged.
   (b) 200 (at point *e*), with the result that unplanned inventory accumulation is equal to 40.
   (c) 280 (at point *f*), with the result that unplanned inventory reduction is equal to 40.
   (d) 200, which is associated with point *d*.

   (e) 40, which is also the level of planned saving.

30. The decrease in desired investment of 40
   (a) will be illustrated by a movement from point *a* to point *c*.
   (b) will decrease real national income ultimately by 80.
   (c) will decrease consumption expenditures ultimately by 40.
   (d) will decrease saving ultimately by 40.
   (e) All of the above.

• • • • • • • • • • • • • •

EXERCISES

1. The consumption function is given by the expression $C = 80 + 0.5Y_d$. The first two columns of the following schedule depict this functional form for various levels of disposable income.

Y_d	C	APC	ΔY_d	ΔC	MPC	S
0	80	n.a.	n.a.	n.a.	n.a.	−80
100	130	1.30				−30
			60	30	0.50	
160	160	1.00				___
				20	0.50	
200	180	___	___			20
					0.50	
400	280	0.70	___	___		120
			350			
750	455	___		___	___	___

(a) Fill in the missing values for the change in real disposable income (ΔY_d).
(b) Using the definition for the average propensity to consume (*APC*), fill in the missing values for *APC*. What did you notice happened to the value of *APC* as the level of Y_d increased?

(c) Fill in the missing values for ΔC.
(d) Using the definition for *MPC*, calculate it for the income change from 400 to 750.
(e) Using the definition for saving, $S = Y_d - C$, fill in the missing values in the table. Using the formula $\Delta S/\Delta Y_d$, prove that the marginal propensity to save is constant and equal to 0.5.
(f) Prove that the algebraic expression for the saving function is $S = -80 + 0.5Y_d$.

(g) What is the break-even level of real disposable income? What is the amount of saving at this level of Y_d?

(h) Plot both the desired consumption (as line *C*) and desired saving (as line *S*) functions in the grid in Figure 23-3. In addition, draw the 45° line and prove that this line intersects the consumption function at a level of Y_d for which $S = 0$.

Figure 23-3

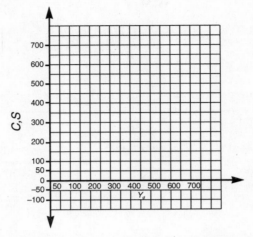

(i) Is desired consumption expenditure both autonomous and induced? Explain

2. The last question was based on a consumption function, $C = 80 + 0.5Y_d$, and a saving function, $S = -80 + 0.5Y_d$. Write the algebraic expression for the following cases:

(a) The consumption function that has autonomous consumption of 100 and a marginal propensity to consume of 0.5.

(b) The consumption function that has autonomous consumption of 80 and a marginal propensity to consume of 0.8.

(c) The saving function for case (b).

(d) The saving function that has autonomous saving of −50 and a marginal propensity to save of 0.6.

(e) The consumption function for case (d).

(f) Plot case (c) on Figure 23-3 and compare this curve with $S = -80 + 0.5Y_d$.

3. This exercise involves real wealth and the consumption function. Suppose that an economy has a consumption function given by $C = 60 + 0.8Y + 0.1(W/P)$. The term W/P is the level of "real" wealth, W is the level of nominal wealth, and P is the price level. C represents desired consumption expenditure, and Y represents the level of real national income. Assume that the price level has a value of 1.0 and is constant and that the economy's total nominal wealth is 400. Therefore, in this case real and nominal wealth are both equal to 400.

   (a) Given that real wealth is 400, rewrite the expression for the consumption function.

   (b) Fill in the missing values in columns 2 and 4 in the following schedule.

(1) Y	(2) C (W/P=400)	(3) C (W/P=2,400)	(4) S (W/P=400)	(5) S (W/P=2,400)
0	100	300	−100	−300
500	____	700	____	−200
1,000	900	1,100	100	−100
1,500	____	____	____	____
2,000	1,700	1,900	+300	+100

   (c) Assume that the economy's real and nominal wealth increases from 400 to 2,400 (the price level remains at 1.0). Write the new consumption function, and fill in the missing values in columns 3 and 5.

   (d) As a result of the wealth increase, what happens to the consumption function? The saving function? Check your answers against Figure 23-2 in the textbook.

4. Answer the following questions using Figure 23-4.

   Figure 23-4

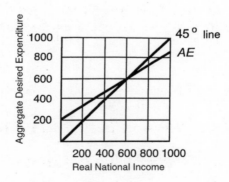

   (a) When national income is 0, desired aggregate expenditure is _____.
   (b) When national income is 600, desired aggregate expenditure is _____.
   (c) If actual national income were 300, desired aggregate expenditure would be (less/greater) than income. Hence, inventories are likely to (fall/rise), and output and national income are likely to (expand/contract).
   (d) If actual national income were 1,000, desired aggregate expenditure would be (less/greater) than national income, inventories would (fall/rise), and hence output and national income are likely to (expand/contract).

(e) In this case, the marginal propensity not to spend is _____ and the marginal propensity to spend is _____ .

(f) The equilibrium level of national income is _____ .

5. The following table summarizes desired levels of aggregate expenditure for an economy where the price level can be assumed constant.

Y	C	I	AE
0	80	120	200
100	140	120	260
200	200	120	320
300	_____	120	_____
400	_____	120	_____
500	_____	120	_____
600	_____	120	_____
700	_____	120	_____

(a) Fill in the missing entries in the consumption and aggregate expenditure columns, assuming that the marginal propensity to consume out of disposable income remains constant.

(b) What is the equilibrium level of income in this economy?

(c) Explain why an output level (Y) of 400 is not an equilibrium situation.

(d) What is the marginal propensity not to spend on domestic goods? What is the simple multiplier for this economy?

(e) If investment were to increase by 60, what would the new equilibrium level of national income become? Show your answer in two ways, by using the table above and by applying the simple income multiplier.

6. Equilibrium national income occurs where desired saving equals desired investment. In this simple economy, $Y = Y_d$.

(a) Using the schedule in question 5, calculate the level of saving at each level of Y.

(b) Since investment is 120, what is the level of Y at which $S = I$?

*7. This exercise involves an algebraic determination of equilibrium national income. You are given the following information about behaviour in an economy:

The consumption function is

$$C = 100 + 0.75Y_d.$$ (1)

The relationship between national income and disposable income is

$$Y_d = Y.$$ (2)

Investment expenditures are

$$I = 50.$$ (3)

(a) What does equation (2) imply?

(b) Aggregate expenditure is the algebraic sum of the various components. Derive the algebraic expression for *AE*.

(c) What is the marginal propensity to spend? The marginal propensity not to spend?

(d) What is the algebraic equivalent to the statement "equilibrium is achieved when the *AE* curve intersects the 45° line"?

(e) Using your answer for part (d), solve for the equilibrium level of *Y*.

(f) What is the value of the simple multiplier?

(g) If investment increased from 50 to 55, what is the new equilibrium level of *Y*?

(h) Now consider a different consumption function. All other equations remain the same. Suppose that the consumption function was $C = 100 + 0.8Y_d$ rather than equation (1). Answer the following questions.
(i) The slope of consumption function has (increased/decreased).
(ii) The slope of the saving function has (increased/decreased).
(iii) The value of the simple multiplier has (increased/decreased).
(iv) The equilibrium level of *Y* has (increased/decreased).

*8. To confirm your answer to part (e) above, use the equilibrium condition that equilibrium occurs when *S* = *I*. (*Hint:* You must prove that the saving function is $S = -100 + .25Y$)

ANSWERS
Multiple-Choice Questions

1. (e)	**2.** (c)	**3.** (b)	**4.** (b)	**5.** (e)
6. (b)	**7.** (a)	**8.** (e)	**9.** (c)	**10.** (d)
11. (c)	**12.** (a)	**13.** (e)	**14.** (c)	**15.** (e)
16. (b)	**17.** (d)	**18.** (a)	**19.** (b)	**20.** (b)
21. (a)	**22.** (e)	**23.** (a)	**24.** (b)	**25.** (a)
26. (a)	**27.** (a)	**28.** (c)	**29.** (b)	**30.** (e)

Exercises

1. (a) 40, 200.
  (b) 0.90, 0.61; the value of APC fell.
  (c) 100, 175.
  (d) $0.50 = 175 \div 350$.
  (e) 0, 295. The marginal propensity to save is 0.50 and is constant. For an increase in Y_d from 0 to 100, saving increases from –80 to –30. The ratio of the change is 0.50.
  (f) Saving is defined as $Y_d - C$, or $Y_d - (80 + 0.5Y_d)$. Hence, the saving function is, $S = -80 + 0.5Y_d$.
  (g) 160, at which $S = 0$.
  (h) **Figure 23-5**

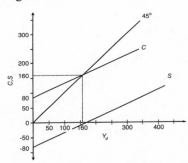

  (i) Consumption expenditure is both autonomous and induced. It has an autonomous component because consumption is 80 when disposable income is zero. Since the marginal propensity to consume is 0.50, consumption is therefore induced as well.

2. (a) $C = 100 + 0.5Y_d$.
  (b) $C = 80 + 0.8Y_d$.
  (c) $S = -80 + 0.2Y_d$.
  (d) $S = -50 + 0.6Y_d$.
  (e) $C = 50 + 0.4Y_d$.
  (f) The new saving function has a smaller slope (0.2), the same intercept (–80), and intersects the income axis at $Y = 400$.

3. (a) When real wealth is 400, the consumption function becomes $C = 60 + 0.8Y + 0.1(400)$ or $C = 100 + 0.8Y$.
  (b) C is 500, 1,300. S is 0, +200.
  (c) The consumption function becomes $C = 60 + 0.8Y + 0.1(2,400)$ or $C = 300 + 0.8Y$. C is 1,500; S is zero.
  (d) The consumption function shifted up in a parallel fashion (an increase of 200 at every level of real national income). The saving function shifted down in a parallel fashion (a decrease of 200 at every level of real national income).

4. (a) 200.
  (b) 600.
  (c) Greater; fall; expand.
  (d) Less; rise; contract.
  (e) 1/3, 2/3.
  (f) 600.

5. (a) C: 260, 320, 380, 440, 500; AE: 380, 440, 500, 560, 620.
  (b) $Y = 500$ since $AE = Y$.
  (c) At $Y = 400$, aggregate expenditure is 440 (320 + 120). Since desired expenditure is greater than actual expenditure, there will be unplanned inventories reductions. Firms adjust to this situation by increasing output until the economy reaches an equilibrium of 500.
  (d) $0.4 = 1 - MPC$. The simple multiplier is $K = 1/1 - z$, where z is the marginal propensity to spend. Hence, $K = 1 \div 0.4 = 2.5$.
  (e) Since the multiplier is 2.5 and investment increases by 60, the total change in real national income is 150. Hence, the new equilibrium real income level is 650 (500 + 150). Using the schedule, the value $Y = 650$ is midpoint between 600 and 700. Hence, $C = 470$ and $I = 180$ for a total of $Y = 650$.

6. (a) –80, –40, 0, +40, +80, +120, +160, +200.
  (b) Saving (120) equals investment at $Y = 500$.

*7. (a) Disposable income equals total income. Hence, there are no net taxes and no business saving.
  (b) $AE = C + I$, or $100 + 0.75Y (=Y_d) + 50$. Hence, $AE = 150 + 0.75Y$.
  (c) Inspecting the expression for the AE function, we see that the slope is 0.75, which is the marginal propensity to spend. In this case, the marginal propensity to spend is equal to the

marginal propensity to consume. The marginal propensity not to spend (or in this case, the marginal propensity to save) is equal to 0.25.

(d) $AE = Y$.

(e) $Y = 150 + 0.75\,Y$ implies $Y = 600$.

(f) $K = 1/1 - z$, where z is the marginal propensity to spend. In this case, the value of the simple multiplier is $1 \div 0.25 = 4.0$.

(g)   An increase in real national income of 20 (5×4.0). Hence, the new equilibrium level is 620 ($600 + 20$).

(h)   Increased, decreased, increased, increased.

*8. $S = Y - (100 + 0.75\,Y)$ or $S = -100 + 0.25\,Y$. Equating this equation to investment (50), we obtain $Y = 600$.

CHAPTER 24

NATIONAL INCOME AND AGGREGATE EXPENDITURE II: AN OPEN ECONOMY WITH GOVERNMENT

CHAPTER OVERVIEW

The previous chapter developed basic principles of national income determination under the restrictive assumptions that the price level was constant and that the economy had no government and no foreign trade. This chapter incorporates foreign trade and fiscal policy.

Fiscal policy includes taxation, transfers, and expenditure policies. Government expenditures on goods and services are an injection of demand that adds to desired aggregate expenditure. Income taxes and transfers affect national income indirectly through their influence on disposable income and hence consumption expenditure. A Public Savings function which incorporates net taxes and government expenditure is developed in this chapter. The slope of the public savings (or budget surplus) function is the *tax rate*.

Net exports, another source of aggregate expenditure, are a negative function of national income because imports rise with income. A larger *marginal propensity to import* increases the slope of the net export function and reduces the size of the simple multiplier.

Equilibrium national income is determined using two approaches: the *aggregate expenditure* approach and the *augmented saving-investment* approach. The latter involves calculating national savings $[S + (T - G)]$ and national asset formation $[I + (X - IM)]$. The simple multiplier now incorporates the tax rate and the marginal propensity to import.

LEARNING OBJECTIVES

After studying this chapter, you should be able to:

- explain the way in which government purchases and net taxes affect desired expenditures and national income;
- derive the budget surplus function and recognize that net taxes typically are an increasing function of income, and thereby reduce the size of the simple multiplier;
- derive the net export function and understand the economic factors that will cause the function to shift;
- derive the aggregate expenditure function which includes consumption, investment, government expenditure, net exports, and the indirect effects of net taxes on disposable income;
- understand the determination of equilibrium national income in terms of aggregate desired expenditure and actual output;
- determine equilibrium national income using the augmented saving-investment approach;
- understand that the value of the multiplier is influenced by the tax rate and the marginal propensity to import.

1. Equilibrium real national income occurs when
   (a) $Y = C + I + G + (X - IM)$.
   (b) the average propensity to spend is one.
   (c) desired aggregate expenditure equals output.
   (d) the AE function intersects the 45° line.
   (e) All of the above.

2. Which of the following items would *not* be considered a government purchase of goods and services?
   (a) The City of Quebec buys additional garbage trucks.
   (b) The Province of British Columbia pays a consulting firm to conduct an ecological study of a new dam proposal.
   (c) The federal government pays for new radar systems for the Canadian Navy.
   (d) The City of Moncton issues welfare payments to needy citizens.
   (e) None of the above.

3. Which of the following is *not* a component of aggregate expenditure?
   (a) Investment.
   (b) Government expenditure on goods and services.
   (c) Net exports.
   (d) Consumption expenditure.
   (e) Personal income taxes paid.

4. In our analytical model, *all but which* of the following are functions of current income?
   (a) Consumption.
   (b) Net exports.
   (c) Investment.
   (d) Personal income taxes.
   (e) Saving.

5. If $Y_d = 0.8\,Y$ and consumption was always 80 percent of disposable income, then the marginal propensity to consume out of total income would be
   (a) 0.8.   (b) 0.75.
   (c) 0.64.   (d) 0.2.
   (e) 1.6.

6. An increase in the tax rate would
   (a) increase disposable income.
   (b) decrease the slope of the AE function.
   (c) shift the AE function downward in a parallel fashion.
   (d) shift the AE function upward in a parallel fashion.
   (e) None of the above.

7. National income is likely to increase as the result of increases in *all but which* of the following, assuming other autonomous variables remain constant?
   (a) The tax rate.
   (b) Net exports.
   (c) Government purchases.
   (d) Investment.
   (e) Autonomous consumption.

8. The simple multiplier will become larger when which of the following variables increases?
   (a) The marginal propensity to save.
   (b) The marginal propensity to import.
   (c) The income tax rate.
   (d) The marginal propensity not to spend.
   (e) The marginal propensity to consume.

9. The balanced budget multiplier for which an increase in government spending is paid for with an equal increase in taxes is likely to be
   (a) equal to the multiplier for an increase in G without tax increases.
   (b) zero under all circumstances.
   (c) greater than the multiplier for an increase in G without tax increases.
   (d) less than the multiplier for an increase in G without tax increases.
   (e) infinitely large.

10. The value of the multiplier will increase if the
    (a) marginal propensity to spend out of disposable income decreases.
    (b) marginal propensity to import falls.
    (c) slope of the AE curve decreases.
    (d) tax rate increases.
    (e) slope of the public saving function increases.

Questions 11 to 14 refer to Figure 24-1.

Figure 24-1

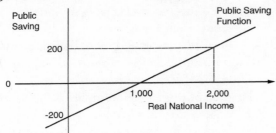

11. The marginal tax rate implied in the diagram is
    (a) zero.   (b) 0.1.
    (c) 0.2.   (d) 0.5.
    (e) 0.4.

12. When national income is 2,000,
    (a) the government has a surplus budget position of 200.
    (b) government purchases exceed taxes net of transfers by 200.
    (c) the government budget is balanced.
    (d) public saving is zero.
    (e) the government has necessarily accumulated more public debt.

13. If the government were to raise the income tax rate, the public saving function would be
    (a) shifted upward parallel to the current function.
    (b) rotated upward from the current intercept.
    (c) shifted downward parallel to the current function.
    (d) unaffected.
    (e) rotated downward from $Y = 1,000$.

14. If the government were to increase its expenditures, the public saving function would be
    (a) shifted upward parallel to the current function.
    (b) rotated upward from the current intercept.
    (c) unaffected.
    (d) rotated downward from the current intercept.
    (e) None of the above.

Questions 15 to 20 refer to Figure 24-2.

Figure 24-2

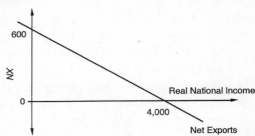

15. The net export function slopes downward because as income increases
    (a) imports increase, thereby reducing net exports.
    (b) exports fall, thereby reducing net exports.
    (c) prices of domestic goods rise, thereby raising the value of exports.
    (d) foreign income falls, thereby reducing net exports.
    (e) the exchange rate appreciates.

16. In a movement along the net export function, an extra dollar of income results in imports
    (a) rising by 60 cents.
    (b) rising by 15 cents.
    (c) falling by 15 cents.
    (d) falling by 40 cents.
    (e) falling by 60 cents.

17. When national income is 3,000, the net export function implies that
    (a) imports are greater than exports.
    (b) net exports are negative.
    (c) net exports are zero.
    (d) exports are greater than imports.
    (e) the marginal propensity to import is zero.

18. A net export function that is represented by a horizontal line would signify that
    (a) imports are not a function of income.
    (b) exports are induced.
    (c) imports are very close substitutes for domestic goods.
    (d) exports are very close substitutes for domestic goods.
    (e) imports are induced.

19. If foreign income rises, the net export function
 (a) becomes steeper.
 (b) becomes flatter.
 (c) shifts upward.
 (d) shifts downward.
 (e) is unaffected.

20. The net export function is most likely to shift downward when, other things being equal,
 (a) prices for the country's exports decrease.
 (b) the exchange rate depreciates.
 (c) domestic prices fall relative to foreign prices.
 (d) foreign income rises.
 (e) tariffs are imposed on imports.

Questions 21 to 30 refer to the following information about an economy. Before attempting these questions, you should calculate the values of aggregate expenditure, the government's budget surplus, and national asset formation for each of the six levels of national income (Y) shown in the schedule.

Y	T	C	I	G	NX
0	0	100	56	50	10
100	20	156	56	50	0
200	40	212	56	50	–10
300	60	268	56	50	–20
400	80	324	56	50	–30
500	100	380	56	50	–40

Getting to know the underlying model: Questions 21 to 25

21. Which of the following statements is correct?
 (a) Autonomous consumption is 100.
 (b) Autonomous exports are 10.
 (c) The marginal propensity to import is 0.1.
 (d) The marginal tax rate is 0.2.
 (e) All of the above.

22. The marginal propensity to consume
 (a) out of disposable income is 0.56.
 (b) out of total income is 0.56.
 (c) out of disposable income is 0.70.
 (d) out of total income is 0.70.
 (e) Both (b) and (c).

23. Which of the following statements is *not* correct?
 (a) Desired aggregate expenditure at $Y = 200$ is 308.

 (b) The marginal propensity to spend out of total income is 0.46.
 (c) At $Y = 500$, there is a budget deficit of 50.
 (d) At an income level of 400, imports are greater than exports.
 (e) At an income level of 300, there is a government budget surplus of 10.

24. The value of the simple multiplier is
 (a) 1.85 approximately.
 (b) equal to the marginal propensity not to spend, which is 0.54.
 (c) equal to the slope of the AE function, which is 0.46.
 (d) 2.17 approximately.
 (e) the reciprocal of the marginal propensity to import.

25. At an income level of 400, the value of national asset formation is
 (a) 26. (b) 50.
 (c) 130. (d) –30.
 (e) 30.

Equilibrium and comparative statics: Questions 26 to 28

26. Which of the following statements is true?
 (a) According to the AE approach, equilibrium national income is 400.
 (b) The average propensity to spend is unity at $Y = 400$.
 (c) Total imports are 40 at $Y = 400$.
 (d) Public saving (budget surplus) is 30 at equilibrium national income.
 (e) All of the above.

27. Which of the following statements is *not* true?
 (a) The value of the simple multiplier is 1.85, approximately.
 (b) An increase in investment from 56 to 83 will increase equilibrium national income from 400 to 450, approximately.
 (c) An increase in the equilibrium value of real national income will have no effect on total taxes collected.
 (d) If exports fall from 10 to 0, real national income will fall by approximately 18.5.
 (e) An increase of 50 in the equilibrium value of real national income will decrease net exports by 10.

28. An increase in the tax rate from 20 to 30 percent will
    (a) decrease the slope of the *AE* curve.
    (b) change the value of the simple multiplier to 1.64, approximately.
    (c) decrease the marginal propensity to consume out of total income to a value of 0.49.
    (d) generate an equilibrium level of real national income that is less than 400.
    (e) All of the above.

Fiscal Policy: Questions 29 and 30

29. Suppose that current equilibrium GDP was 400 and that the target or desired level of GDP was 418.5. Which of the following policies would achieve the target value of GDP?
    (a) Government expenditures should increase by 18.5.
    (b) The tax rate should be increased from 0.20 to 0.30.
    (c) Government spending should increase by 10.
    (d) The government should reduce the money supply and its expenditures by 10.
    (e) None of the above.

30. If the government wanted to reduce real GDP by 15 and the balanced budget multiplier was 0.75, then
    (a) government spending and taxation revenue should increase by 20.
    (b) government spending and taxation revenue should decrease by 15.
    (c) government spending and taxation revenue should increase by 15.
    (d) government spending and taxation revenue should decrease by 20.
    (e) government spending should decrease by 15.

• • • • • • • • • • • • • •

EXERCISES

1. This question deals with the Keynesian consumption: the relationship between consumption and two variants of current income, real disposable income, and total real income. You are given the following information:

Y	Y_d	Desired C	$S = Y_d - C$
0	0	44	−44
100	70	100	−30
200	140	156	−16
300	210	212	−2

   (a) What relationship exists between Y and Y_d? Why is Y_d less than Y?
   (b) Prove that the marginal propensity to consume out of real disposable income is constant and equal to 0.8.

   (c) Derive the algebraic expression for the relationship between C and Y_d.

   (d) Calculate the marginal propensity to consume out of real income (Y).

(e) Derive the algebraic expression for the relationship between C and Y.

(f) Suppose that the marginal propensity to consume out of disposable income remains at 0.8 but that the relationship between income and disposable income becomes $Y_d = 0.6Y$. What economic event might have caused the change? Recalculate the values of C and Y_d for Y values equal to 100, 200, and 300. Recalculate the marginal propensity to consume out of total income.

2. As an economy expands in terms of real income, net exports fall. If $X - IM$ is negative, a deficit in the balance of trade is said to exist. To explain this, we present the following hypothetical schedule, where Y represents levels of real national income, X represents desired exports, and IM represents desired imports.

Y	X	IM	(X – IM)
0	40	0	_____
100	40	10	_____
200	40	20	_____
400	40	40	_____
800	40	80	_____

(a) Exports are assumed to be autonomous (independent of the level of Y). However, what specific relationship exists between IM (imports) and Y? Identify some factors that explain the positive relationship between desired imports and real national income.

(b) Calculate the values for $X - IM$. Does the balance of trade fall (become smaller) as Y increases?

(c) Plot the net export curve on the grid in Figure 24-3.

Figure 24-3

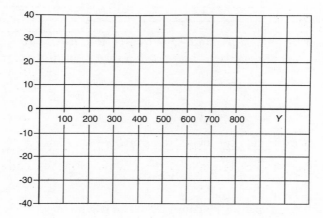

(d) Suppose that exports at each level of Y fell from 40 to 30. Recalculate the value of $X - IM$ at each level of Y, and plot the new net export curve.

(e) Identify three factors that might have caused exports to decline as in (d).

3. This exercise tests your knowledge of the concept of the public saving function. You are given the following information about an economy:

Y	G	T
0	200	0
400	200	100
800	200	200
1,000	200	250
1,200	200	300

(a) Using the expression $(B = T - G)$, calculate the values of public saving (budget surplus) for each of the five national income levels.

(b) What is the value of the tax rate according to the schedule?

(c) If the economy experiences a recession and national income falls from 1,000 to 800, what is the change in public saving, assuming government purchases and tax rates remain unchanged? Explain.

(d) Suppose that the government increased its expenditures from 200 to 250 at each level of real national income. Explain what will happen to the public saving function.

Exercises 4-6 use the following information about an economy. The data labelled "Case A" in this schedule represent the initial situation in the economy. Potential GDP is 450.

Case A						Case B		Case C		Case D	
Y	C	I	G	NX	AE	I	AE	NX	AE	C	AE
0	10	50	10	10	80	60	90	−10	60	10	80
200	190	50	10	−10	240	60	___	−30	___	150	___
300	280	50	10	−20	320	60	___	−40	___	220	___
400	370	50	10	−30	400	60	___	−50	___	290	___
450	415	50	10	−35	440	60	___	−55	___	325	___

4. (a) For case A, determine the equilibrium level of real national income and the marginal propensity to spend.

(b) Graph the aggregate expenditure curve, and indicate the equilibrium level of real national income (case A). What is the value of the output gap?

Figure 24-4

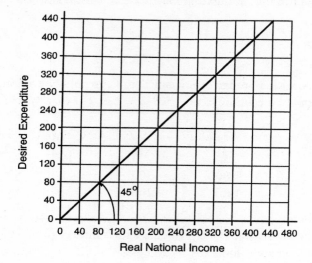

(c) Now assume that a change occurs in the economy so that case B holds. Case B is identical to case A except that investment at *every level of Y* increases from 50 to 60. Fill in the missing values in the table for *AE*, and plot the new aggregate expenditure curve. What has happened to the aggregate expenditure curve? (Compare case A with case B.)

(d) Using the *AE* curve for case B, what is the value of desired *AE* at a level of real national income of 400? What do you predict will happen to the equilibrium level of real national income in this situation? Explain.

(e) What is the equilibrium level of real national income for case B? What has been the total change in real national income (ΔY) between case A and case B? Calculate the ratio $\Delta Y/\Delta I$ from A to B. What is the value of the simple multiplier? What has happened to the value of the output gap?

(f) Calculate the value of the marginal propensity to spend (denoted as z in the text) for case B. Using the formula $K = 1/(1 - z)$, confirm your answer for the value of the simple multiplier in (e).

(g) The total change in income is composed of two parts: the change in the autonomous component of $AE(\Delta A)$, which in this case is ΔI, and the *induced* change in aggregate expenditure (ΔN). What is the value for ΔN?

5. Assume that case A is the initial situation but now net exports at every level of income fall such that $X - IM$ (or NX) has fallen by 20 at every level of Y. This is case C in the schedule above.

(a) Fill in the missing values of *AE* for case C. What is the new equilibrium level of real national income? What is the marginal propensity to spend? What is the value of the output gap?

(b) Comparing case A with case C, what is the total change in *Y*? Calculate the value of the multiplier.

(c)   What happened to the *AE* curve? (Compare case A with case C.)

6.   Assume that case A is the initial situation but that factors in the economy change so that case D in the above schedule applies. Case D is identical to case A except that the consumption function is now quite different.

(a)   Calculate the marginal propensities to consume out of national income for both cases, and indicate the nature of the behavioural change between the two cases.

(b)   Fill in the missing values of *AE* for case D. Graph the new aggregate expenditure curve on the grid in exercise 4(b) and compare it with the one for case A.

(c)   Calculate the marginal propensity to spend for case D, and compare it with that for case A. Calculate the multiplier value, and compare it with the multiplier for case A.

(d)   What is the equilibrium level of real national income for case D?

7.   This exercise enforces your understanding of the augmented saving–investment approach in order to determine equilibrium national income. Refer to the data in the schedule associated with questions 21 to 30 in the **Multiple-Choice** section. Equilibrium national income was 400 according to the aggregate expenditure approach. We want to confirm this answer..

(a)   Calculate the level of private saving at $Y = 400$ using the expression $S = Y_d - C$.

(b)   Calculate the level of public saving at $Y = 400$ using the expression $T - G$.

(c)   Add your answers to (a) and (b) to find the level of national saving.

(d)   Calculate the level of national asset formation at $Y = 400$ using the expression $I + NX$. Confirm that this value is equal to the level of national saving.

8.   A newly elected government inherits an inflationary gap. Record high export sales of one of the country's manufactured goods have created an inflationary gap of 12 billion. The recently appointed minister of finance seeks advice from her advisers. After careful study, they advise her to increase taxes permanently by 3 billion, keeping government spending at its current level. Their recommendation is based on the following assumptions:

(i) The high level of export sales will continue, and potential GDP will remain at 1 trillion.

(ii) The taxation multiplier is 4.

(iii) Within the foreseeable future, changes in both prices and input prices are likely to be negligible.

(iv) Since the government has a large majority, policy changes can be made quickly with few execution lags. Moreover, the advisers are confident that the private sector will respond quickly to this policy change.

The advisers have also been told by the chief economist in the ministry that both the export and government spending multipliers are 6.0.

(a) Assuming that all information is correct, do you agree that the recommended policy will eliminate the inflationary gap? Explain.

(b) The minister accepts the advice, the tax change becomes law, and the size of the output gap begins to decrease. However, shortly after the policy change, exports of one of the country's food products falls unexpectedly by 2.5 billion due to the introduction of a cheaper and higher-quality product by a foreign competitor. Assuming that input prices remain constant and that the chief economist's numbers are accurate, what will happen to the equilibrium level of GDP if no additional fiscal measures are introduced? What is the value of the output gap now?

(c) The finance minister is severely criticized in Parliament. The prime minister insists that she reverse the government's fiscal stance and restore taxes to their original levels (that is, reduce them by 3 billion). Will this reversal in fiscal policy resolve the output gap problem described in (b)? Explain.

(d) The finance minister threatens to resign. She argues that her credibility as minister is at stake. A reversal of policy would be political suicide for her. Moreover, her taxation increase was correct; unforeseen external factors caused the problem. She convinces the prime minister that the government's appropriate stance should be to retain the 3 billion increase in taxation but also increase government spending by 2.5 billion. Comment on this new policy stance.

*9. This exercise involves an algebraic macroeconomic model. You should read the appendix to this chapter before attempting these questions. You are given the following information about behaviour in an economy that has a potential real national income of 300.

The consumption function is

$$C = 30 + 0.9Y_d. \tag{1}$$

The term 0.9 is the marginal propensity to consume out of disposable income and we will denote it as the parameter, b.

The relationship between Y_d and Y is

$$Y_d = 0.8Y. \tag{2}$$

Since equation (2) implies that the tax rate (t) is 0.2, the tax function can be written as

$$T = 0.2Y. \tag{3}$$

Investment expenditure is

$$I = 40. \tag{4}$$

Government expenditure is

$$G = 20. \tag{5}$$

The net export function is

$$X - IM = 20 - 0.12Y. \tag{6}$$

The term 0.12 is the marginal propensity to import and is denoted as m.

The AE expenditure identity is

$$AE = C + I + G + (X - IM). \tag{7}$$

The public saving (B) identity is

$$B = T - G. \tag{8}$$

Using the AE approach, the equilibrium condition is

$$AE = Y. \tag{9}$$

Solving for equilibrium real national income using the AE approach

The key to determining the equilibrium level of real national income is to derive the algebraic expression for the AE function. We do this step by step.

(a) Since AE is a relationship between desired expenditures and Y, it is necessary to express consumption as a function of Y. Hence, substitute equation (2) into (1), and form the new consumption function. Call this function equation (10). What is the marginal propensity to consume out of total income?

(b) The AE function is the algebraic sum of the components of desired aggregate expenditure. Substitute equations (10), (4), (5), and (6) into equation (7), and derive the algebraic expression for the AE function. Make sure you collect all of the autonomous terms as well as all the coefficients for the Y variable.

(c) The slope of the AE function (z) is given by, $z = b - bt - m$. Prove that this value is equal to the value of the coefficient of the Y term in part (b).

(d) Using equation (9), solve for the equilibrium level of Y. What is the value of the simple multiplier? What is the value of the output gap?

(e) What is the value of public saving (budget surplus) at the equilibrium level of GDP?

(f) What is the value of net exports at the equilibrium level of GDP?

Solving for equilibrium real national income using the augmented saving–investment approach

(g) Prove that the private saving function is the expression $S = -30 + .08Y$.

(h) Prove that the public saving function is the expression $B = 0.2Y - 20$.

(i) Prove that the national saving function is the expression $-50 + 0.28Y$.

(j) Prove that national asset formation function is the expression $60 - 0.12Y$.

(k) By equating the national saving function to the national asset formation function, prove that equilibrium national income is 275.

Fiscal Policy Issues

(l) Assume that the government wishes to eliminate the output gap. What change in government expenditures would you recommend?

(m) Eliminating the output gap by changing the tax rate is a much more difficult exercise. We use the *AE* approach to deal with this interesting policy issue. Suppose that equation (2) changed to $Y_d = 0.8367Y$. What has happened to the tax rate? Prove that the new equation for the *AE* function is given by $AE = 110 + .633Y$. Using equation (9) and the new aggregate expenditure function, prove that the new equilibrium level of real national income is approximately equal to 300. Has the tax cut policy eliminated the output gap?

(n) Could the government eliminate the output gap by changing its spending and its taxation by the same amount? This is called a balanced budget policy. This model has a balanced budget multiplier of 0.46 approximately. What is the needed equal change in government spending and taxation revenue that is required to eliminate the current output gap?

ANSWERS

Multiple-Choice Questions

1. (e)	**2.** (d)	**3.** (e)	**4.** (c)	**5.** (c)
6. (b)	**7.** (a)	**8.** (e)	**9.** (d)	**10.** (b)
11. (c)	**12.** (a)	**13.** (b)	**14.** (e)	**15.** (a)
16. (b)	**17.** (d)	**18.** (a)	**19.** (c)	**20.** (b)
21. (e)	**22.** (e)	**23.** (c)	**24.** (a)	**25.** (a)
26. (e)	**27.** (c)	**28.** (e)	**29.** (c)	**30.** (d)

Exercises

1. (a) There is a positive relationship given by the expression $Y_d = 0.7Y$. It is less because taxes outweigh transfer payments; net taxes are positive and are deducted from total income.

   (b) $\Delta C / \Delta Y_d = 0.8$ and is constant. When Y_d increases from 0 to 70, consumption increases by 56.

   (c) Since autonomous consumption (when $Y = 0$) is 44 and the marginal propensity to consume out of disposable income is 0.8, the consumption function is written as $C = 44 + 0.8Y_d$.

   (d) The marginal propensity to consume out of total real income is calculated from the first and the third columns. We observe that every 1 dollar increase in real income generates a 56 cent increase in consumption. Hence, the marginal propensity to consume out of total income is 0.56.

   (e) The consumption function is written as $C = 44 + 0.56Y$.

   (f) Since disposable income is less at every level of income, the tax rate must have increased. In this case, the tax rate has increased from 30 to 40 percent. As real income increases from 100 to 300, disposable income levels become 60, 120, and 180. Consumption levels become 92, 140, 188. The marginal propensity to consume out of total real income becomes 0.48, which is equal to 0.8×0.6.

2. (a) Imports are positively related to national income by the expression $IM = 0.1Y$. As real national income rises, households buy more imported goods; firms, in order to produce more goods, require more imported inputs; and it is possible for governments and firms to import various machines, goods, and services as part of their investment and expenditure programs.

   (b) 40, 30, 20, 0, –40. Yes, because imports rise as income rises.

   (c) **Figure 24-5**

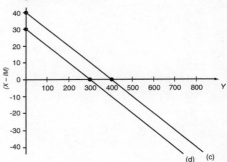

   (d) $Y = 0$, $NX = 30$; $Y = 100$, $NX = 20$; $Y = 200$, $NX = 10$; $Y = 400$, $NX = -10$; $Y = 800$, $NX = -50$.

   (e) The external value of the domestic currency appreciated (or the exchange rate fell); foreign income fell; domestic inflation was higher than foreign inflation.

3. (a) –200, –100, 0, 50, 100.

   (b) The tax rate is 0.25.

   (c) The budget surplus (public saving) falls from 50 to 0. As Y falls, tax revenue falls. Since G is constant, the government's budget surplus (public saving) falls.

   (d) The public saving function shifts down and to the right.

4. (a) $AE = Y$ at 400. The marginal propensity to spend is 0.80 and is constant ($\Delta AE = 160$, $\Delta Y = 200$, $\Delta AE / \Delta Y = 0.80$).

   (b) The AE curve has an intercept value of 80 on the vertical axis, has a slope of 0.80, and intersects the 45° line at an income level of 400. There is an output gap of minus 50 (a recessionary gap).

   (c) AE: 90, 250, 330, 410, 450. The AE curve shifts vertically upward by 10 in a parallel fashion.

   (d) $AE = 410$ when $Y = 400$. Since AE is greater than national income, real income and employment will rise.

   (e) $AE = Y$ at 450. The change in income is 50, and $\Delta Y / \Delta I = 5$. The value of the simple multiplier is 5. The output gap has been eliminated.

   (f) The marginal propensity to spend is 0.80. The marginal propensity not to spend is 0.20. $K = 1/0.2 = 5$.

   (g) Since the total change in income is 50 and $I = 10$, the value of ΔN is 40.

5. (a) *AE*: 60, 220, 300, 380, 420. Equilibrium is $Y = 300$. The marginal propensity to spend remains at 0.80. The output gap is now −150.

(b) Y fell by 100. The multiplier is $\Delta Y/\Delta(X - IM) = -100/-20 = 5$.

(c) The *AE* curve shifts downward by 20 in a parallel fashion.

6. (a) Case A: *MPC* = 0.90; case D: *MPC* = 0.70. Consumers have become more frugal; they are saving a higher proportion of national income.

(b) *AE*: 80, 200, 260, 320, 350. The new *AE* has an intercept of 80 on the vertical axis, has a slope of 0.60, and intersects the 45° line at $Y = 200$. The *AE* curve for case D is flatter than that for case A.

(c) The marginal propensity to spend for case D is 0.60, which is lower than 0.80 for case A. The multiplier for case D is therefore $1/(1 - 0.60) = 2.5$.

(d) $AE = Y$ when $Y = 200$.

7. (a) Private saving equals −4 (= 400 − 80 − 324).

(b) Public saving equals +30 (= 80 − 50).

(c) National saving equals +26 (= 30 − 4).

(d) National asset formation equals +26 (= 56 − 30).

8. (a) The inflationary gap of 12 will be completely eliminated if taxes are increased by 3 billion since the tax multiplier is 4.

(b) GDP declines for two reasons. The increase in taxation will decrease GDP by 12 billion, and the decrease in exports will decrease GDP by 15 billion (2.5 × 6). The total decrease is therefore 27 billion. The economy's initial GDP level must have been 1,012 billion. After the taxation and export changes, the new equilibrium level must be 27 billion less, or 985 billion. Hence, the output (recessionary) gap is −15 billion.

(c) No, a taxation cut of 3 billion will increase GDP by 12 billion, leaving a recessionary gap of −3 billion (997 − 1,000).

(d) If nothing else happens, the minister's amended policy will restore potential GDP. As was discussed before, the taxation increase will eliminate the inflationary gap. The 2.5 billion increase in government spending will counteract the 2.5 billion reduction in food exports.

*9. (a) Equation (10) is C = 30 + 0.72Y. The marginal propensity to consume out of total real income is 0.72.

(b) $AE = 30 + 0.72Y + 40 + 20 + 20 - 0.12Y = 110 + 0.60Y$.

(c) $z = b(= 0.9) - bt(= 0.9 \times 0.2) - m(= 0.12) = 0.6$.

(d) $110 + 0.6Y = Y$ or $Y = 275$. The value of the simple multiplier is $K = 1/1 - z$ or 2.5. The output gap is 275 − 300 or −25. This is a recessionary gap.

(e) $B = 0.2 \times 275 - 20 = 35$.

(f) $(X - M) = 20 - 0.12(275) = -13$.

(g) Private saving is equal to $Y_d - C$ or $Y - 0.2Y - [30 + 0.9(Y - 0.2Y)]$.

(h) Public saving is equal to $T - G$ or $0.2Y - 20$.

(i) National saving is equal to $S + T - G$ or $0.28Y - 50$.

(j) National asset formation is equal to $I + NX$ or $60 - 0.12Y$.

(k) Equating the national saving function to the national asset formation function, we obtain $Y = 275$.

(l) The output gap is −25 (275 − 300). The government spending multiplier in this model is 2.5. Hence, government expenditure should rise by 10.

(m) The new consumption function (expressed as a function of total income) is $C = 30 + (0.836 \times 0.9)Y$ or $C = 30 + .753Y$. Hence, aggregate expenditure is $30 + .753Y + 40 + 20 + 20 - 0.12Y$ or $110 + 0.633Y$. Using the condition that $AE = Y$, we obtain a new equilibrium level of real national income of 299.8 (approximately 300). The output gap has been eliminated.

(n) Both G and total taxation revenue must increase by 54.3. With a balanced budget multiplier of 0.46, GDP will increase by 25.

CHAPTER 25
· · · · · · · · · · · · · · ·

NATIONAL INCOME AND THE PRICE LEVEL IN THE SHORT RUN

· · · · · · · · · · · · · ·
CHAPTER OVERVIEW

The previous two chapters analysed national income determination under the assumption that the price level was fixed. In the next two chapters we consider the simultaneous determination of real national income and the price level. This chapter focuses on the short run, when factor prices are fixed. Equilibrium of national income and the price level occurs at the intersection of the *AD* and *SRAS* curves.

A downward-sloping aggregate demand curve is developed. A rise in the price level lowers private-sector wealth; this leads to a downward shift in the aggregate expenditure curve and a decrease in the equilibrium level of income. Moreover, a rise in the price level shifts the net export function downward, which means a downward shift in the aggregate expenditure curve. Hence, national income equilibrium decreases.

The slope of the short-run aggregate supply curve (*SRAS*) may have three ranges; flat, intermediate, and steep. It may be flat when unemployment is high but becomes progressively steeper as full employment is approached. Although factor prices are constant for any *SRAS* curve, unit costs usually increase as output increases. Hence, firms want higher prices for increased output.

The effects of aggregate demand shocks on real income and the price level depend on the range of the *SRAS* curve in which the demand shock occurs. The steeper the slope of the *SRAS,* the less the increase in real income and the greater the increase in the price level from any increase in aggregate demand. Hence, the value of the multiplier depends on the slope of the *SRAS* curve.

· · · · · · · · · · · · · ·
LEARNING OBJECTIVES

After studying this chapter, you should be able to:

■ explain why changes in the price level, by influencing consumption and net exports, cause the aggregate expenditure curve to shift;

■ derive a downward-sloping aggregate demand curve and recognize what factors cause this curve to shift;

■ explain why the simple multiplier gives the magnitude of the horizontal shift in the *AD* curve in response to the change in autonomous expenditure;

■ understand the economic factors that determine the slope of the short-run aggregate supply curve;

■ explain why a demand shock has a smaller multiplier effect on output when the *SRAS* curve slopes upward;

■ demonstrate how shifts in the *SRAS* curve, especially due to changes in input prices and productivity, affect equilibrium real national income and the price level, and explain how stagflation may result.

MULTIPLE-CHOICE QUESTIONS

1. All other things being equal, an increase in the domestic price level will
   (a) increase the value of real wealth and hence cause an upward shift in the consumption function.
   (b) decrease the value of real wealth and hence cause an upward shift in the consumption function.
   (c) cause exports to increase, thereby causing the net export function to shift downward.
   (d) decrease the value of real wealth and cause the consumption and aggregate expenditure functions to shift downward.
   (e) cause input prices to fall.

2. All other things being equal, a decrease in the domestic price level will shift the net export function
   (a) downward, thus causing the aggregate expenditure function to shift downward.
   (b) upward, thus causing the aggregate expenditure function to shift upward.
   (c) upward, thus causing the aggregate expenditure function to shift downward.
   (d) downward, thus causing the aggregate expenditure function to shift upward.
   (e) downward, thus causing the SRAS curve to shift upward.

3. The aggregate demand (AD) curve relates
   (a) real national income to desired expenditure for a given price level.
   (b) nominal national income to the price level.
   (c) equilibrium real national income to the price level.
   (d) consumption expenditure to the price level.
   (e) real national income to inflation rates.

4. All other things being equal, a fall in the domestic price level causes
   (a) the aggregate expenditure curve to shift upward and hence leads to a movement downward and to the right along the AD curve.
   (b) the aggregate expenditure curve to shift upward and hence leads to a movement upward and to the left along the AD curve.
   (c) the AD curve to shift to the right and a movement upward and to the right along the AE curve.
   (d) the AD and the AE curves to shift upward.
   (e) the SRAS curve to shift downward.

5. An upward-sloping SRAS curve indicates
   (a) firms' willingness to supply more output if the output can be sold at higher prices.
   (b) that expanding output means incurring higher unit costs and higher prices of output.
   (c) that expanding output means higher factor prices and therefore higher output prices.
   (d) Both (a) and (b).
   (e) None of the above.

6. All other things being equal, the AD curve shifts to the right as a result of all but which of the following changes?
   (a) Increased government expenditure.
   (b) Increased autonomous imports.
   (c) Increased autonomous exports.
   (d) Increased investment expenditure.
   (e) Decreased tax rates.

7. If the SRAS curve is horizontal,
   (a) output can be increased at a constant price level.
   (b) any increase in AD will cause real national income and the price level to increase.
   (c) output is constant but the price level is variable.
   (d) the economy is most likely operating beyond its potential level of real national income.
   (e) potential output varies in the short run.

8. If the current price level is below the short-run macroeconomic equilibrium level,

    (a) the desired output of firms is greater than the level of output consistent with expenditure decisions.

    (b) desired aggregate expenditure is less than the amount of goods supplied in the short run.

    (c) the desired output of firms is less than the level of output consistent with expenditure decisions.

    (d) price will tend to adjust such that there will be movement downward and to the right along the *AD* curve.

    (e) price will adjust downward along the *SRAS* curve.

9. All other things being equal, an increase in desired investment expenditures will

    (a) shift the *AE* curve upward.

    (b) shift the *AD* curve to the right.

    (c) cause the equilibrium levels of real national income and price to increase if the economy operates in the intermediate range of the *SRAS* curve.

    (d) All of the above.

    (e) None of the above.

10. A rightward shift in the *SRAS* curve is brought about by

    (a) an increase in factor prices.

    (b) decreases in productivity.

    (c) increases in productivity and/or decreases in factor prices.

    (d) decreases in factor supplies.

    (e) increases in real wealth.

11. With a given aggregate demand curve, a shift in the *SRAS* curve to the left will cause

    (a) increases in real national income and the price level in the short run.

    (b) an increase in the price level but a decrease in real national income in the short run.

    (c) a decrease in the price level but an increase in real national income.

    (d) a decrease in potential real national income.

    (e) a movement down an *AD* curve.

Questions 12 through 19 refer to Figure 25-1.

12. According to the curves AE_0 and AD_0, the equilibrium levels of price and real national income are, respectively,

    (a) 2.0 and 500.   (b) 2.6 and 800.

    (c) 2.0 and 1,000.   (d) 2.6 and 1,000.

    (e) None of the above.

13. Assuming that the *AE* curve shifts upward from AE_0 to AE_1 but the price level remains constant at its initial level, we can say that

    (a) autonomous expenditures must have increased by 250.

    (b) real national income increases by 500.

    (c) the aggregate demand curve shifts to the right so that $Y = 1,000$ at the price level 2.0.

    (d) input prices must have remained constant.

    (e) Any or all of the above.

Figure 25-1

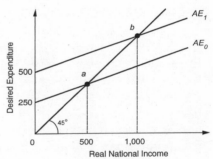

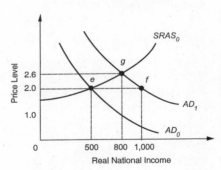

14. According to the diagram, the value of the simple multiplier is

    (a) 5.0.   (b) 0.5.

    (c) 4.0.   (d) 1.2.

    (e) 2.0.

15. Given the aggregate demand curve AD_1 and a price level of 2.0 (point f),
    (a) aggregate demand is less than aggregate supply.
    (b) aggregate demand is equal to aggregate supply.
    (c) firms are unwilling to produce enough to satisfy the existing demand at the existing price level, and hence the price level will rise.
    (d) the price level is likely to fall.
    (e) input prices must rise.

16. Given the increase in autonomous expenditure, moving from point f to point g represents the effect of an increase in the price level that
    (a) reduces both exports and real wealth.
    (b) reduces exports but increases consumption.
    (c) increases both exports and real wealth.
    (d) increases exports and saving.
    (e) increases input prices.

17. The movement from point f to point g implies that
    (a) the AE_1 curve shifts downward to intersect the 45° line at an output level of 800.
    (b) the AE_1 curve shifts downward to intersect the 45° line at an output level 500.
    (c) the economy moves along the AE_1 curve until it reaches an output of 800.
    (d) the economy moves along the AE_1 curve until it reaches an output of 500.
    (e) the economy moves along the AE_0 curve until it reaches an output of 800.

18. Assuming that input prices do not change, the new short-run macroeconomic equilibrium as a result of the increase in autonomous expenditure will be
    (a) at point g.
    (b) at an output level of 800.
    (c) at a price level of 2.6.
    (d) a reduction in the output gap from 500 to 200.
    (e) All of the above.

19. The value of the multiplier after allowing for a price change is
    (a) 1.2.   (b) 2.0.
    (c) 1.0.   (d) 4.0.
    (e) 0.8.

Refer to Figure 25-2 when answering questions 20 through 24. Point a is the initial situation.

Figure 25-2

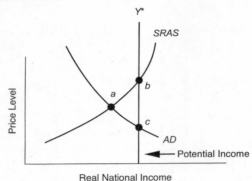

20. When consumers become worried about the future and decide to save more out of additional income,
    (a) the AD curve shifts leftward, causing national income and the price level to fall.
    (b) the AD curve shifts rightward, causing national income and the price level to rise.
    (c) the $SRAS$ curve shifts rightward, causing national income to rise and the price level to fall.
    (d) the $SRAS$ curve shifts leftward, causing national income to fall and the price level to rise.
    (e) the positive output gap will decrease.

21. The dominant short-run effect of an increase in desired investment is to
    (a) shift the $SRAS$ curve to the left.
    (b) shift the $SRAS$ curve to the right.
    (c) shift the AD curve to the left.
    (d) shift the AD curve to the right.
    (e) increase the potential output level.

22. If the AD curve shifts to the right, we expect
    (a) the price level to increase and output to fall.
    (b) the price level to increase and output to rise.
    (c) unemployment to rise.
    (d) productivity to fall.
    (e) input prices to increase in the short run.

23. Rising oil prices would result in stagflation in this economy if the *SRAS* curve
    (a) shifted leftward, causing output and the price level to rise.
    (b) shifted rightward, causing output and the price level to fall.
    (c) shifted leftward, causing output to fall and the price level to rise.
    (d) shifted rightward, causing output to rise and the price level to fall.
    (e) intersected the *AD* curve at a higher output and price level.

24. In order to eliminate the current output gap (shown at point *a*),
    (a) government taxes should be increased such that the *AD* curve shifts from point *a* to point *b*.
    (b) net exports must increase in such a way that the *SRAS* curve shifts from point *a* to point *c*.
    (c) input prices must increase so that the *SRAS* curve shifts from point *a* to point *c*.
    (d) government expenditures must increase so that the new *AD* curve intersects the *SRAS* curve at point *b*.
    (e) input prices must fall so that the new *AD* curve intersects the *SRAS* curve at point *b*.

25. The multiplier value that allows for price changes will be equal to the value of the simple multiplier if the demand shock occurs in the
    (a) flat range of the *SRAS* curve.
    (b) intermediate range of the *SRAS* curve.
    (c) steep portion of the *SRAS* curve.
    (d) range characterized by increasing unit costs.
    (e) inelastic portion of the *AD* curve.

26. Under what circumstances would an aggregate demand increase result in virtually no increase in real income but a large increase in the price level?
    (a) If the demand shock occurred in the flat range of the *SRAS* curve.
    (b) If the demand shock occurred in the intermediate range of the *SRAS* curve.
    (c) If the demand shock occurred in the steep portion of the *SRAS* curve.
    (d) If unit costs were constant before and after the demand shock.
    (e) If input prices decreased.

27. If autonomous investment increased, the multiplier would be zero if
    (a) price increases reduced consumption and net exports by the same amount as the increase in autonomous investment.
    (b) the demand shock occurred in the vertical range of the *SRAS* curve.
    (c) the upward shift in the *AE* curve associated with the increase in investment was completely counteracted by the reduction in net exports and real wealth.
    (d) All of the above.
    (e) None of the above.

28. Assume that the *SRAS* curve slopes upward. After an economic shock, we observe that the price level is lower than before but real output has increased. Which one of the following events, by itself, could explain this observation?
    (a) An increase in input prices.
    (b) An increase in factor productivity.
    (c) An increase in exports.
    (d) A reduction in investment expenditure.
    (e) A decrease in the tax rate.

• • • • • • • • • • • • • •

EXERCISES

1. This exercise involves the derivation of an aggregate demand curve from consumption theory. In making calculations, you should become more familiar with the basis for a downward-sloping *AD* curve. The exercise demonstrates that changes in price affect the level of real wealth, which in turn changes total consumption expenditure. You will also learn some of the factors that cause the *AD* curve to shift.

Desired consumption (C) is shown at two different price levels, P_1 and P_2. The consumption function is given by the expression $C = 100 + 0.8Y + 0.1(W/P)$, where W represents the total nominal wealth in the economy. We assume that nominal wealth is 3,000. All other components of aggregate expenditure are lumped together in one column, labelled $I + G + NX$. Entries in that column are assumed to be unaffected by the price level, but because imports are included in this combination, it is a negative function of real national income.

Y	C_1 (P = 1)	C_2(P = 2)	I + G + NX	AE_1(P = 1)	AE_2(P = 2)
0	400	250	1,200	1,600	1,450
2,500	2,400	2,250	700	3,100	2,950
2,875	_____	_____	625	_____	_____
3,250	_____	_____	550	_____	_____
3,625	_____	_____	475	_____	_____
4,000	_____	_____	400	_____	_____
4,375	_____	_____	325	_____	_____

(a) Use the consumption function above or assume that the marginal propensity to consume that you can derive from the initial data entries remains constant at all levels of national income. Fill in the missing values for C_1, C_2, AE_1, and AE_2.

(b) Plot the aggregate expenditure functions in the uppermost graph in Figure 25-3 and determine the equilibrium level of national income at each price level.

(c) What vertical shift in the AE function occurs as a result of a rise in a price level of $P = 1$ to $P = 2$? What is the change in the equilibrium level of national income after the change?

(d) Use the two values in (b) to plot the aggregate demand curve in the lower graph. Assume that a linear approximation is satisfactory. What is the reason the aggregate demand curve slopes downward?

(e) If government spending rises at all levels of income by 150, by how much does the equilibrium level of national income rise? Plot the new aggregate expenditure function (AE_F) in the upper graph, assuming $P = 1$, and show the new equilibrium level of income. Check your answer by determining the marginal propensity to spend, deriving the simple multiplier, and multiplying it times the autonomous expenditure change.

(f) If government spending rises by 150, explain how that affects the position of the AD curve. How does your answer to (e) provide useful information regarding the size of any shift in the curve? Plot the new AD curve on the lower graph.

(g) In the examples above, if the price level falls from 2 to 1, the AE curve shifts up by 150, and if the government increases spending by 150, the AE curve shifts up by 150. Yet in one case the economy moves along the AD curve, and in the other case the AD curve shifts. Explain why these different results occur.

Figure 25-3

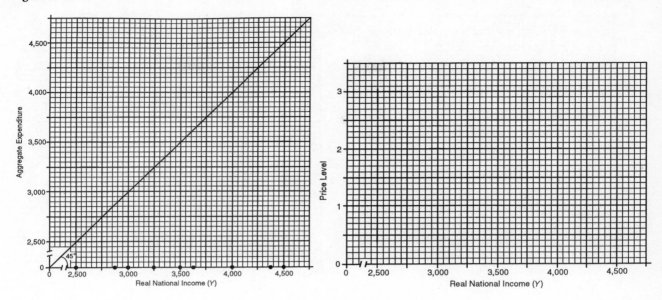

2. Another reason why the *AD* curve slopes downward is that a reduction in the domestic price level (assuming that the foreign price level remains constant) increases the domestic economy's competitiveness internationally, *ceteris paribus*. Thus, net exports (*NX*) should increase if the domestic price level falls. This exercise has the same consumption function as exercise 1. However, now the component *X – IM* depends on relative prices (the ratio of the domestic price level to the foreign price level). For our present purposes, the foreign price is assumed to be equal to 1.0 and constant. Thus, the relative price can be represented by the domestic price level, *P*. The nonconsumption items in aggregate expenditure are now determined by the equation

$$I + G + NX = 1{,}500 - 0.2Y - 300P$$

There are two domestic price levels, $P = 1$ and $P = 2$.

(a) Using the equation just given, fill in the entries for $I + G + NX$ for both price levels. Then calculate AE_1 and AE_2 for all levels of income in the table.

Y	C_1	$(I + G + NX)_1$	AE_1	C_2	$(I + G + NX)_2$	AE_2
0	400	1,200	1,600	250	900	1,150
2,500	2,400	700	3,100	2,250	400	2,650
2,875	2,700	_____	_____	2,550	_____	_____
3,250	3,000	_____	_____	2,850	_____	_____
3,625	3,300	_____	_____	3,150	_____	_____
4,000	3,600	_____	_____	3,450	_____	_____
4,375	3,900	_____	_____	3,750	_____	_____

(b) Plot the two aggregate expenditure functions in the upper panel of the graph on the next page, and determine the equilibrium level of national income at each price level (*P*).

(c) Based on your answer to (b), plot the *AD* curve for this economy in Figure 25-4, assuming that a linear approximation is satisfactory.

Figure 25-4

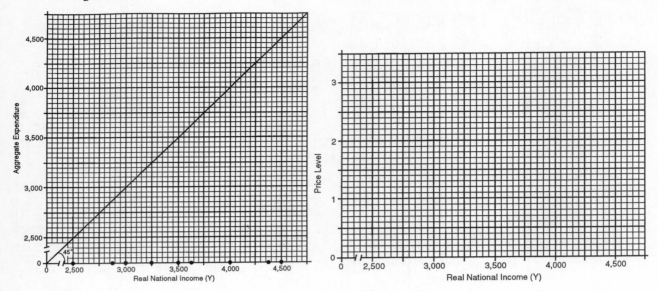

(d) How can you characterize the slope of this *AD* curve compared to the one you derived in exercise 1?

(e) Suppose that the expression for nonconsumption demand expenditures were $I + G + NX = 1,500 - 0.2Y - 600P$. Without solving the model formally, how would you expect this change to affect the slope of the aggregate demand curve?

(f) To summarize your findings, based on a common initial equilibrium price level and national income the more price responsive foreign demand is for domestically produced goods and the more price responsive domestic demand is for foreign goods, the (flatter, steeper) is the slope of the *AD* curve, all other things being equal. Also, the more responsive consumption is to changes in real wealth, the (flatter, steeper) is the slope of the *AD* curve.

*3. This exercise involves an upward-sloping *SRAS* curve. Students who have not studied microeconomics may find it difficult. All students may wish to refer to Chapters 10 and 12 in the text. The text explains that the *SRAS* curve represents the relationship between the price level and the supply of aggregate output when factor prices remain constant. The *SRAS* curve will have a positive slope when increases in output cause increases in unit costs and product prices even though input prices do not change. The *SRAS* curve tends to be relatively flat when the economy operates below its potential output level. However, production increases beyond normal capacity levels will be associated with large increases in unit costs, which in turn generate large price level increases.

The complete explanation of a positively sloped *SRAS* curve is complex; the aggregate relationship between output and the price level reflects the overall behaviour of diverse firms that differ in market structure for products and inputs as well as in their objectives. This exercise deals with the concept of unit costs that increase in response to output increases by profit-maximizing firms that operate in competitive markets for inputs and products.

Short-run theory of competitive firms yields the following principles: (1) A competitive firm's short-run supply curve is that part of its marginal cost curve which lies above the average variable cost curve; (2) a competitive firm maximizes profits (or minimizes short-term losses) by equating marginal cost to product price; and (3) short-run capacity is the level of output that corresponds to the minimum short-run average total cost. A firm that is producing at an output less than the point of minimum average total cost has excess capacity.

Consider a representative firm in the competitive sector. Assume that its total fixed costs (associated with a fixed capital stock) are $100 and that the firm pays $10 for each worker it hires. The following table provides detailed information about its production, employment of labour, and costs.

(1) Labour	Total cost (dollars)				Marginal cost (dollars/unit)	Average cost (dollars/unit)		
	(2) Output	(3) Fixed	(4) Variable	(5) Total	(6) MC*	(7) Fixed	(8) Variable	(9) Total
0	0.0	100	0	100		—	—	—
					0.67			
1	15.0	100	10	110		6.67	0.67	7.33
					0.53			
2	34.0	100	20	120		2.94	0.59	3.53
					0.71			
3	48.0	100	30	130		2.08	0.62	2.71
					0.83			
4	60.0	100	40	140		1.67	0.67	2.33
					5.00			
5	62.0	100	50	150		1.61	0.81	2.42
					10.00			
6	63.0	100	60	160		1.59	0.95	2.54
					20.00			
7	63.5	100	70	170		1.57	1.10	2.68

*Marginal cost (in column 6) is shown between the lines of total cost because it refers to the change in total cost divided by the change in output that brought it about. An MC value of $0.71 is the $10 increase in TC (from $120 to $130) divided by the 14-unit increase in output from (34 to 48).

(a) What output level represents the firm's short-run capacity?

(b) Suppose that the firm considers increasing its production from 41 (the midpoint of the output range 34 to 48) to 54 (the midpoint of the output range 48 to 60). Will its marginal cost increase, decrease, or remain constant? What happens to the firm's average variable costs (unit variable costs)? Recalling that a firm equates product price with marginal cost, what change in price is required to induce the firm to increase its output from 41 to 54? Both output levels (41 and 54) are less than its capacity. Hence, when a firm has excess capacity, increases in output cause (large, small) increases in unit costs; therefore, its short-run supply curve is relatively (flat, steep).

(c) Why did marginal costs increase as output increased from 41 to 54? (*Hint:* What was the incremental contribution to output of hiring the third worker as output increased from 34 to 48 compared with the incremental contribution to output of hiring the fourth worker as output increased from 48 to 60?)

(d) Suppose that the firm considers increasing its output from 54 to 61 (the midpoint of the output range 60 to 62). Will its marginal costs increase, decrease, or remain constant? What happens to its average (unit) variable costs? What price will the firm require to maximize profits for the higher output? An output level of 61 is greater than the firm's short-run capacity. Hence, for output levels that are higher than capacity, the firm's short-run supply curve is relatively (flat, steep).

(e) The text also explains that the *SRAS* curve will shift to the left if input prices increase. Prove that the representative firm's marginal and average variable costs increase at every output level if the wage rate increases from $10 per worker to $20 per worker. Continue to assume that fixed costs are $100.

(f) The *SRAS* curve will shift downward and to the right if factor productivity increases. Prove that the representative firm's marginal cost will decrease at every output level if labour productivity increases by filling in the missing entries in the following table. New output levels refer to those after the productivity change. Continue to assume that the wage rate is $10 per worker.

Labour	Output		Total cost (dollars)	Marginal cost (dollars/unit)	
	Old	New		Old	New
0	0.0	0.0	100		
				0.67	_____
1	15.0	16.0	110		
				0.53	_____
2	34.0	36.0	120		
				0.71	_____
3	48.0	51.0	130		
				0.83	_____
4	60.0	64.0	140		
				5.00	_____
5	62.0	67.0	150		
				10.00	_____
6	63.0	69.0	160		
				20.00	_____
7	63.5	70.5	170		

4. The aggregate demand function is given by $P = 40 - 2Y$, and the short-run aggregate supply function is given by $P = 10 + Y$, where Y refers to real national income and P is the price level.
   (a) Graph the *AD* curve and indicate both intercept values in Figure 25-5.
   (b) Plot the *SRAS* curve and indicate its intercept value on the price axis.

Figure 25-5

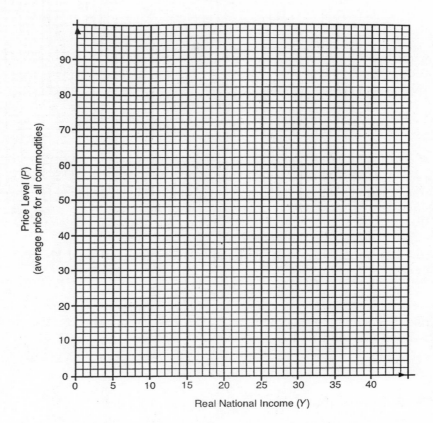

(c) Referring to the graph, what is the macroeconomic equilibrium (equilibrium levels of P and Y)? Prove algebraically that the intersection of the two equations yields these equilibrium values.

(d) Suppose that the expression for the *AD* curve became $P = 70 - 2Y$. Plot this expression in the graph, and discuss the changes that occurred to the levels of P and Y. Comment on the size of the horizontal shift in the *AD* curve in relation to the value of the change in output.

5. This exercise focuses on the value of the multiplier allowing for price changes. You are given the following information about an economy: The aggregate demand function is

$$P = \frac{60}{0.2Y - 25} \quad (1)$$

The short-run aggregate supply function is

$$P = 0.02Y. \quad (2)$$

The *AE* function is

$$AE = 0.8Y + 25 + 0.1(W/P). \quad (3)$$

P represents the price level, Y represents real national income, and W is nominal wealth. The marginal propensity to spend is 0.8, and the nominal value of wealth is 600.

(a) Graph the *AD* and *SRAS* curves.

Figure 25-6

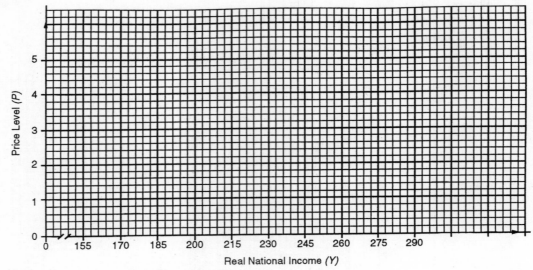

(b) According to the graph, what are the equilibrium values of *P* and *Y*?

(c) Using the equilibrium condition $Y = AE$, prove that your answer for the equilibrium value of *Y* (when $P = 4$) in (b) is confirmed.

(d) What is the value of the simple multiplier?

(e) Suppose that the *AE* function becomes $AE = 0.8Y + 10 + 0.1(W/P)$ because a component of autonomous expenditure decreases by 15. As a consequence, the *AD* function becomes $P = 60/(0.2Y - 10)$. When graphed, this expression lies to the left of the initial *AD* curve. If the price level remains at 4 for the time being, what is the new equilibrium level of *Y* according to the new *AE* function? (*Note:* This is not a permanent equilibrium value, as the next question in this exercise points out.)

(f) What is the quantity of output supplied at a price level of 4 according to the *SRAS* function? What is the quantity demanded at a price level of 4 according to the new *AD* function?

(g) In the situation depicted in (f), the price level will fall. Prove that the new *AD* curve intersects the *SRAS* curve at a price level of 3 and a real income level of 150.

(h) A fall in autonomous expenditure of 15 triggered a decline in the equilibrium level of Y of 50. What is the value of the multiplier that allows for price level changes? How does this value compare with the value of the simple multiplier? Explain.

6. Suppose that you are given the following values for the aggregate supply curve:

P	Aggregate supply	AD_a	AD_b	AD_c	AD_e	AD_f
1.0	0-50	_____	_____	_____	_____	_____
1.2	70	_____	_____	_____	_____	_____
1.4	80	_____	_____	_____	_____	_____
1.6	85	_____	_____	_____	_____	_____
1.8	85	_____	_____	_____	_____	_____
2.0	85	_____	_____	_____	_____	_____

(a) Assume that the aggregate expenditure function is $AE = 30 + 0.5Y - 5P$. Determine the appropriate entries for column AD_a and plot them in Figure 25-7, labelling the curve AD_a. (As a shortcut in deriving the AD curve without plotting the separate AE curves for each price level, note that equilibrium values of national income occur when $Y = 30 - 0.5Y - 5P$, and then simplify by combining the Y terms.) Therefore, the AD curve is a linear function. Also plot the AS curve. What is the equilibrium level of national income?

Figure 25-7

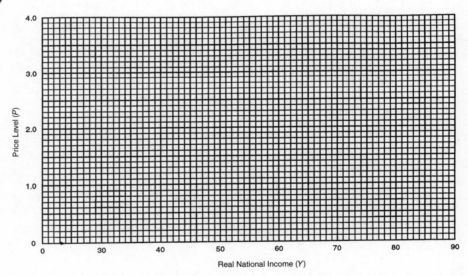

(b) Suppose that business confidence in the economy falls, so that investment declines by 10, and the AE function becomes $20 + 0.5Y - 5P$. Fill in the entries for the new AD curve under AD_b, and plot it on the graph. What is the new equilibrium level of national income?

(c) Suppose instead that business confidence rose, so that the AE function became $40 + 0.5Y - 5P$. Fill in the entries for the new AD curve (AD_c), and plot it on the graph. What is the new equilibrium level of national income?

(d) In (b) and (c), shifts in the AD curve by the same amount but in the opposite direction did not result in the same change in the absolute value of output. Explain why they did not.

(e) If the economy, instead, starts from a position where $AE = 47 + 0.5Y - 5P$, determine the appropriate AD curve entries (AD_e), plot them, and solve for the equilibrium level of income.

(f) Starting from a position where $AE = 47 + 0.5Y - 5P$, suppose that business confidence improves and investment rises by 10. What are the appropriate entries for the AD curve now (AD_f)? How does the resulting shift in the AD curve from (e) compare to the shift you determined from (a) to (c)? How does the change in equilibrium national income compare to what you found from (a) to (c)?

(g) From the various AD shifts you have examined, what can you conclude about the potential error from relying on the simple multiplier to predict changes in national income?

(h) Suppose that productivity in the economy rose with no offsetting increase in factor prices, so that the $SRAS$ curve shifted downward by 0.2 at all points. Based on AD_e, how do the new price level (P) and national income (Y) compare to the solution you found in (c)? What seems to be the dominant effect of the productivity change in this economy?

7. *"I don't give a . . . [expletive deleted] . . . about the slope of the SRAS curve."*

The Finance Minister is under extreme pressure from his caucus, the public, and the opposition parties to reduce unemployment and to eliminate a prolonged recessionary gap. He summons his key economic advisors in the central bank and the Department of Finance to (1) brief him on the current situation and to (2) advise him on various policy options.

After an hour's briefing, the Minister is assured that the officials from the central bank and his ministry have reached consensus on the following:
(1) The output (recessionary) gap is $8 billion.
(2) Private-sector autonomous expenditures are not likely to change in the foreseeable future.
(3) Over the period of the policy change, input (factor) prices will not change.
(4) The preferred policy change is an expansion in government expenditure.

The second hour of the briefing is acrimonious. The central bank officials argue that the slope of the $SRAS$ curve is very steep with the result that the multiplier value is 1.2. Therefore, they recommend a government expenditure increase of $6.67 billion. The Finance officials argue vehemently that the slope of the $SRAS$ curve is quite flat and recommend a government expenditure increase of $3.2 billion. Shouting occurs and accusations of incompetence are made by both parties. The Minister has heard enough! He slams his fist on the conference table and, paraphrasing the words of former President Richard Nixon, he replies "I don't give a . . . [expletive deleted] . . . about the slope of the $SRAS$ curve. Resolve the issue and give me a specific policy recommendation within 24 hours. And, you better be right, or many of you will find yourselves unemployed."

(a) What is the value of the government expenditure multiplier according to the Finance Department officials?

(b) Is the discrepancy between the two estimated multiplier values consistent with the differing views about the slope of the *SRAS* curve? Why might the two separate groups have differing views regarding the slope of the *SRAS* curve?

(c) Suppose that the views of the Department of Finance officials prevail. The Minister of Finance announces an increase in government expenditure of $3.2 billion. After all effects of the expenditure programs have been realized in the economy, it is reported to the Minister that real national income has increased by $3.8 billion and that the price level increase was larger than expected. The Minister is demoted to the backbenches with cabinet responsibility. What went wrong?

• • • • • • • • • • • • • • •

ANSWERS
Multiple-Choice Questions

1. (d)	**2.** (b)	**3.** (c)	**4.** (a)	**5.** (d)
6. (b)	**7.** (a)	**8.** (c)	**9.** (d)	**10.** (c)
11. (b)	**12.** (a)	**13.** (e)	**14.** (e)	**15.** (c)
16. (a)	**17.** (a)	**18.** (e)	**19.** (a)	**20.** (a)
21. (d)	**22.** (b)	**23.** (c)	**24.** (d)	**25.** (a)
26. (c)	**27.** (d)	**28.** (b)		

Exercises

1. (a) The missing entries are:
C_1: 2,700; 3,000; 3,300; 3,600; 3,900.
C_2: 2,550; 2,850; 3,150; 3,450; 3,750.
AE_1: 3,325; 3,550; 3,775; 4,000; 4,225.
AE_2: 3,175; 3,400; 3,625; 3,850; 4,075.

(b) For $P = 1$, national income is 4,000. For $P = 2$, national income is 3,625. See Figure 25-8 for the completed graph.

(c) *AE* shifts down; national income falls by 375.

(d) The *AD* curve slopes downward because consumption is an increasing function of real wealth. The *AD* curves drawn on the basis of two observations only are approximations, because the actual relationship based on the algebraic model is nonlinear, as determined by *W/P*.

(e) National income rises by 375. The marginal propensity to spend is 0.6 and the simple multiplier is 2.5. Note that $2.5 \times 150 = 375$.

(f) Greater government spending shifts the *AE* curve upward by 150 and the *AD* curve rightward by 375.

(g) The *AD* curve relates equilibrium national income to the price level, and therefore the change in the price level leads to a movement along the *AD* curve. The increase in government spending increases desired expenditures at all price levels, and the therefore the *AD* curve shifts rightward.

Figure 25-8

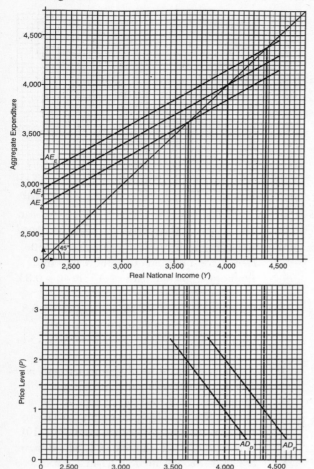

Figure 25-9

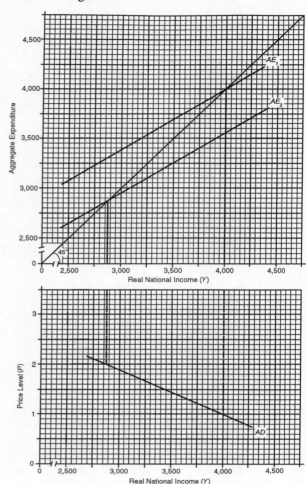

2. (a) Missing entries are as follows:

(I + G + X–IM)₁	(I + G + X–IM)₂	AE₁	AE₂
625	325	3,325	2,875
550	250	3,550	3,100
475	175	3,775	3,325
400	100	4,000	3,550
325	25	4,225	3,775

(b) Equilibrium levels are 4,000 at $P = 1$ and 2,875 at $P = 2$.

(c) See Figure 25-9.

(d) The slope of this AD curve is flatter than the AD curve in exercise 1.

(e) The larger the coefficient for the price term in the net export function (i.e., the more price-responsive net exports are), the flatter the AD curve.

(f) Flatter, flatter.

*3. (a) According to the schedule, the minimum ATC occurs at about 60 units.

(b) Marginal cost increases from 0.71 to 0.83. Average variable cost increases. Price must also rise to (at least) 0.83. Small; flat.

(c) The marginal productivity of labour falls for successive increments of workers; that is, the incremental contribution is falling. This can be shown by computing the ratio of the *change* in output associated with the change in labour. The third worker contributes 14 additional units of output; the fourth worker contributes only 12 additional units of output; the fifth worker contributes 2 additional units; and the sixth contributes only half a unit of output. Thus, marginal and unit costs increase because of diminishing marginal productivity of labour.

(d) Its marginal cost increases from 0.83 to 5.00. Unit variable costs increase as well. Price must rise to (at least) 5.00. Steep.

(e) Total costs are now 100, 120, 140, 160, 180, 200, 220, and 240. The marginal costs are now 1.33, 1.05, 1.42, 1.66, 10.00, 20.00, and 40.00. Unit variable costs are now 1.33, 1.18, 1.25, 1.33, 1.61, 1.90, and 2.20.

(f) The new marginal costs are 0.63, 0.50, 0.67, 0.77, 3.33, 5.00, and 6.67. The firm's new marginal cost curve will be below the original marginal cost curve.

4. (a) and (b)

Figure 25-10

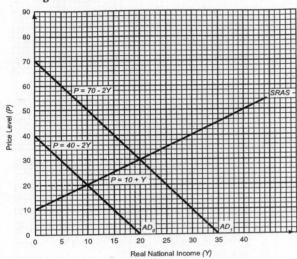

(c) Equilibrium is $P = 20$ and $Y = 10$. They can be solved algebraically by $40 - 2Y = 10 + Y$, which gives $Y = 10$. Substituting $Y = 10$ into either equation gives $P = 20$.

(d) See the graph. The new equilibrium is $P = 30$ and $Y = 20$. A demand shock has caused real income to increase by 10, but the horizontal shift in the AD curve is 15. Some of the stimulus from greater desired aggregate expenditures results in higher prices (a 50 percent increase) rather than greater output, because the expansion in output causes unit costs to increase.

5. (a) **Figure 25-11**

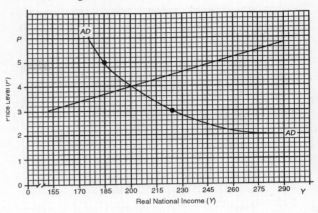

(b) The equilibrium levels are $P = 4$ and $Y = 200$.

(c) When $P = 4$, the value of real wealth is 150. Hence, consumption expenditure plus the autonomous components of AE are $40 + 0.8Y$. $AE = Y$ at $Y = 200$.

(d) Since the marginal propensity to spend is 0.8, the value of the simple multiplier is 5.0.

(e) Equilibrium is given by $Y = 0.8Y + 10 + 15$ or $Y = 125$.

(f) At $P = 4$, the quantity of aggregate supply is 200. At $P = 4$, the quantity of aggregate demand is 125.

(g) For equilibrium, aggregate supply equals aggregate demand or $0.02Y = 60/(0.2Y - 10)$. Substituting $P = 3$ into the $SRAS$ equation, we obtain $Y = 150$. Moreover, when $P = 3$, $Y = 150$ according to the AD function.

(h) The value of the multiplier is $50/15 = 3.33$. This is smaller than the value of the simple multiplier, which in this case is 5.0. This is because the fall in the price level (from 4 to 3) increases the real value of wealth, thereby stimulating more consumption, and the domestic price level falls relative to foreign prices, thereby stimulating more exports and fewer imports.

6. (a) The AD_a entries are 50, 48, 46, 44, 42, 40. Equilibrium national income is 50.

(b) The AD_b entries are 30, 28, 26, 24, 22, 20. Equilibrium national income is 30.

(c) The AD_c entries are 70, 68, 66, 64, 62, 60. Equilibrium national income is a little more than 68 (68.2), and the price level is a little less than 1.2 (1.18).

Figure 25-12

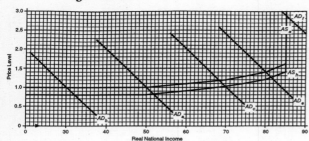

(d) When *AD* shifted leftward, the *SRAS* curve was horizontal and the price remained unchanged. When *AD* shifted rightward, the price level rose because the *SRAS* sloped upward, indicating that costs of production were higher at higher levels of output. The higher price reduces quantity demanded, and the increase in national income is smaller in absolute value than reported in (b).

(e) The *AD* entries are 84, 82, 80, 78, 76, 74. (By extrapolation, *AD* is 70 at *P* = 2.4, a useful point in orienting the *AD* curve for (f). Equilibrium national income is 80, and the price level is 1.4.

(f) The *AD* entries are 90 at *P* = 2.4, 88 at *P* = 2.6, 86 at *P* = 2.8, 84 at *P* = 3.0. Equilibrium national income is 85, and the price level is 2.9. *AD* shifts by the same amount in each case (10 times the simple multiplier, or 20), but here real output increases only from 80 to 85.

(g) Applying the simple multiplier is least likely to result in errors in predicting changes in national income when the economy is operating in the relatively flat portion of the *SRAS* curve. It becomes progressively less appropriate when the economy operates in the (relatively) steep portion of the *SRAS* curve.

(h) The price level falls from 1.18 to 1.0, and equilibrium national income rises from 68 to

70. The primary effect of the productivity increase is to reduce the price level, which increases the purchasing power of a given amount of income.

7. (a) To fill the recessionary gap of $8 billion, they believe that an increase in *G* of $3.2 billion is sufficient; their estimate of the multiplier value must be 2.5.

(b) Yes. A steep slope of the *SRAS* curve implies that any rightward shift in the *AD* curve will have a small effect on *Y* but a large effect on *P*. Hence, the multiplier value of a given increase in *G* will be low for the central bank officials. A steep slope of the *SRAS* curve means that central bank officials believe that unit costs will increase rapidly as output increases are stimulated by expenditure increases.

In contrast, the Finance Department officials must believe that firms have a great deal of excess capacity and hence output increases will invoke only small changes in unit costs and the price level.

(c) Your guess is as good as ours. Several possibilities exist. First, the assumption that private-sector spending was not likely to change might have been wrong. During the period of government expenditure expansion, private-sector spending may have fallen. Second, the assumption of constant input prices might have been wrong. As government expenditure increases triggered price increases, factor prices might have increased also. Hence, the effect of the rightward shift in the *AD* curve might have been countervailed by a leftward shift of the *SRAS* curve. Third, the central bank officials might have been right. The slope of the *SRAS* curve might have been quite steep. Notice that the increase in real national income of $3.8 billion is quite close to their predicted value of $3.28 billion (1.2 × 3.2).

CHAPTER 26

NATIONAL INCOME AND THE PRICE LEVEL IN THE LONG RUN

CHAPTER OVERVIEW

In the previous chapter, we considered the importance of supply conditions in determining national income and the price level, assuming factor prices could not change. In this chapter we allow for factor prices to change in the long run. Hence, a long-run aggregate supply (*LRAS*) is added to the aggregate demand and supply analysis.

For an economy initially producing its potential output, the short-run effect of an increase in aggregate demand is for output and price level to increase. The inflationary gap leads to higher factor prices (wages) and a leftward shift in the *SRAS* curve. The *SRAS* curve will continue to shift leftward until the price level rises enough to eliminate excess demand. Hence, the economy returns to its potential output level. Thus, the *LRAS* curve is vertical at the economy's potential output level. A decrease in aggregate demand causes a recessionary gap, leading to slower wage growth or possibly lower wages. Thus, the *SRAS* curve will shift rightward, thereby generating lower prices and greater output. However, some economists believe that this adjustment process takes a very long time.

Fiscal policies to stabilize the economy may encounter several difficulties. There are lags in recognizing output gaps, making decisions to deal with them, implementing those decisions, and then reversing them when demand conditions change. However, some changes in taxation and transfer payments occur automatically as the economy changes.

LEARNING OBJECTIVES

After studying this chapter, you should be able to:

- indicate how inflationary (positive) output gaps and recessionary (negative) output gaps create pressure for factor prices to change;
- demonstrate that changes in unit labour costs depend on the relationship between the change in labour productivity and the change in the wage rate;
- recognize the asymmetry of wage adjustments, with increases (during inflationary gaps) occurring much more rapidly than decreases (during recessionary gaps);
- explain how wage adjustments shift the *SRAS* curve;
- indicate why, after all input prices have been adjusted to eliminate output gaps, the long-run aggregate supply (*LRAS*) curve will be vertical at the economy's potential level of output;
- explain why prolonged recessionary gaps can result if wages are "sticky" in a downward direction;
- explain the possible roles of discretionary fiscal policy and automatic stabilizers in dealing with recessionary gaps.

MULTIPLE-CHOICE QUESTIONS

1. In an *AD-SRAS* diagram, a recessionary gap is shown by
  (a) the *AD* and *SRAS* curves intersecting at an output level that is to the right of potential GDP.
  (b) the *SRAS*, *AD*, and *LRAS* curves intersecting at the same output level.
  (c) the *AD* and *SRAS* curves intersecting at an output level that is to the left of potential GDP.
  (d) the horizontal distance between the *AD* and *SRAS* curves for any price level.
  (e) the vertical distance between the *AD* and *SRAS* curves for any output level.

2. A recessionary gap is characterized by
  (a) actual output greater than potential output.
  (b) a tendency for wages to rise more rapidly than productivity.
  (c) unemployment greater than the natural rate of unemployment.
  (d) rising input prices and a rising price level.
  (e) falling potential GDP.

3. Starting from a position in which potential national income is constant and equal to actual income, an expansionary demand shock will result in
  (a) short-run increases in both the price level and real GDP.
  (b) a recessionary gap, which creates pressure for factor price increases.
  (c) pressure for a rightward shift of the *SRAS* curve.
  (d) All of the above.
  (e) None of the above.

4. From an initial position where actual output equals potential output, a decrease in aggregate demand is likely to cause
  (a) potential GDP to increase.
  (b) the supply of labour and capital to increase.
  (c) upward pressure on wages.
  (d) the price level to decrease if the *SRAS* curve is horizontal.
  (e) None of the above.

5. A decrease in aggregate demand will, in the long run, cause
  (a) the *SRAS* curve to shift to the left if factor prices are flexible.
  (b) the *SRAS* curve to shift to the right if factor prices are rigid downward.
  (c) persistent unemployment if factor prices are flexible.
  (d) persistent unemployment if factor prices are sticky downward.
  (e) Both (b) and (d).

6. If wages rise 5 percent while productivity rises 3 percent, in the short run
  (a) real wages rise 8 percent.
  (b) the *SRAS* curve shifts to the right.
  (c) the *SRAS* curve shifts to the left.
  (d) real wages fall 2 percent.
  (e) Both (b) and (d).

7. When a large recessionary gap exists, which of the following situations is an economy more likely to face?
  (a) Wages rise 5 percent while productivity rises 3 percent.
  (b) Wages and productivity rise by 3 percent.
  (c) The *AD* curve shifts to the left until the gap is eliminated.
  (d) The *SRAS* curve shifts to the left until the gap is eliminated.
  (e) Wages rise 3 percent while productivity rises 5 percent.

8. With a vertical *LRAS* curve, in the long run
  (a) shifts in aggregate demand affect the price level but not the level of output.
  (b) the price level is determined by demand factors alone.
  (c) the price level depends upon the slope of the *AD* curve alone.
  (d) output is determined by demand factors alone.
  (e) economic growth occurs as the *LRAS* curve shifts to the left.

9. Which of the following depicts economic growth in the long run?
   (a) The *SRAS* curve shifts to the right.
   (b) The *LRAS* curve shifts to the right.
   (c) The *AD* curve shifts to the right.
   (d) Potential GDP increases over time.
   (e) Both (b) and (d).

10. The *LRAS* curve is likely to shift rightward if
    (a) tax changes reduce incentives for investment.
    (b) the nation's supplies of all factors of production increase.
    (c) tax decreases cause higher levels of aggregate demand.
    (d) factor prices increase.
    (e) national saving decreases.

11. From an initial position in which potential and actual income are equal, which of the following causes an inflationary gap, all else equal?
    (a) An increase in taxes.
    (b) A sharp rise in investment expenditure.
    (c) An increase in imports.
    (d) An increase in desired saving at every level of real income.
    (e) A leftward shift in the *SRAS* curve.

12. Which of the following is *not* likely to be associated with the initial stages of an inflationary gap?
    (a) Rising output.
    (b) Increasing unit costs.
    (c) Increasing unemployment.
    (d) A rising price level.
    (e) Rightward shifts in the *AD* curve.

13. If wages were flexible downward,
    (a) leftward shifts in *SRAS* could offset recessionary gaps.
    (b) rightward shifts in *SRAS* could offset recessionary gaps.
    (c) a recessionary shock would be compounded as income fell and the *AD* curve shifted to the left.
    (d) the *AD* would shift to the right, offsetting the recessionary shock.
    (e) prolonged periods of recessionary gaps might occur.

14. The combination of a rising price level and falling real national income (stagflation) most likely results from
    (a) aggregate demand shifts along a given *SRAS* curve.
    (b) automatic adjustments to offset a recessionary gap.
    (c) rightward shifts in the *LRAS* curve along a constant *AD* curve.
    (d) leftward shifts in the *SRAS* curve along a constant *AD* curve.
    (e) productivity gains greater than wage rises.

15. The vertical long-run aggregate supply curve shows that, given full adjustment of input prices,
    (a) potential real income is compatible with any price level.
    (b) output is determined solely by the level of aggregate demand.
    (c) equilibrium real national income is indeterminate.
    (d) the price level is determined solely by aggregate supply.
    (e) output is at its utmost limit.

Questions 16 through 21 refer to Figure 26-1. The curves with the subscript 0 refer to the initial situation.

Figure 26-1

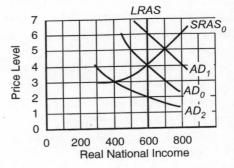

16. Given the *LRAS* curve, at the initial situation
    (a) we know that the economy has reached its potential real income level, and the price level is 4.
    (b) potential income is greater than actual real income, although the equilibrium price level is 4.
    (c) the economy is at a short-run equilibrium in terms of income and the price level, but not in terms of input prices.
    (d) the economy is in equilibrium, but factor use is above normal levels.
    (e) the economy is at its utmost limit of productive capacity.

17. Suppose that the *AD* curve shifts to *AD₁* as government purchases rise. In the short run,
    (a) potential national income increases to 700 and the price level rises to 5.
    (b) real national income increases by 100 and the price level increases to 5 due to wage increases.
    (c) an inflationary gap of 100 occurs, unit costs increase even though factor prices are constant, and the price level increases to 5.
    (d) real national income increases by 200, factor prices remain constant, and the price level remains at 4.
    (e) real national income remains constant, but the price level increases to 6.

18. As a result of the inflationary gap caused by the *AD* shock,
    (a) unit labour costs fall.
    (b) unit labour costs rise.
    (c) the *SRAS* curve shifts to the right.
    (d) the *LRAS* curve shifts to the right.
    (e) the *AD* curve shifts to the left as real wealth falls.

19. The economy's long-run equilibrium after this demand shift will be
    (a) a real income level of 600, higher nominal factor prices, and a price level of 6.
    (b) a real income level of 400 and a price level of 3.
    (c) a price level of 6 and real income of 800, due to an induced rightward shift of the *AD* curve.
    (d) potential and real income equal to 700 and a price level of 6.
    (e) a real income level of 800 and a price level of 4.

20. Suppose that the *AD* curve shifted from *AD₀* to *AD₂* because of a decline in investment expenditure. The short-run impact of this contractionary demand shock is
    (a) a recessionary gap of 200.
    (b) lower unit costs.
    (c) an equilibrium price level of 3.
    (d) an increase in unemployment.
    (e) All of the above.

21. Given the investment decline, the situation described in question 20 will persist, possibly for a long period of time, if
    (a) some other autonomous expenditure component increases.
    (b) factor prices remain constant or decrease very slowly.
    (c) factor prices rise proportionately less than productivity.
    (d) real factor prices fall.
    (e) increases in government expenditure shift the *AD* curve to the right.

22. Constant unit labour costs result when
    (a) wages rise at the same rate as prices.
    (b) wages rise at the same rate as productivity.
    (c) technology improves at the same rate factor supplies grow.
    (d) factor supplies are constant and output increases beyond potential GDP.
    (e) the economy moves up its *LRAS* curve.

23. In the long run when all prices and factor prices have adjusted, the effect of a once-and-for-all increase in government expenditures that creates an initial inflationary gap will be
    (a) an increase in potential GDP.
    (b) a higher price level, but no change in real national income.
    (c) no change in real national income, but probably a higher private-sector share of *AE*.
    (d) Both (b) and (c).
    (e) stagflation.

24. Movements along a budget surplus function indicate
    (a) a discretionary fiscal policy aimed at increasing tax rates.
    (b) a contractionary fiscal policy involving decreases in government expenditure.
    (c) a deliberate change in policy aimed at increasing transfer payments.
    (d) the existence of automatic stabilizers in the net tax system.
    (e) Both (a) and (b).

25. Which of the following are potential limitations of discretionary fiscal policy?
   (a) There may be long decision lags.
   (b) The change in fiscal policy may overshoot its target because factor prices may be working simultaneously to eliminate the gap problem.
   (c) Private-sector decision makers may view the policy to be short-lived and, hence, they do not change their expenditure plans.
   (d) All of the above.
   (e) None of the above.

26. Assuming private expenditure functions do not shift, a decrease in the government's budget surplus due to a discretionary fiscal policy change
   (a) represents contractionary fiscal policy.
   (b) would be an appropriate policy for closing an inflationary gap.
   (c) will shift the aggregate demand curve to the right.
   (d) will have no effect on aggregate demand.
   (e) would not shift the budget surplus function.

27. If there is currently an inflationary gap, an appropriate fiscal policy would be to
   (a) increase taxes.
   (b) increase government spending on goods and services.
   (c) decrease taxes.
   (d) increase transfer payments.
   (e) reduce the budget surplus.

28. If government transfer payments fall when national income expands, it can be said that these payments are
   (a) countercyclical, since they will rise relative to GDP when GDP is rising.
   (b) procyclical, since they fall relative to GDP when GDP is rising.
   (c) countercyclical, since they fall relative to GDP when GDP is rising.
   (d) inconsistent with an upward-sloping consumption function.
   (e) autonomous expenditure.

29. The paradox of thrift implies that
   (a) increased saving directly generates economic growth in the short run.
   (b) increased saving reduces aggregate demand and increases unemployment in the short run.
   (c) reducing the cyclically adjusted budget deficit is an appropriate short-run policy to stimulate the economy.
   (d) individuals lack adequate incentives to save.
   (e) None of the above.

· · · · · · · · · · · · ·

EXERCISES

1. Show graphically and explain the short-run and long-run adjustments that you expect from the following economic changes, given that the economy starts from a position where actual income equals potential income. Assume that the *LRAS* curve is not affected by these events.
   (a) An increase in desired investment due to greater optimism about future economic prospects.

   (b) An increase in the savings rate due to a maturing of the baby-boom generation.

   (c) An increase in the price of imported oil due to political instability in major producing regions.

   (d) An increase in domestic grain production due to favourable weather conditions.

Figure 26-2

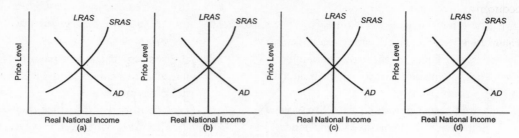

Real National Income
(a)

Real National Income
(b)

Real National Income
(c)

Real National Income
(d)

2. An economy's *SRAS* function is $P = 1 + 0.01Y$, which is presented below in schedule form, where P is the price level and Y is the level of real national income. The long-run aggregate supply curve is vertical at a real national income level of 1,000. Two schedules for the *AD* curve are presented, with case I being the initial situation.

SRAS		LRAS		AD			
				Case I		Case II	
Y	P	Y	P	Y	P	Y	P
0	1.0	1,000	1.0	0	111.0	0	116.5
500	6.0	1,000	6.0	500	61.0	500	66.5
1,000	11.0	1,000	11.0	1,000	11.0	1,000	16.5
1,050	11.5	1,000	11.5	1,050	6.0	1,050	11.5

(a) Taking case I for the *AD* curve, what are the equilibrium levels of P and Y? What is the value of the output gap?

(b) Assume that the *AD* curve shifts right, represented by case II. If the *SRAS* curve does not change immediately, what are the new short-run equilibrium values for P and Y? What type of gap exists, and what is its magnitude?

(c) Given the shift of the *AD* curve, what do you predict will happen in the long run to the equilibrium levels of P and Y? What will happen to the inflationary gap?

(d) Explain what is likely to happen to the *SRAS* curve in the long run. Rewrite the algebraic expression for it, assuming that the slope of the *SRAS* curve does not change.

3. The combination of $Y = 480$ and $P = 1.0$ in Figure 26-3 depicts the initial equilibrium situation in an economy.

Figure 26-3

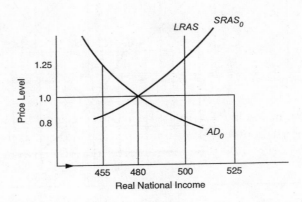

(a) The initial equilibrium reflects what sort of output gap?

(b) If the government chose to wait for factor price changes to eliminate the current gap, what predictions for future values of Y and P, assuming the appropriate factor price changes do occur, would you make?

(c) The government is concerned that the policy stance associated with part (b) will take too long. Thus, the government considers eliminating the gap by increasing its expenditures by 8. It has arrived at this number by knowing that the value of the simple multiplier is 2.5. Show this policy stance in the diagram above. (*Hint:* Draw the new AD curve parallel to AD_0.) Will this policy change eliminate the output gap? Explain.

(d) Demonstrate the consequences of a fiscal policy that expands government expenditures by 18. Draw the corresponding AD curve on the diagram (again, parallel to AD_0) and explain whether you would expect this equilibrium to change in the long run.

(e) What was the value of the multiplier for the policy stance in part (c)? Explain why this multiplier value is less than the simple multiplier.

4. A newly elected prime minister inherits the economic situation depicted in Figure 26-4. Current potential real income is 1,800.

Figure 26-4

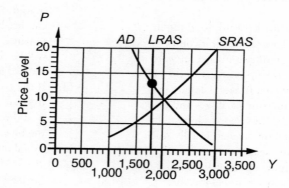

(a) Describe the economic situation that he inherited from the previous government.

(b) If the government does nothing, what is likely to happen to real national income and the price level in future time periods? Assume that aggregate demand (from the private sector) does not change.

(c) The new prime minister believes strongly that appropriate tax policies can increase investment and capital stock in the long run. His government initiates tax changes to affect the *LRAS* curve. Describe the general nature of the tax changes, and explain what this policy action is attempting to do.

(d) The opposition in the House of Commons vehemently objects to the government's policy. What arguments might they muster?

• • • • • • • • • • • • • •

ANSWERS
Multiple-Choice Questions

1. (c)	**2.** (c)	**3.** (a)	**4.** (e)	**5.** (d)
6. (c)	**7.** (e)	**8.** (a)	**9.** (e)	**10.** (b)
11. (b)	**12.** (c)	**13.** (b)	**14.** (d)	**15.** (a)
16. (a)	**17.** (c)	**18.** (b)	**19.** (a)	**20.** (e)
21. (b)	**22.** (b)	**23.** (b)	**24.** (d)	**25.** (d)
26. (c)	**27.** (a)	**28.** (c)	**29.** (b)	

Exercises

1. (a) The *AD* curve shifts rightward in the short run, resulting in greater output and higher prices. Higher prices likely cause wage demands to increase, causing an induced shift in the *SRAS* curve leftward and restoring the initial level of potential income at a higher price level.

(b) The *AD* curve shifts leftward and rotates to become steeper as a result of an increase in the marginal propensity to save. A recessionary gap develops that puts downward pressure on wages and prices. If wages decline, the *SRAS* curve shifts rightward, restoring the initial level of potential income at a lower price level. Due to asymmetric adjustment in the labour market, the recessionary gap may remain for a considerable time.

(c) The SRAS curve shifts leftward, resulting in higher prices and lower national income. Higher prices may induce a further leftward shift in the SRAS, as workers react to the fall in real wages. However, the recessionary gap exerts downward pressure on wages and prices. If wages decline, the SRAS curve shifts rightward, and the economy may eventually reach its potential income again.

(d) The SRAS curve shifts rightward, resulting in lower prices and higher national income. Lower prices may induce a further rightward shift in the SRAS. However, the inflationary gap exerts upward pressure on wages and prices as hours of overtime rise and capacity utilization rates increase. Wages are likely to rise, shifting the SRAS curve leftward, and the economy returns to its long-run potential income.

2. (a) The equilibrium levels are $P = 11$ and $Y = 1,000$. The output gap is 0.

(b) The new equilibrium levels are $P = 11.5$ and $Y = 1,050$. The output gap is a positive value (+50). This is known as an inflationary gap.

(c) Since the economy now tries to operate beyond its potential level, unusually high demand for factors will trigger increases in factor prices. As a consequence, the SRAS curve will shift to the left. In the long run, potential national income will be retored at $Y = 1,000$. According to the new AD curve (case II), $Y = 1,000$ is associated with a price level of 16.5. The short-run inflationary gap will be eliminated in the long run, but the long-run price level will be higher than that which resulted in the short run.

(d) As explained above, the SRAS curve shifts upward and intersects the AD curve and the LRAS curve at $P = 16.5$ and $Y = 1,000$. You can solve algebraically for the amount by which the SRAS curve shifts upward. Initially, $P = 1 + .01Y$, and for given values of P and Y you can determine the intercept term, a: $16.5 = a + .01 \times 1,000$, so $a = 16.5 - 10 = 6.5$ and $P = 6.5 + .01Y$.

3. (a) The initial situation reflects a recessionary gap, since output of 480 is less than potential output of 500, shown by the LRAS curve.

(b) The SRAS curve would shift down along the aggregate demand curve until potential income is reached ($Y^* = 500$) at a price level of 0.8.

(c) An increase in government expenditure of 8

will shift the AD curve to the right by 20. The new AD curve intersects the LRAS curve at $P = 1$ and $Y = 500$, but it intersects the SRAS curve at a level of output less than potential output. Although the size of the recessionary gap has been reduced, a recessionary gap still remains. It is possible that the remaining gap will be eliminated if factor prices decrease, thereby shifting the SRAS curve to the right.

(d) If the government expands its purchases by 18, the new AD curve will shift to the right and pass through the point $P = 1$ and $Y = 525$. If the new AD curve has the same slope as the initial one, it will also pass through the point $P = 1.25$ and $Y = 500$. There will be no need for factor prices to adjust in the long run since the recessionary gap has been eliminated.

(e) The multiplier is calculated by dividing 20 by 18, which is equal to 1.11 and is considerably lower than the simple multiplier value, 2.5. When unit costs and prices rise, some aggregate expenditures are reduced. Specifically, real wealth decreases, and hence some consumption expenditure is reduced. Moreover, as the domestic price increases, net exports are likely to fall.

4. (a) The prime minister has inherited an inflationary gap of 200. Current equilibrium levels of real national income and price are 2,000 and 10, respectively.

(b) If the government does nothing, the economy will adjust by itself. Factor prices will most likely increase, thereby shifting the SRAS curve to the left until it intersects the LRAS curve at $Y = 1,800$ and $P = 13$. As a result, the economy will have an even higher price level, but the inflationary gap will have been eliminated.

(c) The prime minister's policies should involve lower tax rates, which stimulate more investment expenditure, which increases the capital stock. Thus potential real income is affected in the long run. If these policies are totally successful, the LRAS curve will shift to the right, perhaps to $Y = 2,000$ or beyond. Since equilibrium real national income equals the new potential level (2,000), the inflationary gap has been eliminated, and there will be no pressures for the SRAS curve to shift to the left.

(d) The opposition should base their arguments on the fact that tax reductions will stimulate increases in AD. In the short run, there will be even higher pressures for prices and factor prices to increase. Moreover, the added pressures caused by AD increases may prevail for some time, since it is possible that the tax changes may take a long time to shift the LRAS curve to the right.

PART NINE

MONEY, BANKING, AND MONETARY POLICY

CHAPTER 27

THE NATURE OF MONEY AND MONETARY INSTITUTIONS

CHAPTER OVERVIEW

This is first of three chapters that discuss the role of money in the economy. This chapter discusses the functions of money, the evolution of money as a medium of exchange from gold to paper to demand deposits (chequing), and elements of the money supply in the current Canadian economy.

The banking system in Canada consists of two main elements: the Bank of Canada (which is the central bank) and the commercial banks. The Bank of Canada is a publicly owned corporation that is responsible for the day-to-day conduct of monetary policy. Commercial banks are profit-seeking institutions that allow their customers to transfer demand deposits from one bank to another by means of cheques.

When the banking system receives a new cash deposit, it can create new deposits to some multiple of this amount. The amount of new deposits created depends on the banks' target reserve ratio, the amount of cash drain to the public, and whether the banks choose to hold excess reserves.

LEARNING OBJECTIVES

After studying this chapter, you should be able to:

- distinguish the various functions of money;
- explain the historical development of fractionally backed money and fiat money;
- understand the various functions of the Bank of Canada, the nation's central bank;
- understand the structure of the banking system, which includes the Bank of Canada, Schedule A (chartered), B, and C banks, and other financial intermediaries such as trust companies and credit unions;
- distinguish among target, required, and excess reserves in the context of a fractional reserve banking system;
- explain the process by which the banking system can increase and decrease deposit money, given a set of assumptions regarding the target reserve ratio and cash drain from the banking system;
- distinguish among money, money substitutes, and near money as well as among various types of deposit money.

MULTIPLE-CHOICE QUESTIONS

1. For money to serve as an efficient medium of exchange, it must have *all but which* of the following characteristics?
   (a) General acceptability.
   (b) Convertibility into precious metals.
   (c) High value relative to its weight.
   (d) Divisibility.
   (e) Very difficult to counterfeit.

2. The value of money depends primarily on
   (a) the gold backing of the currency alone.
   (b) the gold backing of both currency and deposits.
   (c) its purchasing power.
   (d) who issues it.
   (e) a government decree.

3. To be a satisfactory store of value, money must have
   (a) a relatively stable value.
   (b) a direct relationship to national income.
   (c) a highly volatile value over time.
   (d) no interest payments for holding it.
   (e) the backing of a precious metal, typically gold.

4. "Debasing" the coinage had the effect of
   (a) causing prices to fall in the economy.
   (b) changing relative prices.
   (c) increasing the purchasing power of each coin.
   (d) a loss to the person issuing the coins.
   (e) causing inflation.

5. A fractionally backed paper money system exists when claims against banks' reserves
   (a) have 100 percent backing in precious metals such as gold.
   (b) exceed the value of actual reserves.
   (c) have a direct relationship to national income.
   (d) have a fixed relationship to the quantity of coinage.
   (e) are less than the value of actual gold reserves.

6. Today, paper money in Canada is issued by
   (a) all Schedule A banks.
   (b) the federal Department of Finance.
   (c) Schedule A and Schedule B banks, including some trust companies.
   (d) the central bank of Canada (the Bank of Canada).
   (e) the Privy Council.

7. All Canadian currency (coins and paper notes) is
   (a) fractionally backed by gold reserves.
   (b) totally backed by gold.
   (c) interest-bearing.
   (d) fiat money.
   (e) backed by deposits in the commercial banks.

8. Which of the following is not an asset of a commercial bank?
   (a) Foreign currency holdings.
   (b) Reserves.
   (c) Loans.
   (d) Government of Canada securities.
   (e) Deposits of households.

9. The reserve ratio is the fraction of a bank's
   (a) deposits that it must hold in the form of currency.
   (b) deposits that it holds as reserves either in currency or as deposits with the Bank of Canada.
   (c) assets that it holds in the form of reserves.
   (d) reserves that it must hold in the form of deposits with the Bank of Canada.
   (e) None of the above.

10. Which one of the following is *not* a function of the Bank of Canada?
    (a) Providing banking services for the federal government.
    (b) Acting as a lender of last resort to the banks.
    (c) Controlling the supply of money and credit.
    (d) Lending to business firms.
    (e) Supporting money markets.

11. The deposits of banks at the Bank of Canada, which constitute their reserves, appear as
    (a) a liability on the Bank of Canada's balance sheet.
    (b) an asset on the Bank of Canada's balance sheet.
    (c) a liability on the balance sheet of the banks.
    (d) an asset on the balance sheet of the banks.
    (e) Both (a) and (d).

12. Purchase and resale agreements (PRA) involve
    (a) sales and purchases of government securities among banks.
    (b) sales and purchases of government securities between the Bank of Canada and the banks.
    (c) sales of government securities by investment dealers to the Bank of Canada with agreement to repurchase them at a later date.
    (d) sales of government securities by investment dealers to the Government of Canada with agreement to repurchase them at a later date.
    (e) guaranteed loans by the federal government to private businesses.

13. Which of the following is *not* an asset of the Bank of Canada?
    (a) Government of Canada deposits.
    (b) Government of Canada securities.
    (c) Advances to banks.
    (d) Government of Canada securities held under PRA.
    (e) Foreign currency holdings.

14. The process of creating deposit money by banks
    (a) is possible because of the fractional reserve system.
    (b) is consciously undertaken by each bank.
    (c) must occur if there are excess reserves.
    (d) permits only small, gradual changes in the money supply.
    (e) None of the above.

15. A reduction in bank reserves by payments of currency to foreigners will
    (a) always cause a multiple contraction in deposits.
    (b) cause a multiple contraction in deposits only if there are no excess reserves.
    (c) never affect domestic deposits.
    (d) never affect the availability of domestic credit.
    (e) never affect GDP in the short run.

16. If a bank currently holds $600 million in deposits and $40 million in reserves and has a target reserve ratio of 6 percent, this bank has
    (a) excess reserves of $36 million.
    (b) required reserves of $4 million.
    (c) target reserves of $2.4 million.
    (d) target reserves of $40 million.
    (e) excess reserves of $4 million.

17. Suppose a bank has a target reserve ratio of 4 percent. It loses $10 million of its initial deposits of $100 million. Which of the following statements is true?
    (a) To maximize profits, the bank must have been holding initially $40 million in reserves.
    (b) After the loss in deposits, target reserves are $4 million.
    (c) After the loss in deposits, the bank has deficient reserves.
    (d) After the loss in deposits, the bank has excess reserves.
    (e) To maximize profits, the bank initially had more than $4 million in reserves.

18. Assuming a fixed target reserve ratio (v) of 10 percent in a banking system and no cash drain out of the banking system, a banking system that receives $1.00 in new reserves can increase new deposits ultimately by
    (a) $10.00, which is $1/v$ times $1.00.
    (b) 10 cents, which is 10 percent of $1.00.
    (c) the ratio $1/(1 - v)$, which in this case is approximately $1.11.
    (d) $1.10, which is $(1 + v)$ times $1.00.
    (e) $1.00 times $1/1 - z$.

19. The existence of a currency drain from the banking system will, other things being equal,
    (a) reduce the ability of the banking system to expand or contract the money supply.
    (b) have no effect on the ability of the banking system to contract the money supply.
    (c) have no effect on the ability of the banking system to expand the money supply.
    (d) increase the ability of the banking system to expand or contract the money supply.
    (e) increase the marginal propensity to save.

Questions 20 through 23 refer to the following information about a banking system.
(i) There is a banking system in which each bank has a fixed target reserve ratio of 5 percent.
(ii) There is no currency drain from the banking system, and all banks are assumed to hold no excess reserves for a prolonged period of time.
(iii) Banks experiencing excess (deficient) reserves respond by increasing (decreasing) loans.
(iv) The current status of the balance sheet of all banks is as follows:

Assets		Liabilities
Reserves:	$_____	Deposits: $300 million
Loans:	$270 million	
Securities:	$_____	

20. If all banks initially had no excess reserves,
    (a) the reserves of the banks must have been $30 million.
    (b) the holdings of securities by the banks must have been $15 million.
    (c) the reserves of the banks must have been 5 percent of loans, or $13.5 million.
    (d) the reserves of the banks must have been $300 million.
    (e) the reserves of the banks must have been 5 percent of securities.

21. If all banks initially had $16 million of actual reserves, then
    (a) excess reserves are $15 million.
    (b) the banks have $1 million in deficient reserves (negative excess reserves).
    (c) excess reserves are $1 million.
    (d) target reserves are equal to actual reserves.
    (e) the banks must borrow from the Bank of Canada.

22. Assuming that the banking system begins with no excess reserves, a loss of $1 million of deposits from the system will ultimately lead to
    (a) a reduction in the money supply of $19 million.
    (b) a reduction in the money supply of $500,000.
    (c) an increase in the money supply of $20 million.
    (d) deposit liabilities in the banking system of $280 million.
    (e) an increase in the money supply of $19 million.

23. Assuming that the banking system begins with no excess reserves, a gain of $1 million of deposits will ultimately lead to
    (a) increased deposits of $19 million.
    (b) increased loans of $20 million.
    (c) increased loans of $1 million.
    (d) a $5 million increase in the money supply.
    (e) increased deposits of $20 million.

24. The doctrine of the neutrality of money states that the quantity of money influences
    (a) the level of money prices but has no effect on the real part of the economy.
    (b) the real part of the economy but has no effect on the money part of the economy.
    (c) both the real and money parts of the economy in an identical fashion.
    (d) neither the real nor the money part of the economy.
    (e) only M2.

25. Different definitions of the money supply include different types of deposits. The narrowly defined money supply, called M1, includes currency and
    (a) term deposits.
    (b) demand deposits.
    (c) all deposits of Schedule A banks.
    (d) personal savings deposits.
    (e) foreign currency deposits.

26. A money substitute is something that serves as a
    (a) store of value.
    (b) unit of account.
    (c) temporary medium of exchange but not as a store of value.
    (d) temporary medium of exchange and also as a store of value.
    (e) medium of exchange and a unit of account.

27. A rise of the Consumer Price Index from 100 to 110 would change the store of value represented by $1,000 in currency to
    (a) $1,100.   (b) $900.
    (c) $909.   (d) no change ($1,000).
    (e) $9.09.

28. The multiple expansion of deposits triggered by a $1 new deposit into the banking system will be reduced if
    (a) there is no cash drain at every stage of the process.
    (b) every bank increases its target reserve ratio.
    (c) every bank lowers its target reserve ratio.
    (d) the Bank of Canada lowers a required reserve ratio.
    (e) None of the above.

Questions 29 to 31 are based on the following monetary aggregate (billions of dollars) for October 1995.

Chartered bank net demand deposits	33.8
Nonpersonal notice deposits and personal savings deposits	322.1
Currency outside banks	26.0
Deposits at non-bank financial institutions	231.5

Source: *Bank of Canada Review*, Fall 1995.

29. The value of M1 at this date was (in billions)
    (a) 33.8.   (b) 26.0.
    (c) 381.9.   (d) 613.4.
    (e) 59.8.

30. The value of M2 at this date was (in billions)
    (a) 59.8.   (b) 381.9.
    (c) 355.9.   (d) 348.1.
    (e) 613.4.

31. The component of M3 at this date (in billions) *not* included in either M1 or M2 was
    (a) 33.8.   (b) 26.0.
    (c) 322.1.   (d) 231.5.
    (e) Both (a) and (b).

• • • • • • • • • • • • •

EXERCISES

1. Indicate which of the three functions of money is demonstrated in each of the following transactions. Use the appropriate number: (1) medium of exchange, (2) store of value, (3) unit of account.
    (a) Farmer Brown puts cash in a mattress. _____
    (b) Storekeeper Jones adds up the total sales for the day. _____
    (c) Plumber Smith makes $500 per week. _____
    (d) Travelling salesperson Lee buys $100 of gasoline per week. _____
    (e) The Blacks buy a good oriental rug with the thought that it will keep its value for a long time.

    _____

2. Which of the following might be regarded in Canada as money, which as near money, and which as neither? Explain your answers briefly.
    (a) A share of stock in Bell Canada. _____

    (b) A $10 Bank of Canada note. _____

(c) A Canada Savings Bond maturing in 2001. _____

(d) A bank note issued by a Saskatchewan bank in 1897. _____

(e) An ounce of gold in a Krugerrand (South African coinage provided for hoarders and speculators). _____

(f) A fixed-term account at a trust company. _____

(g) A personal chequing deposit at the Bank of Montreal. _____

3. Arrange the following items on the proper side of a bank's balance sheet.
   (a) Demand deposits   2,000,000
   (b) Savings and time deposits   4,080,000
   (c) Currency in vaults   60,000
   (d) Deposits in the Bank of Canada   1,000,000
   (e) Loans to the public   4,000,000
   (f) Security holdings (Canadian government,
        provincial, municipal, and other)   1,500,000
   (g) Bank building and fixtures   360,000
   (h) Capital and surplus   920,000
   (i) Foreign currency assets   80,000

Assets	Liabilities

4. We use "T-accounts," abbreviated balance sheets for a bank, to show changes in a bank's reserves, loans, and deposits. Make the entries on the following T-accounts, using + and − signs to show increase or decrease, for each of the following independent events. (Remember that all changes must balance.)

		Assets	Liabilities
(a)	You deposit your paycheque of $100 at your bank.	Reserves: Loans and securities:	Deposits:
(b)	A bank sells $10,000 of government bonds in the open market to replenish its reserves.	Reserves: Loans and securities:	Deposits:
(c)	A bank makes a loan of $5,000 to a local business and credits it to its chequing account.	Reserves: Loans and securities:	Deposits:
(d)	A bank sells $50,000 of securities to the Bank of Canada and receives deposits in the Bank of Canada.	Reserves: Loans and securities:	Deposits:
(e)	A business uses $5,000 of its demand deposits to pay off a loan from the same bank.	Reserves: Loans and securities:	Deposits:
(f)	A banks orders $5,000 in currency from the Bank of Canada.	Reserves: Loans and securities:	Deposits:

5. Suppose that Bank A, a Canadian bank, begins with the T-account shown here. The target reserve ratio is assumed to be 10 percent. Joe Doe, a holder of a deposit in Bank A, withdraws $1,000 and deposits this amount in a commercial bank in a foreign country. Thus, $1,000 has been taken out of the Canadian banking system.

Bank A (initial situation)		Bank A (after the withdrawal)	
Reserves: $10,000 Loans: $90,000	Deposits: $100,000	Reserves: Loans:	Deposits:

(a) What were Bank A's target reserves? Did it have excess reserves initially?

(b) Show the immediate effect of the withdrawal from Bank A.

(c) What is the status of Bank A's reserves now?

(d) Bank A reacts by calling in a loan that it had made to Mary Smith equal to the amount of its reserve deficiency. Mary repays the loan by writing a cheque on her account in Bank B, another Canadian bank that also has a fixed target reserve ratio of 10 percent. Bank B's initial T-account is shown next. Fill in the T-accounts for the effects of Bank A's receiving the payment from Mary and of Bank B's losing Mary's deposit.

Bank B (initial situation)		Bank B (after losing Mary's deposit)	
Reserves: $5,000 Loans: $45,000	Deposits: $50,000	Reserves: Loans:	Deposits:

Bank A	
(after receiving loan repayment)	
Reserves:	Deposits:
Loans:	

(e) After this transaction, does Bank A have deficient reserves? Does Bank B?

(f) In fact, Bank B has a deficiency of reserves. It reacts by calling in a loan made to Peter Piper equal to the amount of the deficiency. Peter cashes in a deposit that he held in Bank C; that is, Bank C loses a deposit and Peter repays Bank B. Bank C's initial situation is shown next; its target reserve ratio is also 10 percent. Fill in the T-accounts for the effects of Bank B's receiving the loan repayment and Bank C's losing Peter's savings deposit.

Bank C		Bank C	
(initial situation)		**(after losing Peter's deposit)**	
Reserves: $7,000	Deposits: $70,000	Reserves:	Deposits:
Loans: $63,000		Loans:	

Bank B	
(after receiving loan repayment)	
Reserves:	Deposits:
Loans:	

(g) After this transaction, does Bank B have deficient reserves? Does Bank C?

(h) After this transaction, the reduction in the money supply has been Joe's original withdrawal plus $ _____ in other deposits. Loans have been reduced by $_____ .

(i) Assuming a 10 percent target ratio of all banks, the process will continue until the total reduction in the money supply will be $_____ . The total reduction in loans will be $_____ .

6. Suppose that a foreign company withdraws money from its account in a foreign country, buys $1 million of Canadian currency, and deposits this sum into the Canadian banking system. The target reserve ratio for each bank is assumed to be 8 percent, and there is no currency drain from the banking system. The initial situation in the Canadian banking system is depicted as follows:

All banks	
(after receiving loan repayment)	
Reserves: $ 72 million	Deposits: $900 million
Loans: $728 million	
Securities: $100 million	

(a) According to the initial scenario, target reserves are $_____ and excess reserves are $_____.

(b) After the $1 million deposit, target reserves are $_____ and excess reserves are $_____.

(c) Assuming that all excess reserves are used to expand loans, the final (increase, decrease) in the money supply will be _____ times the new $1 million deposit, which is equal to _____.

(d) The final (increase, decrease) in loans will be $_____.

7. Star Bank, a Schedule A Canadian bank that currently has $300 million in deposits, has been operating with a target reserve ratio of 8 percent. Judy Kupferschmidt has just inherited the equivalent of $1 million Canadian from a relative living in Florida and deposits this sum in this bank.

   (a) If the bank continued to operate on an 8 percent target reserve basis, what is the magnitude of its excess reserves after Judy's deposit? (Assume Star Bank had no initial excess reserves.)

   (b) If other Canadian banks also had 8 percent target reserve ratios and there was no cash drain from the banking system, what might be the final change in the Canadian money supply?

   (c) Suppose that Star Bank considers the risk of extending new loans from the excess reserves created by Judy's deposit to be too high. It decides to hold all of Judy's deposits in reserves. What is its new target reserve ratio, approximately? Will a multiple expansion in bank deposits occur?

   (d) Assume that the scenario in (a) holds; Judy deposits $1 million in Star Bank. All Canadian banks, including Star, have a constant target reserve ratio of 8 percent. However, the Canadian public normally holds 2 percent of its money holdings in the form of currency (Bank of Canada notes and coins). If all banks used all of their excess reserves to extend loans, what would be the maximum possible change in the Canadian money supply?

• • • • • • • • • • • • •

ANSWERS

Multiple-Choice Questions

1. (b)	2. (c)	3. (a)	4. (e)	5. (b)
6. (d)	7. (d)	8. (e)	9. (b)	10. (d)
11. (e)	12. (c)	13. (a)	14. (a)	15. (b)
16. (e)	17. (c)	18. (a)	19. (a)	20. (b)
21. (c)	22. (d)	23. (e)	24. (a)	25. (b)
26. (c)	27. (c)	28. (b)	29. (e)	30. (b)
31. (d)				

Exercises

1. (a) 2.　(b)　1 and 3.
   (c) 3.　(d)　1.
   (e) 1, and the rug serves as function 2.

2. (a) Neither.　　　　(b) Money.
   (c) Near money; it is easily convertible to money.
   (d) Neither; once money but now a collector's item.
   (e) Neither, but readily convertible into money and considered by some to be a good store of value.
   (f) Near money.
   (g) Money.

3.	Assets		Liabilities	
Currency in vaults	$ 60,000	Demand deposits	$2,000,000
Deposits in Bank of Canada	1,000,000	Savings deposits	4,080,000
Loans to public	4,000,000		
Security holdings	1,500,000		
Bank building and fixtures	360,000	Capital and surplus	920,000
Foreign currency assets	80,000		
	$7,000,000		$7,000,000

4. (a) Reserves +$100; deposits +$100.
   (b) Reserves +$10,000; securities −$10,000.
   (c) Loans +$5,000; deposits +$5,000.
   (d) Reserves +$50,000; securities −$50,000.
   (e) Loans −$5,000; deposits −$5,000.
   (f) Total reserves unchanged; currency +$5,000; reserve deposits with the Bank of Canada, −$5,000.

5. (a) Target reserves = $10,000; no.
   (b) Deposits −$1,000 to $99,000; reserves −$1,000 to $9,000.
   (c) Target reserves = $9,900; actual reserves = $9,000; hence, its reserves are deficient by 900.
   (d) Bank A: reserves +$900; loans −$900
       Bank B: reserves −$900 to $4,100; deposits −$900 to $49,100.
   (e) Bank A does not, but Bank B has a deficiency of $810.
   (f) Bank B: reserves +$810; loans −$810
       Bank C: reserves −$810 to $6,190; deposits −$810 to $69,190.
   (g) No, but Bank C has a deficiency of $729.
   (h) −$900 + (−$810) + (−$729) = −$2,439; loans down by $1,710.
   (i) $10,000; $9,000.

6. (a) $72 million (0.08 × $900 million); 0.
   (b) $72.08 million (0.08 × $901 million); $920,000.
   (c) Increase; 12.5 (1/0.08); $12.5 million.
   (d) Increase; $11.5 million (12.5 − 1.0).

7. (a) $920,000.
   (b) $12.5 million (= 1/0.08 × $1 million).
   (c) Its initial reserve holdings were $24 million. After Judy's deposit, reserves are $25 million and total deposits are $301 million. Therefore, the new target reserve ratio is 8.3 percent. No; Star has no excess reserves to lend out. Thus, no other bank receives additional reserves.
   (d) $10 million increase. This is obtained by multiplying $1 million by 1/(0.08 + 0.02). The value 0.08 is the reserve ratio and 0.02 is the cash drain.

CHAPTER 28

• • • • • • • • • • • • • • •

THE ROLE OF MONEY IN MACROECONOMICS

• • • • • • • • • • • • • • •

CHAPTER OVERVIEW

This chapter considers the transmission mechanism by which changes in the money supply influence macroeconomic variables such as the interest rate, real national income, and the price level. An important chain of causation is as follows: an increase in the money supply causes an initial disequilibrium in the money and bond markets, which leads to a decline in the equilibrium level of the interest rate. The lower interest rate causes an increase in desired aggregate expenditure (particularly investment) and hence in aggregate demand. Two important determinants of the size of this effect are the extent to which the demand for money and the amount of desired investment respond to changes in the interest rate. Also, you should read Extension 28.2 which outlines the transmission mechanism in an open economy. Changes in domestic interest rates can affect the external value of the domestic currency, which in turn affects net exports.

The chapter discusses three motives for holding money. The negative relationship between the quantity demanded for money and the interest rate is called the *liquidity preference function*. Bonds represent another asset that can be held in one's wealth portfolio. The relationship between the yield (interest) of a bond and its price is outlined at the beginning of the chapter.

The chapter concludes by demonstrating the short-run effects of a change on the money supply on real income and the price level in an *AD-SRAS* framework. Once again, the slope of the *SRAS* curve determines the extent to which a shift in the *AD* curve (caused by a change in the money supply) changes Y and P.

• • • • • • • • • • • • • • •

LEARNING OBJECTIVES

After studying this chapter, you should be able to:

■ explain the relationship between the market price of a bond and its interest rate;

■ identify three alternatives for holding money;

■ explain the demand for money as a function of interest rates, national income, and the price level;

■ distinguish between real and nominal money balances;

■ explain why the slopes of the marginal efficiency of investment curve and the liquidity preference curve determine the effect that a change in the money supply has on national income;

■ understand that the effect of a monetary change on national income also depends on the slope of the *SRAS* curve triggered by changes in input prices;

■ explain the negative slope of the aggregate demand curve using the monetary transmission mechanism.

1. In a free market, the equilibrium market price of a bond will be
   (a) the present value of the income stream it produces.
   (b) unaffected by changes in the interest rate.
   (c) the sum of the annual returns, compounded to their value at the end of the asset's useful life.
   (d) positively related to its yield.
   (e) the same as its face value, or its principal value.

2. A bond promises to pay $1,000 one year from now. At an interest rate of 8 percent, the bond's present value is $_____. If the interest rate were 10 percent, the market value of the bond would be $_____.
   (a) $926; $909.   (b) $1,000; $1,000.
   (c) $920; $900.   (d) $1,080; $1,100.
   (e) $556; $500.

3. The opportunity cost to firms and households of holding money balances is
   (a) zero, since all economic transactions require the use of money.
   (b) the forgone interest that could have been earned on other assets.
   (c) low when interest rates are high.
   (d) the interest rate received on chequing accounts.
   (e) zero, since the Bank of Canada pays no interest for holding commercial bank reserves.

4. A bond that pays interest forever and never repays the principal is called a
   (a) perpetuity.   (b) preferred share.
   (c) fixed-term bond.   (d) treasury bill.
   (e) junk bond.

5. When the interest rate on an annual basis is 7 percent, the present value of a bond that promises to pay $114.49 one year hence is equal to
   (a) $1,635.57.   (b) $122.50.
   (c) $107.00.   (d) by definition, $114.49.
   (e) $8.01.

6. If Sue pays $95.238 for a one-year bond that promises to pay $100 at the end of the year, the interest rate on this bond, if Sue holds it to maturity, is
   (a) 5.24 percent.   (b) 5.00 percent.
   (c) 4.76 percent.   (d) 9.52 percent.
   (e) 23.8 percent.

7. The amount of money held for transaction balances will
   (a) vary positively with national income measured in current prices.
   (b) vary positively with interest rates.
   (c) vary negatively with the value of national income.
   (d) be larger with shorter intervals between paydays.
   (e) be zero if there are interest-bearing assets.

8. Precautionary balances would be expected to increase if
   (a) business transactions were to become much less certain.
   (b) interest rates increased.
   (c) people were expecting securities prices to rise.
   (d) prices and incomes fell.
   (e) the market prices of bonds fell.

9. The speculative motive for holding money balances
   (a) applies to bonds but not other interest-earning assets.
   (b) varies positively with national income.
   (c) assumes that the opportunity cost of holding cash balances is zero.
   (d) suggests that individuals will hold money in order to avoid or reduce the risk associated with fluctuations in the market prices of bonds.
   (e) deals with the uncertainty of future transactions.

10. If there is an excess supply of money, households and firms will
    (a) sell bonds and add to their holdings of money, thereby causing the interest rate to fall.
    (b) purchase bonds and reduce their holdings of money, thereby causing the interest rate to rise.
    (c) purchase bonds and reduce their holdings of money, thereby causing the interest rate to fall and bond prices to rise.
    (d) purchase bonds and reduce their holdings of money, thereby causing the price of bonds to fall.
    (e) sell bonds and add to their holdings of money, thereby causing the price of bonds to fall.

11. Suppose that the real and nominal value of *M1* was $16.7 billion in 1975 and that prices doubled between 1975 and 1983. What would be the nominal value of M1 in 1983 that maintains a constant real supply of money over this period?
    (a) $8.35 billion.   (b) $33.4 billion.
    (c) $16.7 billion.   (d) $14.7 billion.
    (e) None of the above.

12. Changes in interest rates caused by monetary disequilibrium
    (a) are usually of little consequence in influencing economic activity in the short run.
    (b) will have little effect on the prices of long-term bonds.
    (c) cause the liquidity preference function to shift, thus affecting desired investment expenditures.
    (d) cause a change in the money supply, thereby affecting interest-sensitive expenditures.
    (e) provide the link between changes in the money supply and changes in aggregate demand.

13. Other things being equal, a fall in the interest rate will cause
    (a) a shift in the *MEI* function to the left.
    (b) a shift in the *MEI* function to the right.
    (c) a movement down the *MEI* function.
    (d) a movement up the *MEI* function.
    (e) the market price of bonds to fall.

14. The marginal efficiency of the investment curve illustrates the
    (a) positive relation between investment and the rate of interest.
    (b) negative relation between investment and the rate of interest.
    (c) negative relation between the capital stock and the rate of interest.
    (d) positive relation between the capital stock and the rate of interest.
    (e) rate of return on bonds for various maturity dates.

15. A movement from excess demand for money balances to monetary equilibrium
    (a) tends to increase aggregate demand.
    (b) has an unpredictable effect on aggregate demand.
    (c) tends to decrease aggregate demand.
    (d) will affect aggregate demand but not the interest rate.
    (e) will increase the demand for bonds.

16. If the Bank of Canada increases the money supply, we would expect the
    (a) interest rate to fall, the *AE* curve to shift upward, and the *AD* curve to shift to the left.
    (b) interest rate to fall, the *AE* curve to shift downward, and the *AD* curve to shift to the right.
    (c) interest rate to rise, the *AE* curve to shift upward, and the *AD* curve to shift to the left.
    (d) interest rate to fall, the *AE* curve to be unaffected, and the *AD* curve to become flatter.
    (e) interest rate to fall, the *AE* curve to shift upward, and the *AD* curve to shift rightward.

17. A rise in the price level, other things being equal, will tend to shift the *AE* function downward because of
    (a) reduced demand for money balances.
    (b) a rise in the demand for nominal money balances, which increases interest rates.
    (c) an excess supply of money balances, which decreases interest rates.
    (d) the fact that interest rates will fall.
    (e) the fact that real wealth increases.

18. The monetary adjustment mechanism will eliminate an inflationary gap by
(a) raising interest rates, reducing investment, and increasing aggregate expenditure.
(b) lowering interest rates, increasing investment, and increasing aggregate expenditure.
(c) raising interest rates, reducing investment, and moving leftward along the *AD* curve.
(d) raising interest rates, reducing investment, and shifting the *AD* curve.
(e) increasing the exchange rate.

19. A given change in the money supply will exert a larger effect on real national income in the short run
(a) the flatter the *LP* curve is and the steeper the *MEI* curve is.
(b) the flatter both the *LP* and *MEI* curves are.
(c) the steeper both the *LP* and *MEI* curves are.
(d) the steeper the *LP* curve is and the flatter the *MEI* curve is.
(e) if the economy operates with the steep portion of the *SRAS* curve.

20. A sufficiently large rise in the price level will eliminate an inflationary gap provided that
(a) the nominal money supply remains constant.
(b) the nominal money supply increases.
(c) the Bank of Canada validates the inflation.
(d) government expenditures are financed by increases in the money supply.
(e) the liquidity preference curve is flat.

21. An inflation is said be *validated* when
(a) the money supply increases at the same rate as the price level rises.
(b) the nominal supply decreases at the same rate as the price level rises.
(c) the monetary adjustment mechanism is unaffected by Bank of Canada policy.
(d) Statistics Canada releases the inflation data to the federal government.
(e) wages rise with the rate of inflation.

22. Bond X matures in 2 years and bond Y matures in 10 years. An increase in the interest rate
(a) causes a larger percentage decline in the price of bond Y than in that of bond X.

(b) causes a smaller percentage increase in the price of bond Y than in that of bond X.
(c) causes the same percentage change in the price of both bonds.
(d) has no effect on the price of either bond.
(e) must also change the face value of each bond.

Questions 23 through 27 refer to Figure 28-1. An initial equilibrium at point *a* is changed by an increase in the money supply. The new short-run equilibrium is shown by point *b*.

Figure 28-1

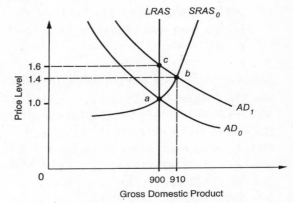

23. Point *b* represents
(a) an inflationary gap of 10, but constant factor prices.
(b) a recessionary gap of 10, but higher unit costs.
(c) a negative output gap of 10, but higher factor costs.
(d) long-run equilibrium, since input prices will never change.
(e) higher factor prices than at point *a*.

24. An increase in the money supply shifted the *AD* curve to the right because
(a) an excess demand for money was created in the money market; thus interest rates and investment expenditure will both increase.
(b) consumption expenditure increased as real GDP increased.
(c) real wealth decreased.
(d) a decline in interest rates stimulated more investment expenditures.
(e) None of the above.

25. The gap situation depicted at point *b* is likely to cause further adjustment. Specifically, we would expect
(a) input prices to rise.
(b) the *SRAS* curve to begin shifting leftward.
(c) the price level to increase beyond 1.4.
(d) a movement upward along AD_1.
(e) All of the above.

26. As the adjustment described in question 25 occurs, we would expect
(a) the nominal demand for money to increase.
(b) the interest rate to rise as long as the central bank does not expand the money supply beyond the initial increase.
(c) a decrease in investment expenditure as interest rates increase.
(d) a decrease in consumption and net exports as prices rise.
(e) All of the above.

27. As long as input price changes completely offset the price change, the long-run impact of the monetary expansion will be
(a) at point *b*, since real wages do not change.
(b) increases in both real GDP and the price level.
(c) a price level of 1.6 and GDP of 900, or point *c*.
(d) at point *a*, since price increases cause the *AD* curve to shift leftward to its initial position.
(e) higher real and nominal GDP.

28. The short-run impact of a decrease in the money supply on real national income will be high if
(a) the economy operates in the steep portion of its *SRAS* curve.
(b) the liquidity preference curve is perfectly elastic.
(c) the *MEI* curve is perfectly inelastic.
(d) factor prices fall causing the *SRAS* curve to shift rightward.
(e) None of the above.

29. If there is 10 percent inflation while interest rates, real wealth, and real national income are constant,
(a) the demand for real money balances will increase by 10 percent.

(b) the demand for nominal money balances will fall by 10 percent.
(c) the demand for real money balances will decrease by 10 percent.
(d) the demand for nominal money balances will increase by 10 percent, leaving real money balances unchanged.
(e) the demand for nominal money balances will be unchanged.

30. Between 1986 and 1990, *M2* increased by $189.2 billion to $254.4 billion while the consumer price index increased from 100 to 119.5. Over this period, we observe that the real value of *M2*
(a) increased from $1.89 billion to $2.29 billion.
(b) increased from $189.2 billion to $254.4 billion.
(c) increased by about 19.5 percent.
(d) decreased by about 19.5 percent.
(e) increased by about 12.5 percent.

Questions 31 to 33 refer to the material in Extension 28.2.

31. Increases in Canadian interest rates relative to those in the rest of the world
(a) will increase Canadians' demand for foreign assets.
(b) will decrease foreigners' demand for Canadian assets.
(c) will decrease Canadians' and foreigners' demand for Canadian assets.
(d) will increase Canadians' and foreigners' demand for Canadian assets.
(e) Both (a) and (b).

32. If Canadian interest rates rise relative to those in other countries,
(a) the demand for Canadian dollars in international exchange markets will increase.
(b) the demand for Canadian dollars in international exchange markets will fall.
(c) the exchange rate will rise.
(d) the external value of the Canadian dollar will rise.
(e) Both (a) and (d).

33. The transmission mechanism of a money increase on real national income is potentially greater in an open economy than a closed economy if
(a) domestic interest rates are tied to foreign interest rates.
(b) the domestic currency depreciates thereby stimulating exports and discouraging imports.
(c) the external value of the domestic currency rises thereby stimulating exports and discouraging imports.
(d) domestic interest rate decreases cause the exchange rate to fall.
(e) if net exports are perfectly inelastic with respect to price changes.

● ● ● ● ● ● ● ● ● ● ● ● ● ●

EXERCISES

1. Using Table 17.1 in the Study Guide, calculate the present value for each of the following assets:
(a) A bond that promises to pay $100 three years from now and has a constant annual interest rate of 2 percent.

(b) A bond that promises to pay $100 two years from now and has a constant annual interest rate of 6 percent.

(c) A perpetuity that pays $100 a year and has an annual interest rate of 15 percent.

(d) An investment that pays $100 after one year, $150 after two years, and $80 after three years and has an annual interest rate of 10 percent.

2. If you are not convinced that interest rates and present value are negatively related, perhaps this exercise will eliminate your doubt. The present value of a bond is the market equilibrium price of the bond. Consider two bonds, A and B. Bond A promises to pay $120 one year hence, and bond B promises to pay $120 two years from now.
(a) Calculate the present value for bond A when the interest rate is 8 percent. Calculate the present value for interest rates of 10 percent, 20 percent, and 25 percent. What happened to the market price when interest rates rose?

(b) If you were told that the market price (present value) of bond A increased, what would you conclude is happening to the interest rate on bond A?

(c) Calculate the present value for bond B for interest rates of 10 percent, 20 percent, and 25 percent.

(d) Which of the two bonds had the larger percentage change in its price when the interest rate rose from 10 to 20 percent?

(e) If the current rate of interest on both bonds were 20 percent, which bond would currently be selling for the higher market price? Why?

(f) An individual who insists on receiving a 14 percent return on all assets would be prepared to pay what market price for bond A? For bond B?

3. Suppose that a household is paid $1,000 at the beginning of each month. The household spends all of its income on the purchase of goods and services each month. Furthermore, assume that these purchases are at a constant rate throughout the month. Consequently, payments and receipts are not perfectly synchronized.

(a) What is the value of currency holdings at the beginning of the month? At the end of the first week? At the end of the third week? At the end of the month?

(b) What is the magnitude of the *average* currency holdings over the month?

(c) Suppose that the household's income increases to $1,200 and purchases of goods and services during a month are equal to this amount. What is the *average* currency holding?

(d) Suppose that the household is paid $1,000 over the month but in instalments of $500 at the beginning of the month and $500 at the beginning of the third week. What is the magnitude of the *average* currency holdings per month?

4. Two liquidity preference curves are illustrated in Figure 28-2.

Figure 28-2

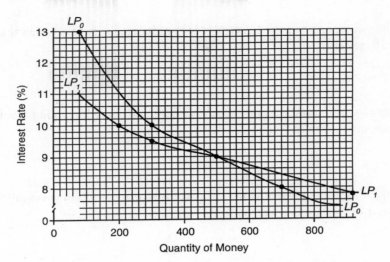

(a) Using your knowledge of the transactions and speculative motives for money, explain why the quantity of money demanded falls when interest rates rise.

(b) If the money supply is 500 and constant at all levels of interest rates, what interest rate is associated with monetary equilibrium? Plot the supply of money function in the graph, and indicate the monetary equilibrium interest rate.

(c) Suppose that the monetary authority decreased the money supply from 500 to 300. At an interest rate of 9 percent, what kind of situation exists in the money market? Would households and firms tend to buy or sell bonds? Explain. Predict what is likely to happen to bond prices and interest rates.

(d) As interest rates rise, what happens to the quantity of money demanded? Predict the new equilibrium level of interest rates first using LP_0 and then using LP_1.

(e) What increase in the money supply (from 500) would be necessary to achieve an equilibrium interest rate of 8 percent if LP_0 applies? If LP_1 applies? Comment on how the shape of the LP curve affects the effectiveness of monetary policy to achieve an interest rate target.

5. (a) Explain and illustrate graphically an excess demand for money, and predict the effect on interest rates.

Figure 28-3

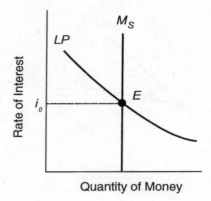

(b) Explain and illustrate graphically an excess supply of money, and predict the effect on interest rates.

Figure 28-4

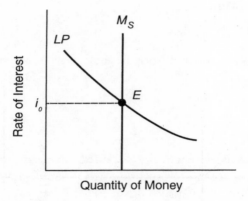

(c) Predict the effect of an increase in the money supply by the Bank of Canada on the rate of interest and desired investment expenditure. Initial equilibrium is M_{SO}, i_0, P_0, and I_0.

Figure 28-5

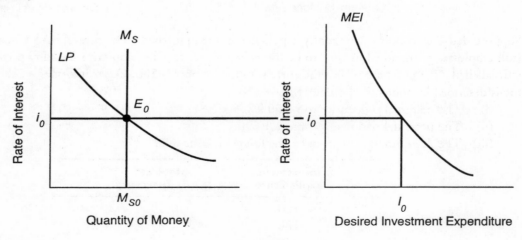

(d) Assuming a constant price of P_0, show the effect of an increase in desired expenditure on the equilibrium level of real national income. Initial equilibrium is E_0 in both graphs.

Figure 28-6

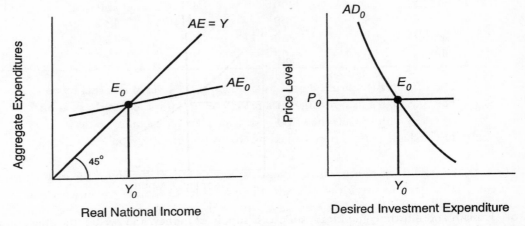

(e) Show the effect of an increase in the price level, other things being equal, on the rate of interest and investment expenditure. Start from equilibrium at E_0, i_0, and I_0, and assume that the supply of money remains constant.

Figure 28-7

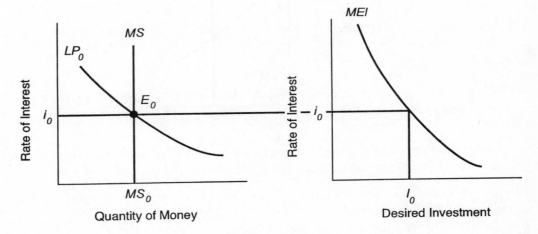

6. Suppose that the economy is currently experiencing unemployment. The central bank considers potential (full-employment) national income to be the policy objective. The economy's liquidity preference curve is that labelled LP_0 in exercise 4, and the current money supply is 500. Other information about the economy is described in points (i) through (vii).
   (i) The marginal propensity to spend is 0.50.
   (ii) The potential national income is 1,600.
   (iii) The *MEI* function is given by the following schedule:

Investment expenditure	Interest rate (percent)
160	13
180	11
200	9
210	8

(iv) Aggregate expenditures are depicted by the following schedule:

Y	C	I	G	NX	AE
1,520	912	200	300	138	1,550
1,540	924	200	300	136	1,560
1,560	936	200	300	134	1,570
1,580	948	200	300	132	1,580
1,600	960	200	300	130	1,590

(v) The *LP* curve is not influenced by changes in the level of national income.

(vi) The *SRAS* curve is horizontal at a price level of 2.0 for all levels of national income less than potential national income (1,600), at which level it becomes vertical.

(vii) The exchange rate is not affected by changes in monetary policy.

The central bank sets its research department to work in order to establish accurate information about the current situation and to suggest what it should do in order to eliminate unemployment.

(a) Referring to the LP_0 curve in exercise 4, what is the current equilibrium level of the interest rate?

(b) Given the interest rate, what is the level of desired investment expenditure according to the *MEI* schedule?

(c) What is the current equilibrium value of real national income? What is the value of the output gap?

(d) What is the value of the simple multiplier? What change in autonomous expenditure is required for the economy to achieve the potential national income level without inflation?

Based on the information in (a) through (d), the research department is in a position to recommend policy changes for the central bank.

(e) Should the money supply be increased or decreased? Should the interest rate be increased or decreased?

(f) Changes in the money supply and the interest rate will change the level of investment. How much must investment be increased from its current level in order to achieve potential national income?

(g) To achieve this higher level of investment, what is the required level of the interest rate? (Refer to the *MEI* schedule.)

(h) Given the required level of the interest rate, what must the money supply be in order to achieve equilibrium in the money market at that interest rate? Refer to the LP_0 curve in exercise 4. What change in the current money supply is necessary?

Now suppose that the central bank is successful in lowering the interest rate and increasing investment by the appropriate magnitudes. It follows that real national income should increase by a multiple and attain a level of 1,600.

(i) Calculate the new level of consumption expenditure and calculate the aggregate level of expenditure at $Y = 1,600$. Is this an equilibrium situation?

(j) Illustrate the change in the AE and AD functions in Figure 28-8.

Figure 28-8

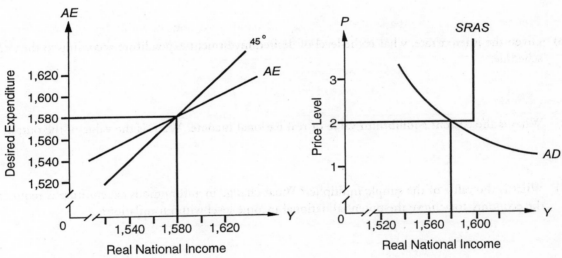

7. **"Failures of the Transmission Mechanism"**
   Question 6 was based upon many assumptions that affect the ability of the central bank to eliminate gap situations. We review some of them in separate cases in this question.

   (a) Suppose that the liquidity preference curve was flat at an interest rate of 9 percent instead of that portrayed in exercise 4. What are the implications for the central bank's ability to eliminate the recessionary gap of 20?

   (b) Now suppose that the LP_0 curve in question 4 holds, but that the MEI schedule [assumption (iii)] changes to one that indicates that investment expenditure remains at 200 regardless of interest rate. Explain what this means and note the implications for the central bank's ability to eliminate the recessionary gap of 20.

(c) Assume that the *LP* and *MEI* schedules are those indicated in question 6. Now, however, assumption (vi) changes so that the *SRAS* curve is upward sloping rather than flat. Indicate the implications of this new assumption on the ability of the central bank to eliminate the recessionary gap. (*Hint:* Part of your answer should deal with the assumption of constant factor prices.)

(d) Let's change assumption (vii). If prices rise because of the change in the money supply and the exchange rate is free to move (up or down), how will the exchange rate (or the external value of the domestic currency) be affected? Will this help or hinder the efficacy of the transmission mechanism?

Appendix Exercise

The following exercise is based on the material in the appendix to this chapter. Read the appendix before attempting this exercise.

8. This exercise focuses on the shape of the aggregate demand curve and the monetary adjustment mechanism. The following two tables show the effects of changes in the price level on desired investment.

	LP Schedule	
	Quantity of money demanded	
Interest rate	P = 1	P = 2
4	80	100
6	70	90
8	60	80
10	50	70
12	40	60
14	30	50

MEI Schedule	
Rate of interest	Desired investment expenditure
10	180
11	179
12	177
13	174
14	170

Assume that the nominal supply of money is fixed at a value of 50.

(a) Assume that the price level is 1.0, what is the equilibrium interest rate? What is desired investment expenditure?

(b) Assume that the price level becomes 2.0. For a given level of real national income, what will happen to the demand for money? What will happen in the bond market? Explain.

(c) Using the *LP* schedule for *P* = 2, determine the new equilibrium interest rate.

(d) Given this change in the interest rate, what is the new level of desired investment expenditure?

The following table shows the effects of changes in desired investment (*I*) on real national income (*Y*).

Y	C	I (i = 10%)	AE (i = 10%)	AE (i =14%)
340	170	180	350	_____
350	175	180	355	_____
360	180	180	360	_____
370	185	180	365	_____

(e) What is the equilibrium level of real national income (*Y*) associated with an interest rate of 10 percent and a price level of 1.0?

(f) Given the interest rate increase because of a doubling of the price level, what is the level of desired investment? Fill in the values for the new level of aggregate expenditure. What is the new equilibrium level of *Y*?

Now we synthesize the relationship between *P* and *Y*.

(g) Graph the *AD* curve, plotting the negative relationship between *P* and *Y* for this exercise. Use your answers to (e) and (f).

Figure 28-9

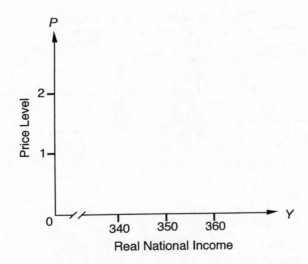

ANSWERS
Multiple-Choice Questions

1. (a)	**2.** (a)	**3.** (b)	**4.** (a)	**5.** (c)
6. (b)	**7.** (a)	**8.** (a)	**9.** (d)	**10.** (c)
11. (b)	**12.** (e)	**13.** (c)	**14.** (b)	**15.** (c)
16. (e)	**17.** (b)	**18.** (c)	**19.** (d)	**20.** (a)
21. (a)	**22.** (a)	**23.** (a)	**24.** (d)	**25.** (e)
26. (e)	**27.** (c)	**28.** (e)	**29.** (d)	**30.** (e)
31. (d)	**32.** (e)	**33.** (b)		

Exercises

1.
(a) PV = $100/(1 + 0.02)3 = $94.23.
(b) PV = $100/(1 + 0.06)2 = $89.00.
(c) PV = $100/0.15 = $666.67.
(d) PV = $100/(1.10) + $150/(1.10)2 + $80/(1.10)^3.
   PV = $90.91 + $123.97 + $60.11 = $274.99.

2.
(a) PV at 8 percent is $120/(1.08) = $111.11; PV at 10 percent is $120/(1.10) = $109.09; PV at 20 percent is $120/(1.20) = $100.00; PV at 25 percent is $120/(1.25) = $96.00. As the interest rate increased, the market price (present value) of bond A fell.
(b) Other things being equal, the interest rate must have been falling.
(c) PV at 10 percent is $120/(1.10)^2 = $99.17
   PV at 20 percent is $120/(1.20)^2 = $83.33
   PV at 25 percent is $120/(1.25)^2 = $76.80
(d) The price of bond A fell from $109.09 to $100.00, a 8.3 percent decrease. Bond B, having a longer maturity period, had a 16.0 percent decline in its price.
(e) Bond A has the higher market price (compare $100.00 with $83.33). The further in the future that dollars are received, the lower the present value of those dollars, other things being equal. For bond A, $120 was received one year from now, whereas bond B paid $120 two years from now.
(f) The person should be prepared to pay $105.26 for bond A, $92.34 for B.

3.
(a) $1,000, $750, $250, $0.
(b) $1,000/2 = $500.
(c) $1,200/2 = $600.
(d) $500/2 = $250.

4.
(a) As the opportunity cost of money rises, people will tend to economize on their transactions

demand for money. In addition, they are prepared to take more risk (and therefore buy more bonds) since the return on bonds has risen.
(b) Demand (either LP_1 or LP_0) equals supply at 9 percent. The supply of money is a vertical line at 500.
(c) At an interest rate of 9 percent, an excess demand for money exists. Households and firms would sell bonds to satisfy their excess demand for money. Hence bond prices would fall and interest rates would rise.
(d) As interest rates rise, the quantity demanded falls until demand equals the lower value of the money supply. Interest rates would equal 10.0 percent for LP_0 and 9.5 percent for LP_1.
(e) If LP_0 applies, the money supply must be 700. If LP_1 applies, the money supply must be 900. Monetary policy aimed at lowering interest rates would be more effective if LP_0 applied, since it takes only an increase in the money supply of 200 (700 − 500) rather than 400 (900 − 500) to reduce the interest rate by one percentage point.

5.
(a) Excess demand for money at i; interest rates should rise to equilibrium at i_0 and E as individuals sell bonds, thereby driving down the price of bonds and raising the interest rate.

Figure 28-10

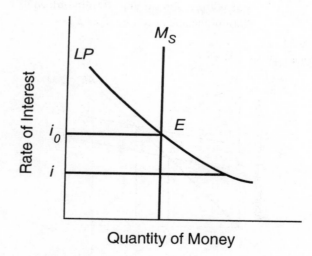

(b) Excess supply of money at i; interest rates should fall to equilibrium at i_0 and E as individuals buy bonds, thereby increasing bond prices and lowering the interest rate.

Figure 28-11

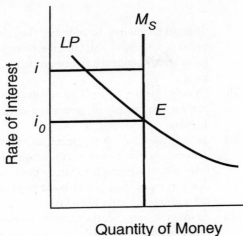

(c) Interest rate drops from i_0 to i_1; investment expenditures rise from I_0 to I_1.

Figure 28-12

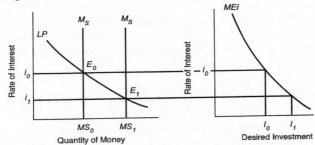

(d) Upward shift in AE caused by more desired expenditure, also shifting AD outward; equilibrium income rises from Y_0 to Y_1.

Figure 28-13

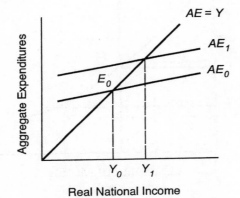

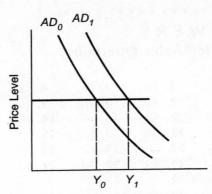

Desired Investment Expenditure

(e) An increase in the price level increases demand for money (for transactions purposes primarily) from LP_0 to LP_1; this raises interest rates from i_0 to i_1 and lowers investment from I_0 to I_1.

Figure 28-14

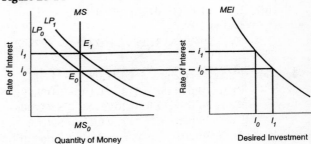

6. (a) 9 percent, at which demand is equal to supply.
    (b) 200.
    (c) When $Y = 1,580$, $AE = Y$. The output gap (recessionary gap) is $1,580 - 1,600 = -20$.
    (d) 2.0. Autonomous expenditure must increase by 10 to achieve an increase in Y of 20.
    (e) Since AE must increase, the interest rate must fall and hence the money supply must rise.
    (f) 10.
    (g) The interest rate must fall from 9 percent to 8 percent.
    (h) According to the graph in exercise 4, the money supply must increase from 500 to 700, an increase of 200.
    (i) Consumption now equals 960, an increase of 12 ($20 \times$ MPC of 0.6). When $Y = 1,600$, $C = 960$ and $AE = Y$. This is equilibrium.

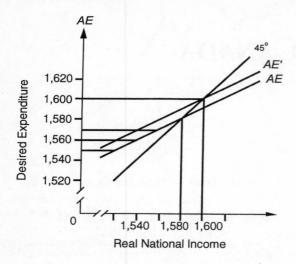

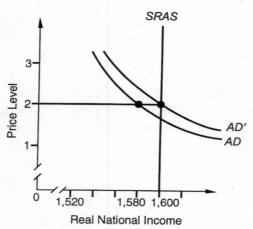

increase in the money supply is likely to be much larger than in question 6. There is a second important factor possibly at work. As the increase in aggregate demand increases the price level, workers may form expectations of inflation. As a result, they bid up wages which shifts the *SRAS* curve to the left. Thus, the positive stimulus of monetary policy is counteracted by the leftward shift of the *SRAS* curve.

(d) If domestic prices rise (assuming foreign prices stay constant), imports become relatively cheaper and exports become relatively more expensive. Thus, the external value of the domestic currency should fall (the exchange rate falls). As the exchange rate falls, net exports should rise with the result that the stimulus of the money increase is helped by the increase in net exports.

8. (a) Demand equals supply (50) at an interest rate of 10 percent. Desired investment expenditure is therefore 180.

(b) If price increases, the *LP* curve shifts upward or rightward (the demand for money increases at every interest rate). Hence, bonds will be sold, lowering their price. As a consequence, the interest rate increases.

(c) The new equilibrium interest rate is 14 percent.

(d) The new level of investment is 170.

(e) $Y = AE$ at 360 (10 percent interest rate and $P = 1.0$).

(f) Investment is now 170. *AE:* 340, 345, 350, 355. Since the new equilibrium level of national income is 340, income has fallen by 20.

(g) **Figure 28-16**

7. (a) Monetary policy is totally ineffective since any change in the money supply has no effect on the interest rate. Since investment is not affected and the multiplier process does not come into play.

(b) The *MEI* is perfectly inelastic with respect to the interest rate. Presumably firms are not at all sensitive to the interest rate when making investment decisions. Thus, even though interest rates change with monetary policy, investment is constant. The multiplier process will not occur (including any change in investment).

(c) As you have seen, the multiplier which allows price changes is less than the value of the simple multiplier. This, in itself, should not hinder monetary policy. However, the required

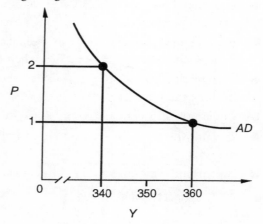

CHAPTER 29

MONETARY POLICY IN CANADA

CHAPTER OVERVIEW

This chapter concerns the policy instruments of monetary policy by the Bank of Canada that influence key macroeconomic variables and, hence, attempt to achieve certain policy variables (such as real national income and the price level). Certain *intermediate targets* (the money supply, the interest rate, and the *Monetary Conditions Index*) help guide the Bank when implementing monetary policy in the short run.

The major tool that the Bank of Canada uses to control the supply of money is control of reserves of the commercial banking system through open-market operations, and by switching government deposits between itself and the chartered banks. Purchases of bonds on the open market by the Bank of Canada or switching government deposits to the banks increases the reserves of the banking system. These policy stances increase the money supply, reduce interest rates, and shift the aggregate demand curve to the right.

The transmission mechanism may take a long time to influence policy variables such as real income and the price level. Changes in reserves are more-or-less immediate, but deposit creation (destruction), switching between assets, changes in investment plans, and the multiplier process all take time. Moreover, change in the demand for money may counteract or thwart monetary policy. Hence, some economists believe that monetary policy involves long and variable lags, and its outcome may be uncertain.

The chapter concludes by reviewing twenty-five years of monetary policy in Canada.

LEARNING OBJECTIVES

After studying this chapter, you should be able to:

- understand how the Bank of Canada can affect the reserves of the banking system by conducting open-market operations and by switching government deposits between itself and the banking system;
- understand that one of the costs of banks running deficit reserve positions is the *bank rate* which is the interest rate that the Bank charges when commercial banks borrow from it;
- recognize that monetary policy in the short run is generally not capable of pursuing two objectives of pushing the price level and real GDP toward independently determined targets;
- explain the distinctions among policy variables, policy instruments, and intermediate targets;
- explain why the full effects of monetary policy on economic activity may be subject to long and variable lags;
- understand why shifts in the demand for money make intermediate targets unreliable indicators on which to base monetary policy.

MULTIPLE-CHOICE QUESTIONS

1. Open-market operations are
   (a) purchases and sales by the Bank of Canada of government securities in financial markets.
   (b) purchases and sales among the commercial banks of securities in financial markets.
   (c) sales of government securities by chartered banks to their customers.
   (d) total purchases and sales of government securities in the bond market.
   (e) switching government deposits between the banks and the Bank of Canada.

2. Which one of the following is *not* a policy instrument of the Bank of Canada?
   (a) Raising the tax rate on interest income received from government bonds.
   (b) Buying bonds from the commercial banks.
   (c) Switching government deposits between itself and the banking system.
   (d) Sale of bonds to the commercial banks.
   (e) Changes in the bank rate.

3. If the Bank of Canada purchases bonds in the open market,
   (a) bank reserves will be reduced.
   (b) bank reserves will be increased.
   (c) the money supply will fall by a maximum of $1/v$ times the value of the purchase (v is the reserve ratio).
   (d) interest rates are likely to rise.
   (e) bond prices are likely to fall.

4. If the Bank of Canada sold $10 million of securities to bank customers in the open market,
   (a) reserves and securities in banks would each rise by $10 million.
   (b) deposits and reserves of banks would initially fall by $10 million.
   (c) the money supply would eventually increase by $1/v$ times the value of the sale (v is the reserve ratio).
   (d) deposits in the banking system would initially rise by $10 million.
   (e) the price of bonds would rise.

5. If the Bank of Canada purchases bonds in the open market, it is likely that
   (a) the price of bonds would fall and the interest rate would rise.
   (b) both the price of bonds and the interest rate would rise.
   (c) both the price of bonds and the interest rate would fall.
   (d) the price of bonds would rise and the interest rate would fall.
   (e) reserves in the banks would fall.

6. To eliminate an inflationary gap, the Bank of Canada might
   (a) sell bonds in the open market.
   (b) purchase bonds in the open market.
   (c) transfer government deposits into the banking system.
   (d) increase the monetary base.
   (e) lower the bank rate.

7. The bank rate is defined as the interest rate
   (a) charged on preferred-customer loans by a bank.
   (b) charged by banks for overdrafts of large corporations.
   (c) on credit card accounts.
   (d) on three-month treasury bills.
   (e) at which the Bank of Canada makes loans (advances) to the banks.

8. If the Bank of Canada transfers $10 million of government deposits from the banking system to itself,
   (a) reserves and government deposits in the banking system will increase by $10 million.
   (b) reserves and government deposits in the Bank will increase by $10 million.
   (c) reserves of the banks will fall by $10 million and government deposits in the Bank will increase by $10 million.
   (d) the money supply is likely to increase by $1/v$ times the amount of the transfer.
   (e) it is a signal to the financial system that the Bank is attempting to increase nominal national income.

9. Which of the following statements is *not* true in Canada?
   (a) Banks must have non-negative average reserves over a four-week averaging period.
   (b) The true cost of a bank borrowing from the Bank of Canada is twice the bank rate.
   (c) The Bank of Canada's assets include government securities.
   (d) The value of the exchange rate is excluded from the *Monetary Conditions Index.*
   (e) The Bank of Canada manages some government accounts in the banks.

10. If the Bank of Canada purchases government bonds in the open market,
    (a) an excess supply of money balances is created, higher bond prices will prevail, and aggregate expenditure will be higher than before.
    (b) an excess demand for money balances is created, higher bond prices will prevail, and aggregate expenditure will be lower than before.
    (c) an excess supply of money balances is created, lower bond prices will prevail, and aggregate expenditure will be lower than before.
    (d) an excess demand for money balances is created, lower bond prices will prevail, and aggregate expenditure will be higher than before.
    (e) None of the above.

11. If the Bank of Canada purchases government bonds in the open market,
    (a) the aggregate demand curve will shift to the right.
    (b) the aggregate demand curve will shift to the left.
    (c) the aggregate expenditure curve will shift downward and to the right.
    (d) there will be a movement up the *MEI* curve.
    (e) Both (b) and (c).

12. Which of the following have been considered intermediate targets by the Bank of Canada?
    (a) The interest rate.
    (b) Nominal GDP.
    (c) The price level.
    (d) Real GDP.
    (e) The inflation rate.

13. If the demand for money falls by a greater degree than the money supply is being restricted,
    (a) interest rates will fall.
    (b) the quantity demanded for money will be greater than the quantity supplied.
    (c) interest rates will rise.
    (d) money supply expansion is necessary for achieving the initial target interest rate.
    (e) None of the above.

14. An important implication of long and variable execution lags associated with monetary policy is that
    (a) national income can be easily fine-tuned with open-market operations.
    (b) monetary policy is never capable of eliminating an inflationary gap.
    (c) discretionary monetary policy may prove to be destabilizing.
    (d) a stable monetary rule, regardless of demand instability, guarantees monetary stability.
    (e) monetary policy does not have short-run effects on nominal GDP.

15. The experience of "monetary gradualism" in the period 1975-1980 in Canada indicated that
    (a) shifts in the demand for money were unimportant when setting a monetary growth rule.
    (b) monetary growth rules ran into problems because of decreases in the demand for money.
    (c) interest rates as the main intermediate target were reasonably easy to achieve.
    (d) the demand for M1 was quite stable even though the demand for M2 was quite volatile.
    (e) increases in the demand for money counteracted monetary policy.

16. Which of the following did *not* occur in Canada during 1987-1990?
    (a) The inflation rate decreased.
    (b) The Bank of Canada's policy stressed long-term price stability.
    (c) The differential between Canadian and U.S. interest rates increased.
    (d) The external value of the Canadian dollar was high.
    (e) A "tight money" policy was pursued by the Bank of Canada.

Questions 17 through 20 refer to Figure 29-1.

Figure 29-1

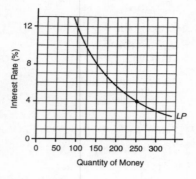

17. If the central bank chose an intermediate interest-rate target of 12 percent,
    (a) both the money supply and the quantity of money demanded must be 100.
    (b) it can set the monetary base at whatever level it wishes.
    (c) a money supply of 150 would create an excess supply of bonds at an interest rate of 12 percent.
    (d) a money supply of 250 would cause bond prices to rise at an interest rate of 12 percent.
    (e) Both (a) and (c).

18. If the money supply were 150 and the central bank's interest rate target were 12 percent, the central bank
    (a) need do nothing since a money supply of 150 achieves its interest-rate target.
    (b) must sell bonds in the open market, thereby lowering bond prices.
    (c) will lower the bank rate to indicate its intentions to decrease the supply of money.
    (d) must increase government deposits in the banks in order to increase their reserves.
    (e) must buy bonds in the open market.

19. If the central bank set a monetary supply target of 150, then according to the *LP* (the demand for money) curve,
    (a) there would be an excess supply of money at an interest rate of 12 percent.
    (b) there would be an excess supply of bonds at an interest rate of 4 percent.

    (c) the equilibrium interest rate must be 8 percent.
    (d) All of the above.
    (e) None of the above.

20. If the central bank reduced its monetary supply target from 150 to 100,
    (a) it would have to increase its monetary base target.
    (b) the equilibrium interest rate would rise from 8 to 12 percent, provided that the *LP* (demand for money) curve did not shift.
    (c) it would have to increase the price of bonds by purchasing bonds in the bond market.
    (d) it must have agreed to assist the federal government in financing additional spending.
    (e) it should transfer government deposits from itself to the commercial banks.

Questions 21 through 24 refer to Figure 29-2. The current situation is depicted at point *a*. Assume that both the *SRAS* and *LRAS* curves do not shift for the period under consideration.

Figure 29-2

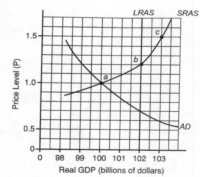

21. Which of the following combinations of policy objectives by a central bank are feasible in the short run?
    (a) A price level of 1.1 and real GDP of 100.
    (b) Potential GDP of 102 and a price level of 1.2.
    (c) Potential GDP and a price level of 1.0.
    (d) Real GDP of 99 and a price level of 1.0.
    (e) All of the above are feasible if appropriate monetary base policies were adopted.

22. Suppose that central bank policy is designed to eliminate the current output gap. Its monetary policy involves
  (a) a policy trade-off, since the elimination of the output gap is accompanied by an increase in the price level.
  (b) either an increase in its monetary base target or a decrease in its interest-rate target.
  (c) increasing the reserves of the banking system.
  (d) transferring government deposits from itself to the banks.
  (e) All of the above.

23. Information concerning the strength of the transmission mechanism indicates that every $500 million increase in the money supply increases real GDP by $1 billion. If the reserve ratio is 10 percent, the output gap will be completely eliminated if the central bank
  (a) increases reserves in the banking system by $100 million.
  (b) increases the money supply by $500 million.
  (c) increases the reserves in the banking system by $10 billion.
  (d) increases the money supply by $2 billion.
  (e) None of the above.

24. Given the policy outlined in question 23, which of the following might explain why the economy might achieve a short-run equilibrium at point *c* rather than point *b*?
  (a) The central bank's policy is accompanied by an unexpected increase in household saving.
  (b) The government increased the tax rate to complement the central bank's policy.
  (c) The central bank's policy is accompanied by an unexpected decline in export sales.
  (d) Actual import purchases are lower than forecasted levels used to design the required change in the money supply.
  (e) High interest rates reduced investment expenditures more than was anticipated.

• • • • • • • • • • • • • • •

EXERCISES

1. The Bank of Canada decides to purchase $100 million of Canadian government securities from the non-bank public in open-market operations.
  (a) Show the effect of this first step on the banking system. (Be sure to use + and – to indicate changes, not totals.) Assume that the public holds all their money in bank deposits.

| Bank of Canada | | All banks | |
Assets	Liabilities	Assets	Liabilities
Securities:	Bank reserves:	Reserves:	Demand deposits:

  (b) If the target reserve ratio is 10 percent, it is now possible for deposits to increase by a total of _____ (including the original increase).
  (c) What is likely to happen to the level of interest rates?

  (d) Will the money supply necessarily increase by the full amount in (b)? Explain.

2. Suppose that each bank in the banking system has achieved its target reserve position. Now the Bank of Canada transfers a total of $300 million of government deposits from the banking system to itself.
  (a) Show the effect of this transaction in the following balance sheets. Use + for an increase and – for a decrease.

Bank of Canada	
	Government deposits: Bank reserves:

Banking system	
Reserves:	Government deposits:

(b) Is the policy designed to combat a recessionary or an inflationary gap situation? Explain.

(c) If the target reserve ratio is 5 percent, what is the possible *final* change in the money supply?

(d) Discuss the factors that determine the time it takes for the change in the money supply to eliminate the output gap problem.

3. Use Figure 29-3 to illustrate the effects of the following Bank of Canada monetary policies, and answer questions (a), (b), and (c).

Figure 29-3

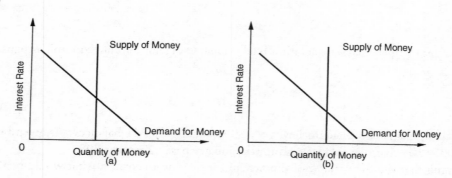

(a) Use graph (a) for this question. The Bank of Canada sells government securities.
Total reserves will (increase, decrease).
The money supply curve should shift to the _____ .
This policy is (expansionary, contractionary).
The quantity of money demanded will (increase, decrease).
Interest rates will tend to _____ .

(b) Use graph (b) for this question. The Bank of Canada transfers government deposits into the banks.
Excess reserves will initially (increase, decrease).
The money supply curve should shift to the _____ .
This policy is (expansionary, contractionary).
The quantity of money demanded will (increase, decrease).
Interest rates will tend to _____ .

(c) Use graph (a) for this question. The demand for money curve shifts farther to the left than the supply of money curve does.
Interest rates will tend to _____ .
Investment expenditure will tend to _____ .
National income will tend to _____ .

4. Suppose that the demand for money (liquidity preference) function was $D_M = 300 - 20i$, where D_M is the quantity of money demanded and i is the rate of interest in percentage terms. The supply of money is 100.
   (a) What is the equilibrium value for the interest rate?

   (b) Suppose, because of expansion in the economy, that the demand curve for money becomes $D_M = 400 - 20i$, but the supply of money remains at 100. If the interest remained at 10 percent, what situation exists in the money market? What is likely to happen to the equilibrium level of the interest rate in the future? Be specific.

   (c) Given the circumstances described in (b) and assuming that the Bank of Canada was determined to maintain an interest-rate target of 10 percent, what change in the money supply would be required? Be specific.

   (d) What type of open-market operations would be appropriate for the change in the money supply discussed in (c)?

   (e) Is this type of open-market operation likely to encourage or curtail economic expansion?

5. Suppose that the Bank of Canada believed that the demand for M1 balances was given by the expression DM1 = $300 - 20i$. Its previously announced monetary base target was 200.
   (a) Assuming that the Bank's view of the demand for M1 were correct, what would be the equilibrium interest rate?
   (b) Now, the Bank reduces its monetary base target from M1 = 200 to M1 = 150, but the interest rate does not change. Explain what may have happened.
   (c) Was the change in the policy stance of the Bank consistent with fighting high unemployment or high inflation? Comment on the effectiveness of the Bank's policy in terms of what actually occurred in the money and bond markets.

6. Suppose that you are an advisor to the governor of the central bank of the country of Montand. The governor has committed the Bank of Montand to a policy of zero inflation. The situation in the recent past is depicted by point a in Figure 29-4. Now, quite unexpectedly real national income and the price level rise to point b. Your research indicates that this situation is likely to prevail for some time. The governor asks you to outline some of the policy options open to her.

Figure 29-4

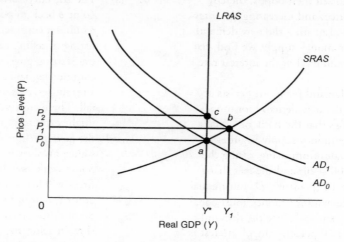

(a) **Policy Option I:** Reverse the trend and get the economy back to point *a*. What policy recommendations would you make? What reservations might you express to the governor?

(b) **Policy Option II:** No central bank intervention. What arguments would you make to support this stance? If this "policy" is pursued, what reservations would you express to the governor?

● ● ● ● ● ● ● ● ● ● ● ● ●

ANSWERS
Multiple-Choice Questions

1. (a)	**2.** (a)	**3.** (b)	**4.** (b)	**5.** (d)
6. (a)	**7.** (e)	**8.** (c)	**9.** (d)	**10.** (a)
11. (a)	**12.** (a)	**13.** (a)	**14.** (c)	**15.** (b)
16. (a)	**17.** (a)	**18.** (b)	**19.** (d)	**20.** (b)
21. (b)	**22.** (e)	**23.** (a)	**24.** (d)	

Exercises

1. (a) Bank of Canada: Securities +100, Bank reserves +100; All banks: Reserves +100, Demand deposits +100.

   (b) $1 billion (10 × $100 million). The value 10 is obtained from 1 divided by 0.10.

   (c) Other things being equal, interest rates are likely to fall because banks wish to make new loans and, hence, reduce the loan rate. All interest rates will fall because other institutions will want to be competitive with the banks.

   (d) Excess reserves make money (demand deposit) creation possible. However, the actual effects on the money supply depend on the willingness and ability of banks to lend their excess reserves (change their excess reserves) and whether there are any cash drains from the banking system.

2. (a) Bank of Canada: Government deposits: + $300 million; Bank reserves: −$300 million. Banking system: reserves −$300 million; Government deposits: −$300 million.

   (b) Since the Bank of Canada's policy reduces reserves in the banking system, the policy is directed to decreasing economic activity, which is an anti-inflationary policy. Assuming a stable demand for money function, interest rates will rise and investment will fall.

   (c) A $6 billion reduction. This is equal to $300 million times 1/0.05, where the value 0.05 is the reserve ratio.

   (d) A reduction in the money supply increases the interest rate. Firms would not necessarily revise their investment expenditures immediately. Moreover, when investment does decline, the effects on the induced components of aggregate expenditure may not be instantaneous; that is, the final effect of the multiplier process is achieved only after several time periods have elapsed.

3. (a) decrease; left; contractionary; decrease; rise.

   (b) increase; right; expansionary; increase; fall.

   (c) fall; increase; increase.

4. (a) Equating demand with supply, we obtain an equilibrium level of the interest rate of 10 percent.

   (b) At an interest rate of 10 percent, there would be an excess demand for money. Firms and households would sell their bonds, thereby reducing bond prices and increasing the interest rate on bonds. Equating the new demand function with the money supply, we find that the new equilibrium level of the interest rate is 15 percent.

(c) Since an excess demand for money exists at $i = 10$ percent with the new demand for money function, it follows that the Bank of Canada must increase the money supply in order to prevent interest rates from rising. Using the function $D_M = 400 - 20i$ and the fact that i must be equal to 10 (percent), D_M must equal 200. Since the demand for money must equal the supply of money, and since the demand for money with a 10 percent rate of interest is 200, it follows that the supply of money must be increased from 100 to 200, an increase of 100.

(d) The Bank of Canada should buy bonds in the open market to provide additional reserves for banks.

(e) Given the increase in the demand for money with a fixed supply of money, the resulting interest-rate increase would have reduced some investment expenditure, thereby curtailing some of the economic expansion. However, with the Bank of Canada's interest-rate target policy and the expansionary open-market operation, economic expansion would be sustained or perhaps increased.

5. (a) Equating demand to supply, the interest rate should be 5 percent.

(b) A lower monetary base target should have increased the equilibrium interest rate to 7.5 percent. If the interest rate did not change, the demand curve for *M1* must have shifted leftward; i.e., the demand for *M1* balances declined at every interest rate. In fact, assuming the new demand curve for *M1* is parallel to the initial demand curve, the new equation must be $250 - 20i$ with a supply of 150.

(c) A reduction in the money supply and an intended increase in the interest rate are consistent with combating inflation. Since the interest rate did not change, aggregate expenditures will not be reduced. Hence, the Bank's policy is likely to fail.

6. (a) The *AD* curve must be shifted leftward from point *b* back to point *a*. Such a change requires a contractionary monetary policy consisting of selling bonds in the open market or transferring government deposits from the commercial banks to the Bank of Montand. As a result, reserves of the commercial banks will fall. There are several reservations that you might express, but we discuss only three. First, the governor must be warned that this policy stance involves reducing real national income. Some workers will lose their jobs and some firms will lose profits in the process. The governor is bound to be criticized by these groups. Second, the transmission mechanism may be slow in achieving the Bank's goal. Will banks react by reducing loans; will interest rates rise; will firms and perhaps consumers downsize their expenditures; how long will the multiplier process take to reduce real national income by the value of the output gap? Third, you hope that neither the *SRAS* curve nor the *AD* curves shifts unexpectedly while the transmission mechanism is in operation. Otherwise, your recommended reduction in bank reserves may be an overkill or inadequate.

(b) Policy option II requires that the Bank of Montand does not change the nominal money supply and that private-market forces eliminate the inflation gap. The inflationary gap should be characterized by wage rises that are greater than productivity gains. Hence, the *SRAS* curve will shift upward until it reaches point *c*. Critics are sure to point out that inflation is higher than before (compare $P_2 - P_0$ with $P_1 - P_0$). As real national income falls back to its potential level, the governor must be warned to avoid the temptation to increase the nominal supply of money. Notice, that the movement from point *b* to point *c* involves rising prices and falling real output (*stagflation*). Critics are likely to notice the inactivity of the central bank and perhaps not appreciate that although the prices will rise, the inflationary gap will be eliminated ultimately by the reductions in real wealth, higher interest rates, and lower net exports (a movement up along AD_1). As the next chapter will explain, you hope that the process from points *b* to *c* does not generate *inflationary expectations*.

PART TEN

MACROECONOMIC PROBLEMS AND POLICIES

CHAPTER 30

INFLATION

CHAPTER OVERVIEW

Inflation is triggered by a decrease in short-run aggregate supply (a supply shock) or an increase in aggregate demand (a demand shock). Both shocks can be once-and-for-all or repeated. Actions by the central bank (validation) are especially important in determining whether inflationary shocks are temporary or sustained.

Wages are an important factor price. Wage rate increases that exceed productivity increases will cause the *SRAS* curve to shift upward because unit costs increase. Wage rate increases matched by equal productivity gains do not change unit costs. Wage rate demands are also conditioned by expected inflation, and the chapter discusses two alternative ways that expectations are formed: backward-looking expectations and rational expectations. Hence, expectations of inflation can also shift the *SRAS* curve to shift upward.

Inflationary shocks that are not validated by increases in the money supply by the central bank tend to be self-correcting, although the time of adjustment may be long. By way of contrast, inflationary shocks that are validated can create sustained inflation. Validated inflation may also trigger expectations of continued inflation.

The process by governments, particularly the monetary authority, to eliminate sustained inflation is extremely difficult. There are no quick fixes. The text outlines three important phases that are required to eliminate a sustained (or entrenched) inflationary situation.

The consequences of inflation are both real and monetary. In the short run, demand-shock inflation tends to increase real income above its potential level whereas supply-shock inflation is accompanied by a decrease in real income below its potential level. In the long run, unvalidated and validated inflations are purely monetary phenomena.

LEARNING OBJECTIVES

After studying this chapter, you should be able to:

- distinguish between once-and-for-all and sustained inflation;
- list several reasons for aggregate supply and demand shocks and explain how they cause inflation;
- understand what is meant by monetary validation of inflationary shocks;
- explain the pressure on unit costs when actual unemployment is above, below, and at the NAIRU;
- understand why expectational forces shift the *SRAS* curve;
- explain the three phases of breaking a sustained inflation;
- explain why accelerating inflation will occur when there is persistent inflationary gap and rising inflationary expectations.

MULTIPLE-CHOICE QUESTIONS

1. Which of the following characterizes an inflationary gap situation?
   (a) Money wages rise more rapidly than productivity is rising.
   (b) Actual real GDP is less than potential GDP.
   (c) Current unemployment exceeds the NAIRU.
   (d) Points on the Phillips curve associated with levels of unemployment that are greater than the NAIRU.
   (e) None of the above.

2. Which of the following events is likely to cause the *SRAS* curve to shift upward?
   (a) Expectations of future inflation.
   (b) Productivity rises by 3 percent and wages rise by 2 percent.
   (c) Productivity and wages rise by 4 percent.
   (d) Productivity rises by 1 percent and wages rise by 2 percent.
   (e) Both (a) and (d).

3. If productivity increases by 1 percent, wages increase by 3 percent, and expectations of future inflation are 1.5 percent, then the predicted overall change in unit labour costs is
   (a) 1.5 percent.
   (b) 3.5 percent.
   (c) 5.5 percent.
   (d) 2 percent.
   (e) 4 percent.

4. If the demand effect is –2 percent and the expectational effect is 4 percent, then
   (a) the *SRAS* curve is likely to shift leftward.
   (b) there will be a movement up along the *SRAS* curve.
   (c) wages will rise at 6 percent.
   (d) the *AD* curve has most certainly shifted to the right.
   (e) current unemployment is less than the NAIRU.

5. When the measured unemployment rate is below the NAIRU rate,
   (a) current national income is less than potential national income.
   (b) there is a recessionary gap.
   (c) frictional and structural unemployment are zero.
   (d) there will be upward pressure on unit costs.
   (e) the Phillips curve analysis predicts negative percentage changes in wage rates.

6. Which one of the following could not be the initiating cause of a demand shock inflation?
   (a) An increase in the money supply.
   (b) An increase in exports.
   (c) An increase in the prices of imported goods and services.
   (d) A decrease in tax rates.
   (e) An increase in investment expenditures.

7. Which of the following does not describe the effects of an isolated demand-shock inflation without monetary validation or expectational effects?
   (a) At the initial stage, Y rises above Y^* and the price level increases.
   (b) As money wages rise relative to productivity, the *SRAS* curve shifts rightward.
   (c) As the *SRAS* curve shifts, Y falls back to Y^*.
   (d) As the *SRAS* curve shifts, P rises further.
   (e) In the long run, real income will not change and the price level, although higher than before, will be stable.

8. An inflationary process is said to be validated when
   (a) at least two federal government departments agree on the magnitude of price increase.
   (b) the initial cause of the inflation was an expansion of government expenditure.
   (c) the Bank of Canada maintains a constant nominal money supply during the inflationary process.
   (d) an increase in the nominal money supply accompanies inflationary shocks.
   (e) the *SRAS* curve shifts leftward because of inflationary expectations.

9. A supply-shock inflation could be caused by
   (a) a rise in the price of imported raw materials.
   (b) an increase in wages relative to productivity.
   (c) a depletion of resources that causes their prices to rise.
   (d) an increase in the GST and/or provincial sales tax.
   (e) Any of the above.

10. Which of the following does not describe an isolated supply-shock inflation without validation or expectational effects?
    (a) As the *SRAS* curve shifts upward, prices rise.
    (b) As the *SRAS* curve shifts upward, the actual unemployment rate decreases below the NAIRU.
    (c) Initially output falls, but as wages fall relative to productivity, output increases back to its potential level.
    (d) The initial phase is described as stagflation.
    (e) Desired aggregate demand decreases initially as interest rates increase with prices.

11. If the final effects of an inflation are characterized by continuous price rises and output level above Y^*, this is categorized as a
    (a) isolated demand shock with no validation.
    (b) repeated supply shock with validation.
    (c) isolated supply shock with validation.
    (d) repeated demand shock with validation.
    (e) None of the above.

12. Which of the following is not a characteristic or implication of backward-looking expectations?
    (a) Backward-looking expectations tend to change slowly.
    (b) If inflation has been 5 percent over the last two years, people will expect it to be 5 percent next year.
    (c) People revise their expectations in light of the mistakes that they made in estimating inflation in the past.
    (d) People will not continue to make persistent, systematic errors in forming expectations.
    (e) None of the above.

13. If an isolated supply-shock inflation is not validated, which of the following statements is true?
    (a) The *AD* curve will shift rightward as the nominal money supply increases.
    (b) As long as wages do not fall relative to productivity, the economy may experience a prolonged recession.
    (c) There will be a continuous increase in prices.
    (d) Real national income never deviates from its potential level.
    (e) All of the above.

14. Which one of the following statements about inflation is true?
    (a) Price level increases must eventually come to a halt, unless monetary expansion occurs.
    (b) Inflations that are not validated are always of short duration.
    (c) An isolated inflation must have been caused by a monetary expansion.
    (d) Assuming that actual national income was initially at its potential level, demand-stock inflation never can have short-run effects on real national income.
    (e) From the point of view of long-run equilibrium, inflation is never sustained.

Questions 15 through 18 refer to Figure 30-1.

Figure 30-1

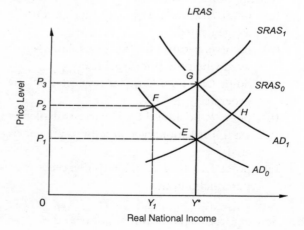

15. Starting from equilibrium at point E, if a supply shock shifts the $SRAS$ curve from $SRAS_0$ to $SRAS_1$ and there is no monetary validation,
    (a) the recessionary gap puts downward pressure on wages and prices, slowly shifting $SRAS$ back downward to $SRAS_0$.
    (b) aggregate demand will increase from AD_0 to AD_1.
    (c) the long-run equilibrium will be at point G.
    (d) the long-run equilibrium will be at point F as long as wages rise less than productivity.
    (e) the long-run equilibrium will be at point F since the $LRAS$ must shift leftward.

16. Starting from equilibrium at point E, if the short-run aggregate supply curve shifts from $SRAS_0$ to $SRAS_1$ and there is complete monetary validation,
    (a) real national income would temporarily fall to Y_1, then be restabilized at Y^*.
    (b) the aggregate demand curve will shift to the right to pass through point G.
    (c) the price level will rise to P_3, assuming that no inflationary expectations are generated.
    (d) in the long run, inflation is a monetary phenomenon.
    (e) All of the above will occur.

17. Starting from equilibrium at point E, the aggregate demand curve shifts from AD_0 to AD_1. If there is no monetary validation, long-run equilibrium will be at
    (a) point H, if no inflationary expectations are generated.
    (b) point E, because the AD curve shifts leftward when the price level rises.
    (c) point G, if no inflationary expectations are generated.
    (d) point F, because the AD curve shifts leftward if inflationary expectations are generated.
    (e) point H, where actual output exceeds potential output.

18. Starting from equilibrium at point E, the aggregate demand curve shifts from AD_0 to AD_1. If there is no monetary validation,
    (a) the price level may temporarily increase to more than P_3 because of inflationary expectations.

    (b) a recessionary gap may be temporarily created because of inflationary expectations.
    (c) long-run equilibrium will be at point G, even though short-run inflationary expectations have been created.
    (d) the actual unemployment rate temporarily may be above the NAIRU if expectations cause a recessionary gap.
    (e) Any or all of the above.

19. The duration of the recession that develops when a central bank stops validating an entrenched inflation
    (a) depends on inflationary expectations and wage momentum.
    (b) is determined by coincidental leftward shifts of the AD curve.
    (c) will typically be very short according to Keynesians.
    (d) will typically be very long according to monetarists.
    (e) must be extremely short if expectations are backward-looking.

20. A sustained, constant rate of inflation occurs when
    (a) Y is consistently above Y^*.
    (b) there is a demand component to inflation.
    (c) the nominal money supply is increased at a constant rate, and there is no demand component to inflation.
    (d) there is no expectational inflation.
    (e) Both (a) and (b).

21. Which of the following does the textbook identify as Phase 2 of breaking a sustained (or entrenched) inflation?
    (a) Slowing the rate of monetary expansion below the current rate of inflation.
    (b) An initial demand and expectational inflation becomes a pure expectational inflation.
    (c) Productivity rises more than wages.
    (d) At the end of the stagflation, unit costs fall, thus shifting the $SRAS$ curve downward.
    (e) At the end of the stagflation, the central bank may increase the money supply to shorten the recessionary gap phase.

22. In which one of the following cases would an incomes policy be most successful in controlling inflation?

(a) In conjunction with an expansionary money policy, to break entrenched inflation.

(b) Alone, as a permanent solution to demand shock inflation.

(c) As a way of stopping or moderating the upward shift in the *SRAS* curve during Phase 2 of an entrenched inflation.

(d) Alone, as a well-publicized substitute for contractionary money and fiscal policy.

(e) Whenever governments consistently choose full employment as their top policy priority.

• • • • • • • • • • • • • • •

EXERCISES

1. Briefly explain each concept and illustrate it on the graph. Assume *no* expectational effects.

(a) A single supply shock that is validated thereafter.

Figure 30-2

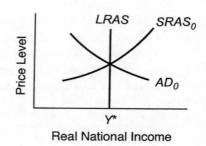

(b) A single supply shock with no monetary validation.

Figure 30-3

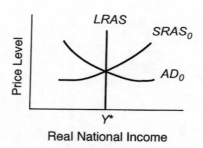

(c) A demand shock with no monetary validation.

Figure 30-4

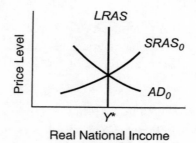

(d) A demand-shock inflation that is validated thereafter.

Figure 30-5

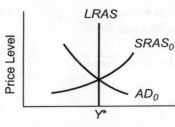

2. For each of the four parts of question 1, indicate the initial (first stage) effects and the final (second stage) effects of inflation in the following table. For the first stage effects, indicate the difference between the new price and the starting price $(P_1 - P_0)$, unemployment at the initial stage in relation to the NAIRU $(U_1 - U^*)$, and the difference between potential output and first-stage output $(Y_1 - Y^*)$. For the final stage effects, indicate the differences between the final (second stage) price, income, and unemployment levels in relation to the first stage levels. If the *SRAS* curve shifts during the final stage, indicate the effect on $\dot{W} - \dot{g}$ the difference in percentage wage changes and percentage productivity changes. Use the notation + (for increase), − (for decrease), and 0 (for no change). Always assume that E_0 is the starting situation at which price is P_0, real national income is Y^*, and the unemployment rate is U^*.

Case	Initial (First stage)	Final (Second stage)	Adjustment
(a)	$P_1 - P_0$ _____ $Y_1 - Y^*$ _____ $U_1 - U^*$ _____	$P_2 - P_1$ _____ $Y_2 - Y_1$ _____ $U_2 - U_1$ _____	$\dot{W} - \dot{g}$ _____
(b)	$P_1 - P_0$ _____ $Y_1 - Y^*$ _____ $U_1 - U^*$ _____	$P_2 - P_1$ _____ $Y_2 - Y_1$ _____ $U_2 - U_1$ _____	$\dot{W} - \dot{g}$ _____
(c)	$P_1 - P_0$ _____ $Y_1 - Y^*$ _____ $U_1 - U^*$ _____	$P_2 - P_1$ _____ $Y_2 - Y_1$ _____ $U_2 - U_1$ _____	$\dot{W} - \dot{g}$ _____
(d)	$P_1 - P_0$ _____ $Y_1 - Y^*$ _____ $U_1 - U^*$ _____	$P_2 - P_1$ _____ $Y_2 - Y_1$ _____ $U_2 - U_1$ _____	$\dot{W} - \dot{g}$ _____

3. This exercise focuses on eliminating entrenched inflation. Suppose that an economy has for some time been experiencing inflation that has been validated by monetary policy. The starting point for this example is point *A* in Figure 30-6.
    (a) If the central bank stops expanding the money supply, what do you predict will happen during Phase 1 to the levels of real national income and the price level? What will happen to the *SRAS* curve? Draw the new *SRAS* curve and label it *SRAS₁*.

    (b) During Phase 2, inflationary expectations are still present such that the *SRAS* curve shifts to *SRAS₂*. Indicate the new (temporary) equilibrium point on the graph. What is the value of the recessionary gap? What are the values for real national income and the price level?

Figure 30-6

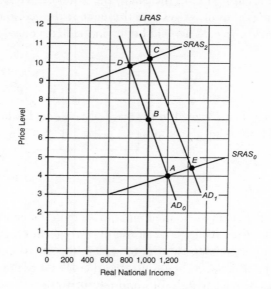

(c) After expectations are reversed, and assuming no changes in the money supply (*AD* remains at *AD₀*), what are your predictions for the equilibrium levels of real national income and price?

(d) Suppose in Phase 3 that expectations are reversed but the central bank increases the money supply sufficiently to shift the *AD* curve to *AD₁*. What will be the equilibrium levels of real national income and price?

4. The following graph illustrates an initial equilibrium at point *E* with real national income *Y₀* and price level *P*. *Y** is potential national income.

Figure 30-7

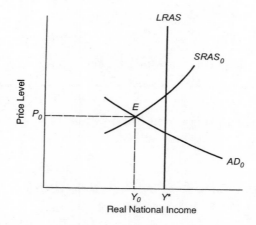

(a) If an increase in the money supply stimulated demand enough to achieve potential national income, draw the new aggregate demand curve and indicate the new price level.

(b) Suppose that the resulting rise in the price level in (a) caused expectations that inflation would occur in the future, and as a result, wages rose throughout the economy. Show on the graph what would happen to the *SRAS* curve. What will be the immediate consequence for real national income and the price level?

(c) If the supply shock that occurred in (b) was fully validated, what would happen to the aggregate demand curve? Illustrate on the graph.

5. A country has been experiencing sustained inflation and an increasing unemployment rate above the NAIRU. Claude Fortin, the finance critic of the major opposition party in parliament rises in his place and asks the finance minister, Yves Moreau, to explain the situation and to indicate what the government intends to do about the situation. The minister responds that the problem has been caused initially by repeated supply shocks of higher prices of imported manufacturing goods that the domestic economy cannot produce. Moreau is pleased to announce that no further supply shocks are anticipated and assures Fortin that his government has been quite responsible by keeping its expenditures and the nominal money supply constant. To be fair, he does express concern that the most recent data indicate that wages are rising faster than productivity.

Fortin, an avid monetarist, jumps to his feet once again and demands that Moreau instruct the central bank to decrease the nominal stock of money. The minister responds that he is not prepared to do any such thing. Hopefully, with the elimination of these supply shocks, the economy will adjust back to full employment with price stability. He also alludes to the fact that he is prepared to consider increasing the money supply to speed up the process to full employment.

From across the floor of parliament, Fortin yells to Moreau, "Shame, resign."

(a) Explain why wages are rising relative to productivity.

(b) Comment on why Fortin believes that a decrease in the nominal money supply is an appropriate policy stance.

(c) Provide some economic reasons for Moreau's policy stance.

• • • • • • • • • • • • •

ANSWERS
Multiple-Choice Questions

1. (a)	**2.** (e)	**3.** (b)	**4.** (a)	**5.** (d)
6. (c)	**7.** (b)	**8.** (d)	**9.** (e)	**10.** (b)
11. (d)	**12.** (d)	**13.** (b)	**14.** (a)	**15.** (a)
16. (e)	**17.** (c)	**18.** (e)	**19.** (a)	**20.** (c)
21. (b)	**22.** (c)			

Exercises

1. (a) Monetary validation of a single supply shock causes costs, the price level, and money supply all to move in the same direction. The supply shock is represented in the leftward shift of the *SRAS* curve; monetary validation shifts the *AD* curve rightward. Equilibrium shifts from E_0 to E_2.

Figure 30-8

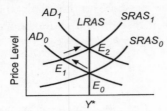

(b) The supply curve shifts to the left as a result of the supply shock, but without monetary validation, unemployment puts downward pressure on wages and costs, shifting the *SRAS* curve back to *SRAS₀*.

Figure 30-9

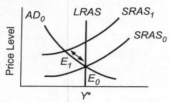

(c) The demand shock shifts the *AD* curve and creates an inflationary gap; this causes wages to rise, shifting the *SRAS* curve to the left. The monetary adjustment mechanism causes movement along the *AD* curve, with the rise in price level eliminating the inflationary gap (at E_2).

Figure 30-10

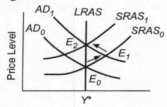

(d) The adjustment process in (c) is frustrated with monetary validation; increases in the money supply shift the *AD* curve to the right, and inflation is sustained. The economy moves along the vertical path indicated by the arrow.

Figure 30-11

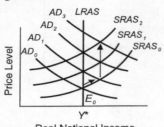

2. (a) Initial effects: The price level rises above P_0 as the *SRAS* curve shifts upward. A recessionary gap is created, and so $Y_1 - Y^*$ is negative and $U_1 - U^*$ is positive.
Final effects: The monetary validation increases prices further, so that $P_1 - P_2$ is positive. The recessionary gap is eliminated such that $Y_2 - Y_1$ is positive while $U_2 - U_1$ is negative. Notice that final values of Y and U are Y and U, respectively. Since the *SRAS* curve does shift,
$\dot{W} - \dot{g}$ is zero.

(b) Initial effects: The same answer as the initial effect in part (a).
Final effects: The recessionary gap creates pressure for wages to fall relative to productivity. Hence, $\dot{W} - \dot{g}$ is negative and the *SRAS* curve shifts downward until potential GDP is reached. Prices fall ($P_2 - P_1$ is negative) and output increases ($Y_2 - Y_1$ is positive). Output returns to its potential level and the unemployment rate is equal to the NAIRU. The final value of the price level is the starting value, P_0.

(c) Initial effects: An inflationary gap is created and so $Y_1 - Y$ is positive, $U_1 - U$ is negative, and $P_1 - P_0$ is positive.
Final effects: The inflationary gap triggers wage increases relative to productivity and so $\dot{W} - \dot{g}$ is positive. The *SRAS* curve shifts up and hence $P_2 - P_1$ and $U_2 - U_1$ are positive while $Y_2 - Y_1$ is negative. Both unemployment and income are at their potential levels, but the price level is permanently higher than P_0.

(d) Initial effects: The same answer as the initial effect in part (c).
Final effects: The same answer as in part (c) except that the price level and real national income do not stabilize at P_2 and Y, respectively. The money validation creates another inflationary gap, and the process begins again. Inflation is now sustained and real output is greater than its potential level.

3. (a) Under the combined influence of an inflationary gap and expectation of continued inflation, wages continue to rise, and the *SRAS* curve, thus, continues to shift. In terms of the graph, the *SRAS* curve shifts leftward to $SRAS_1$ and intersects the *LRAS* curve at point *B*. At this point, real national income is at its potential level (1,000) and the price level is 7.

(b) Continuing price expectations shift the *SRAS* curve up to $SRAS_2$. This curve intersects AD_0 at point *D*. A recessionary gap of 200 has been created. Real national income is 800, and the price level is approximately 10.

(c) The recessionary gap is likely to reduce inflationary expectations and, therefore, wage rates. Hence, the *SRAS* curve will tend to shift rightward (slowly) to point *B* ($SRAS_1$). There will be a movement along AD_0 from point *D* to point *B*, at which the price level is 7 and the economy is producing at its potential level.

(d) This question differs from (c) in that the central banking authority increases the money supply, perhaps to speed up the process of attaining potential national income. The *AD* curve shifts rightward with monetary expansion. The new equilibrium point is point *C*, at which the price level is approximately 10 and real national income is 1,000.

4. (a) The new *AD* curve is AD_1 and the price level is P_1. (See Figure 30-12.)

(b) The *SRAS* would shift to the left, for example, $SRAS_1$ in the graph, and the price level would rise further (along AD_1) to P_2. Real national income would decline to Y_1.

(c) The aggregate demand curve would shift to AD_2. (See Figure 30-12.)

Figure 30-12

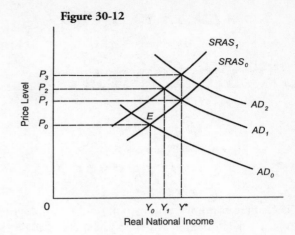

5. (a) The repeated supply shocks that increased domestic prices likely have generated expectations of future inflation. Thus, money wage increases are greater than productivity increases.

(b) We suspect that Fortin believes that a decreased money supply will dampen inflationary expectations at a faster rate. Moreover, the contractionary money policy would certainly increase the value of the recessionary gap and workers might be more prone to lower their wages. Thus, although unemployment would be higher than before, the speed at which the economy adjusts back to price stability at potential output may be increased.

(c) Moreau does not want to increase the recessionary gap as Fortin suggests. Perhaps, he believes that prices will soon fall as workers lower their wages during the recessionary period. Alternatively, when he is convinced that inflationary expectations have subsided and that wages are falling, he may be prepared to speed up the process to full employment by increasing the money supply. During the monetary expansion, prices will rise as the *AD* curve shifts to the right. Hopefully, the price increases will not rekindle inflationary expectations.

CHAPTER 31

● ● ● ● ● ● ● ● ● ● ● ● ●

UNEMPLOYMENT

● ● ● ● ● ● ● ● ● ● ● ● ●

CHAPTER OVERVIEW

This chapter examines employment and unemployment in Canada. Several kinds of unemployment are discussed; cyclical unemployment, which occurs when there is a recessionary gap; structural unemployment, which results from the need to reallocate resources due to changing patterns of demand and supply; and frictional unemployment, which occurs as people move from job to job as a normal part of labour turnover. These distinctions are important in determining what policies will be effective in reducing unemployment.

The components of the NAIRU are outlined, and the economic and demographic factors that cause it to change are discussed.

The chapter outlines the opposing views of the New Classical and New Keynesians schools concerning the flexibility of wages to adjust to cyclical unemployment and the existence of involuntary unemployment. The efficiency wage theory also explains why firms might choose to pay wages higher than the minimum amount that would induce workers to work for them.

● ● ● ● ● ● ● ● ● ● ● ● ●

LEARNING OBJECTIVES

After studying this chapter, you should be able to:

- ■ distinguish voluntary from involuntary unemployment;
- ■ define frictional, structural, and cyclical unemployment and indicate their relative importance during various periods in the Canadian economy;
- ■ understand the factors that determine each type of unemployment;
- ■ explain the factors that can change the level of Canada's natural rate of unemployment (NAIRU);
- ■ describe the effects of demographic and structural changes on unemployment;
- ■ identify different types of policy measures for reducing unemployment.

MULTIPLE-CHOICE QUESTIONS

1. The measured unemployment rate will rise if
  (a) the percentage increase in employment is greater than the percentage increase in the labour force.
  (b) the percentage increase in total unemployment is less than the percentage change in the labour force.
  (c) with a constant labour force, the number of new jobs created is less than the number of jobs lost.
  (d) actual income rises temporarily from its potential level.
  (e) more discouraged, unemployed workers leave the labour force.

2. Which of the following is a potential cost of unemployment?
  (a) The potential output of valuable resources is wasted.
  (b) Workers who would like to work at prevailing wages may stay out of the labour force.
  (c) The unemployed contribute to social unrest in some societies.
  (d) Workers who are unemployed for prolonged periods miss job training opportunities.
  (e) All or any of the above.

3. Voluntary unemployment
  (a) occurs when there is a job available but the unemployed person is unwilling to accept it at the existing wage.
  (b) occurs when workers in declining industries lose jobs permanently.
  (c) will tend to increase as the costs of searching for a job increase, other things equal.
  (d) occurs when a person is willing to accept a job at the going wage rate but no such job can be found.
  (e) occurs when highly skilled jobs are available but an unskilled worker is not qualified to be hired.

Questions 4 through 6 refer to Figure 31-1, which depicts aggregate labour demand and supply in an economy: The initial equilibrium situation is point *a*.

Figure 31-1

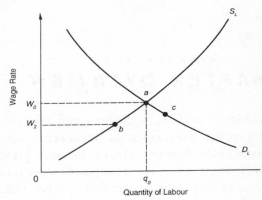

4. Which of the following statements is true?
  (a) At wage rates above W_0, there is an excess demand for labour.
  (b) Job vacancies are equal to the number of unemployed at point *a*.
  (c) If the wage rate is fully flexible, involuntary unemployment occurs when the wage is below W_0.
  (d) At wage rates less than W_0, there is an excess supply of labour.
  (e) All of the above.

5. If the labour demand curve shifts leftward and intersects the labour supply curve at point *b*,
  (a) all of the laid-off workers are involuntarily unemployed when the wage rate falls to W_2.
  (b) there will be involuntarily unemployed workers if the wage rate remains at W_0.
  (c) providing the wage rate falls to W_2, employment falls but there are no involuntarily unemployed workers.
  (d) some workers will involuntarily withdraw from the labour force as the wage rate falls.
  (e) Both (b) and (c).

6. Assuming that the wage rate is fully flexible and that the labour supply curve shifts downward and intersects the labour demand curve at point *c*, then
   (a) both employment and involuntary unemployment increase.
   (b) both employment and involuntary unemployment decrease.
   (c) both employment and involuntary unemployment remain constant.
   (d) employment increases, but there is no involuntary unemployment.
   (e) involuntary unemployment decreases and employment increases.

7. Unemployment that occurs as a result of the normal turnover of labour as people move from job to job is called
   (a) involuntary unemployment.
   (b) structural unemployment.
   (c) cyclical unemployment.
   (d) frictional unemployment.
   (e) real-wage unemployment.

8. The existence of structural unemployment means that
   (a) there is an inadequate number of jobs in the economy.
   (b) the building tradesworkers, particularly those in structural steel, are suffering high rates of unemployment.
   (c) the composition of the demand for labour does not match the composition of available supply.
   (d) cyclical unemployment must also be present.
   (e) all unemployment is voluntary.

9. Search unemployment
   (a) may be a form of voluntary frictional unemployment.
   (b) will tend to increase if search costs are low.
   (c) occurs when members of the labour force look for more suitable jobs.
   (d) occurs because workers do not have perfect knowledge of job availability.
   (e) All or any of the above.

10. The unemployment rate is defined as the percentage of
   (a) unemployed to employed workers.
   (b) the adult population that is unemployed.
   (c) the labour force that is unemployed.
   (d) the labour force that is collecting unemployment insurance.
   (e) the labour force that is registered at a Canada Employment Centre.

11. Which of the following does *not* usually explain the creation of structural unemployment?
   (a) Economic adjustments created by changes in input mixes.
   (b) Changes in the composition of the labour force.
   (c) Disequilibrium structures of relative wages across markets.
   (d) Contractionary monetary policy.
   (e) New labour force entrants with inadequate training for available jobs.

12. The unemployment that exists when there is a recessionary gap is called
   (a) structural unemployment.
   (b) natural unemployment.
   (c) cyclical unemployment.
   (d) frictional unemployment.
   (e) voluntary unemployment.

13. If an economy has achieved its NAIRU, it follows that
   (a) the measured unemployment rate is necessarily zero.
   (b) the economy operates in a recessionary gap.
   (c) the value of the output gap is zero.
   (d) there is neither structural nor frictional unemployment in the economy.
   (e) all unemployment is involuntary.

14. The measured unemployment rate may underestimate the actual unemployment rate because
   (a) it includes people who have voluntarily withdrawn from the labour force.
   (b) part-time workers are not counted as members of the labour force.
   (c) it omits discouraged workers who have voluntarily withdrawn from the labour force.
   (d) it omits those who are actively searching for work but who are unable to find work.
   (e) not all unemployed workers receive employment insurance payments.

15. Which of the following is *not* correct?
  (a) Employment insurance likely increases search unemployment.
  (b) It is neither possible nor perhaps desirable to reduce unemployment to zero.
  (c) Frictional unemployment in an economy such as Canada's is inevitable.
  (d) Long-term relationships between employers and workers help to explain the lack of wage adjustments during economic downturns.
  (e) The NAIRU in Canada has not changed over the last half century.

16. Which of the following will increase the NAIRU?
  (a) An improvement in the educational attainment of the labour force.
  (b) A slowdown in the pace at which the structural demand for labour is changing.
  (c) Less barriers to the flow of labour from a declining to an expanding labour sector.
  (d) A decrease in the speed at which labour adapts to structural changes in labour demand.
  (e) The Bank of Canada buys bonds in the open market.

17. Which of the following policies would be appropriate for reducing the level of cyclical unemployment?
  (a) The Bank of Canada sells large volumes of government bonds in the open market.
  (b) The federal government increases personal income taxes.
  (c) The province of Alberta cuts back on its expenditures to education.
  (d) The city of Moncton increases its expenditures on public housing construction.
  (e) The Bank of Canada transfers government deposits from the banks to itself.

18. Which of the following would be appropriate for reducing structural unemployment in the long run?
  (a) More effective job training programs.
  (b) Increases in the minimum wage in all provinces.
  (c) Policies designed to promote more labour-saving technological change.
  (d) More interprovincial agreements to restrict labour migration.

  (e) Increasing government subsidies to declining industries.

19. Which one of the following statements concerning demographic characteristics and unemployment rates is incorrect?
  (a) Workers with the least education tend to have the highest unemployment rates.
  (b) In the recent past, there has been a large increase in the number of households with more than one income earner.
  (c) An increasing percentage of households with two earners tends to increase search unemployment.
  (d) An increasing number of inexperienced workers in the labour force decreases frictional and structural unemployment.
  (e) Workers in the Atlantic provinces traditionally have had the highest unemployment rates.

20. *Hysteresis* means that an increase in cyclical unemployment may
  (a) decrease the level of frictional and structural unemployment.
  (b) increase the probability that new labour force participants will receive job training during and after a recession.
  (c) increase the level of the NAIRU.
  (d) Both (a) and (b).
  (e) lead to the creation of new jobs in certain economic regions.

21. Efficiency wage theories suggest that
  (a) wages readily fall in response to excess supply in labour markets.
  (b) employers may get a more efficient work force when labour is paid more than the minimum amount that would induce workers to work for them.
  (c) wages must be competitively determined for workers to be efficient.
  (d) workers are paid primarily on the basis of the efficiency of management and supervisors.
  (e) workers are paid primarily on the basis of their annual productivity increases.

22. New Keynesian theories about the persistence of involuntary unemployment
   (a) stress the importance of adverse supply shocks.
   (b) start with the observation that wage rates do not respond quickly to changes in demand and supply in labour markets.
   (c) imply that most unemployment is caused by fluctuations in the willingness of people to supply labour.
   (d) is based on the premise that all unemployment workers cannot be retrained.
   (e) None of the above.

• • • • • • • • • • • • • •

EXERCISES

1. Classify the following situations as frictional unemployment, structural unemployment, search unemployment, or cyclical unemployment, and briefly explain your choice.
   (a) An auto assembly worker is laid off because auto sales decrease during a slowdown in economic activity.

   (b) An engineer refuses a job offer and decides to look for another job that has a higher rate of remuneration.

   (c) A social worker is laid off because the city of Toronto cancels one of its social welfare programs.

   (d) A brewery worker in Regina is laid off when the firm relocates its production to Saskatoon.

   (e) Stenographers are laid off as Vancouver firms introduce word processing equipment into their offices.

   (f) Systems analysts lose their jobs as firms curtail projects due to slumping sales.

2. What specific government policy would you recommend for each of the following causes of unemployment? Explain briefly.
   (a) Structural unemployment caused by sectoral shifts in demand.

   (b) Cyclical unemployment.

(c)   Longer search unemployment caused by generous employment insurance benefits.

(d)   Frictional unemployment.

• • • • • • • • • • • • • •

ANSWERS
Multiple-Choice Questions

1.	(c)	**2.**	(e)	**3.**	(a)	**4.**	(b)	**5.**	(e)
6.	(d)	**7.**	(d)	**8.**	(c)	**9.**	(e)	**10.**	(c)
11.	(d)	**12.**	(c)	**13.**	(c)	**14.**	(c)	**15.**	(e)
16.	(d)	**17.**	(d)	**18.**	(a)	**19.**	(d)	**20.**	(c)
21.	(b)	**22.**	(b)						

Exercises

1. (a) Cyclical, because of the slowdown in economic activity.
    (b) Search or voluntary frictional unemployment. The engineer refused a job because of the expectation of finding another job with a higher rate of remuneration.
    (c) Frictional if short term, structural if the social worker is unable to find work after a prolonged search.
    (d) Frictional if short term, structural if the brewery worker cannot find work in Regina or refused to move to Saskatoon.
    (e) Structural; stenographers may have to undergo retraining in order to acquire skills required by word processing equipment or other types of occupation. It would be frictional if the stenographers could find office work elsewhere.

(f) If the reduction in sales is a result of a general economic recession, cyclical unemployment exists. Conversely, the sales reduction may be due to a sectoral shift away from these firms, in which case the unemployment is frictional if the system analysts find work elsewhere easily or structural if their unemployment is of long duration.

2. (a) Retraining and relocation grants to make movement of labour easier; policies to improve information about existing and (possibly) future employment opportunities.
    (b) Expansionary fiscal and monetary policies.
    (c) Any policy changes are bound to be controversial. Current provisions may be enforced more strictly, or you may recommend changes in unemployment provisions such as reduced weeks or lower weekly benefits.
    (d) Increasing knowledge that workers have about market opportunities would reduce frictional unemployment. Also, the government may wish to provide workers with relocation subsidies.

CHAPTER 32
••••••••••••••••
GOVERNMENT DEBT AND DEFICITS

••••••••••••••••
CHAPTER OVERVIEW

The government's budget deficit is equal to total government expenditure (including interest payments on its debt) minus total government revenue. Since the government must borrow to finance any shortfall in its revenues, the annual deficit is equal to the increase in the stock of government debt during the course of a year. Whenever the deficit is positive, the stock of government debt is growing. The primary budget deficit is equal to the excess of the government's program spending over total tax revenues. The difference between the total budget deficit and the primary deficit is the debt service payments.

The actual value of the budget deficit is a poor measure of the stance of fiscal policy, since its value fluctuates during various phases of the business cycle. Changes in the value of the cyclically adjusted budget deficit reflect changes in the stance of fiscal policy. A rise in the cyclically adjusted budget deficit reflects expansionary fiscal policy.

Changes in the debt-to-GDP ratio depend on the real interest rate, the growth rate of real GDP, and the size of the primary budget deficit. If the real interest rate exceeds the growth rate of real GDP, then stabilizing the debt-to-GDP ratio requires that the government run a primary budget surplus.

Three possible effects of government debt and deficits are discussed: "crowding out" of private economic activity; the potential harm of government debt to future generations; and limitations that debt puts on the conduct of economic policy. There are two possible crowding-out effects in an open economy: private-sector investment is reduced if government borrowing increases the interest rate, and net exports are reduced if increased domestic interest rates cause an increase in the external value of the domestic currency.

••••••••••••••••
LEARNING OBJECTIVES

After studying this chapter, you should be able to:

- review recent trends in the federal government budget deficit, the deficit as a share of GDP, and the debt-to-GDP ratio;
- understand that government deficits can be caused by large debt service payments created by the accumulation of national debt;
- explain why deficits influence the economy through their short-run stabilizing or destabilizing role and through their potential to affect income and welfare adversely in the long run;
- understand the two potential crowding-out effects of deficits;
- explain why the size of debt may hamper economic policy;
- explain the economic and political economy implications of measures to reduce the budget deficit or control its growth.

MULTIPLE-CHOICE QUESTIONS

1. The value of the Canadian federal (national) debt as a share of GDP in the 1990s was
   (a) somewhere between 60 and 70 percent.
   (b) lower than its value in the 1960s.
   (c) greater than its value during World War II.
   (d) equal to the value of the federal government deficit as a share of GDP.
   (e) slightly less than 90 percent.

2. Which one of the following statements is true?
   (a) An overall budgetary deficit implies a primary budget deficit.
   (b) A budgetary deficit means that government borrowing does not change.
   (c) Higher real interest rates imply lower debt service payments.
   (d) A budgetary deficit necessitates an increase in government borrowing.
   (e) Transfer payments are excluded from the category "program spending."

3. The primary federal deficit is defined as
   (a) the total federal deficit minus the value of outstanding debt.
   (b) the total federal deficit generated by transfer payments to primary industries.
   (c) the total federal deficit excluding debt service payments.
   (d) the cyclically adjusted deficit at potential national income.
   (e) the federal deficit attributable to debt service payments.

4. Compared with the 1970 period, debt service-payments in the 1990s
   (a) comprised a higher share of total government revenue.
   (b) were a higher proportion of total government expenditures.
   (c) represented a higher share of GDP.

   (d) All of the above.
   (e) None of the above.

5. Which of the following events by itself will increase the debt-to-GDP ratio?
   (a) The real interest rate exceeds the growth rate of real GDP.
   (b) The government runs a primary budget surplus.
   (c) The real interest rate is equal to the real growth rate of GDP and government runs a primary budget surplus.
   (d) Tax rates increase.
   (e) Both (c) and (d) are correct.

6. Some economists worry that the growing deficit is likely to result in higher inflation
   (a) as the government buys a disproportionately large share of total output.
   (b) if the Bank of Canada increases its purchases of government securities from the federal government in order to finance deficits.
   (c) if the Bank of Canada increases its sales of government securities in the open market.
   (d) if the Bank of Canada refuses to validate the deficit.
   (e) if the deficit completely crowds out private investment.

7. One of the "crowding-out" effects of a larger government budget deficit refers to the outcome of
   (a) higher interest rates and less private investment.
   (b) higher interest rates and more saving.
   (c) lower interest rates and more investment.
   (d) lower interest rates and less saving.
   (e) lower exports because of a higher exchange rate value.

Use Figure 32-1 to answer questions 8 through 10. Assume that potential real national income is 600 and that the curve labelled with the subscript 0 is the initial situation.

Figure 32-1

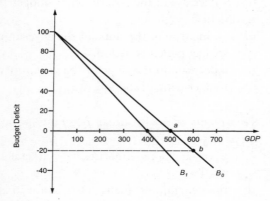

8. Which one of the following statements is *not* true for the deficit function B_0?
  (a) The tax rate is equal to 20 percent.
  (b) The cyclically adjusted deficit is 20.
  (c) There is a balanced budget at $Y = 500$.
  (d) The cyclically adjusted deficit is –20, i.e., a surplus.
  (e) When $Y = 0$, the budget deficit is 100.

9. For the curve B_0, which one of the following statements is true?
  (a) A movement from point a to point b represents an increase in tax rates.
  (b) The decrease in the budget deficit depicted by a movement from point b to point a must have been caused by an increase in government expenditure.
  (c) Since the budget deficit increased when national income fell from 500 to 400, the government must have increased its discretionary spending.
  (d) Changes in discretionary fiscal policy are shown by movements along the budget deficit function.
  (e) Movements along the function represent the automatic stabilizing influence of the tax system.

10. If the budget deficit function changes to B_1, then
  (a) the cyclically adjusted deficit increases to 50.

  (b) the tax rate increased from 20 to 25 percent.
  (c) the tax rate decreased from 20 to 15 percent.
  (d) government expenditures must have decreased at every level of national income.
  (e) the budget deficit decreases at every level of national income because the private saving ratio has increased.

11. If the capital stock falls as a result of a larger government budget deficit,
  (a) the current standard of living is likely to decline, but the future standard of living will improve.
  (b) the future standard of living is likely to decline.
  (c) the current generation bears the burden of the debt.
  (d) the concept of Ricardian neutrality holds.
  (e) future generations will be unaffected so long as consumption expenditure increases offset the effects of the deficit.

12. Some economists are concerned that a large and growing budget deficit
  (a) reduces the government's flexibility to use fiscal policy as a stabilization tool.
  (b) results in high interest payments, leaving less revenue for other public needs.
  (c) requires higher taxes to make rising interest payments.
  (d) will erode the competitiveness of the export sector as the exchange rate depreciates.
  (e) All or any of the above.

13. An annually balanced budget would be destabilizing because
  (a) it would lead to too large a government sector and greater economic inefficiency.
  (b) it would lead to too small a government sector and inadequate provision of public goods.
  (c) aggregate demand would grow faster at all stages of the business cycle.
  (d) government expenditure (hence, aggregate demand) would be increased in expansions and reduced in contractions.
  (e) the debt-to-GDP ratio must increase through time.

14. A deficit will crowd out net exports if
  (a) an interest rate increase depresses the exchange rate.
  (b) there is a large outflow of international capital.
  (c) the deficit attracts more foreign capital, thereby increasing the exchange rate.
  (d) international capital flows are totally insensitive to interest rate changes.
  (e) the deficit stimulates less imports.

15. In an open economy, persistent government budget deficits that are financed by foreign investors
  (a) inevitably reduce the capital stock of the economy.
  (b) have the same economic consequences for both current generations and future generations as would result if the deficits were financed domestically.
  (c) mean that foreigners must be paid interest and principal payments.
  (d) will cause inflation.
  (e) All of the above.

16. If GDP grows over time, the goal of a stable debt-to-GDP ratio requires
  (a) a constant value of outstanding debt.
  (b) a declining value of outstanding debt over time.
  (c) budget deficits so that debt grows at the same rate as GDP.
  (d) declining government deficits.
  (e) annually balanced budgets.

17. Without any policy changes, a rise in real national income leads to
  (a) a downward shift in the budget deficit function.
  (b) an upward shift in the budget deficit function.
  (c) a decrease in the government's budget deficit.
  (d) an increase in the slope of the government budget deficit function.
  (e) a decrease in the slope of the government budget deficit function.

18. Proponents of the Ricardian neutrality position argue that
  (a) government expenditures have no effect on the economy.
  (b) financing government deficits with foreign capital is equivalent to financing the deficits domestically.
  (c) issuing government bonds to finance government expenditures distorts the economy less than raising taxes by an equivalent amount.
  (d) government expenditures have the same effect on the economy whether financed by raising taxes or by issuing bonds if informed taxpayers recognize government borrowing as a future tax liability.
  (e) growing public debt always increases permanent disposable income.

• • • • • • • • • • • • •

EXERCISES

1. You are given the following data about the planned fiscal activity of the government of a hypothetical economy in 1996. All data are in billions of the domestic currency.
Real GDP in 1995 and 1996 is 200.
Government expenditure on goods and services during 1996 is 20.
Transfer payments during 1996 are 5.
Outstanding government debt at the beginning of 1996 is 100.
Taxation revenue during 1996 is 30.
Interest on outstanding debt is 10 percent.

(a) Calculate the value of debt service payments in 1996, assuming that the interest on any newly created debt in 1996 is not paid until 1997.

(b) Calculate the value of program spending during 1996.

(c) Calculate the value of the primary budget deficit and the value of the overall budget deficit.

(d) What is your estimate of the level of government borrowing required in 1996?

(e) Estimate the debt-to-GDP ratio at the beginning of 1996 and at the end of 1996.

(f) What is the deficit-to-GDP ratio at the end of 1996?

2. The minister of finance tables her 1998 budget forecast in the House of Commons. The budget includes a graph of the budget deficit function labelled B_{1998}; see Figure 32-2. Reluctantly, she reveals an anticipated downturn in the economy such that the 1998 real income level will fall by $10 billion from the 1997 level of $160 billion (which is equal to potential GDP). The government's 1998 fiscal policy measures, which will be outlined in detail at a later date, will not change the 1997 federal debt-to-GDP ratio of 60 percent. Maude Walker, an energetic member of one of the opposition parties, decides to do some serious homework to understand the 1998 budget and its relationship with 1994's budget.
   (a) She prepares the following check list for the 1998 budget. Calculate the 1998 magnitudes for her and fill in the missing entries.
   The forecasted level of real national income _____ .
   The value of the output gap _____ .
   The forecasted deficit-to-GDP ratio _____ .
   The tax rate as a percentage _____ .
   The estimated value of federal debt outstanding _____ .
   Best estimate of the level of government expenditure _____ .
   The value of the cyclically adjusted deficit _____ . (Use the formula $B = 30 - 0.2Y$.)
   (b) Next, Walker retrieves 1994 budget information that includes a graph of the budget surplus function labelled as B_{1997} in Figure 32-2. Assuming that the function depicts actual values, calculate the 1997 values below and fill in the 1997 missing entries.

Figure 32-2

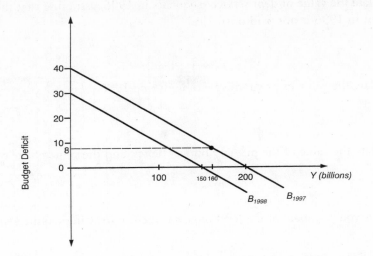

The level of real national income _____ .

The value of the output gap _____ .

The deficit-to-GDP ratio _____ .

The tax rate as a percentage _____ .

The value of federal government debt outstanding _____ .

Best estimate of the level of government expenditure _____ .

The value of the cyclically adjusted deficit. _____ . (Use the formula $B = 40 - 0.2Y$.)

(c) By comparing 1997 and 1998 figures, what should Walker conclude about the change in the fiscal policy stance of the government?

(d) During a question period, Walker asks the minister why government policy for 1998 appears to be procyclical rather than countercyclical. The minister acknowledges that Walker's analysis is correct. However, she replies that, although her policies are painful in the short term, the economy will be better off in the long run. Discuss this statement.

3. This exercise focuses on the crowding-out effect in a closed economy. The country of Zed has a domestic market for financial funds (denominated in zees, abbreviated z). At present, all borrowing and lending occurs in the private sector. The government of Zed plays a completely passive role; it has no expenditures, owes no debt, and collects no tax. The supply of funds (S) arising from private saving in the private sector is given by the equation $S = 30 + i$. The private-sector demand for funds for investment purposes (D) is $D = 60 - 5i$. Both curves represent demand and supply conditions each year; thus, they are flow equations. Current GDP is 1,000 and i ($=r$) is the real rate of interest.

(a) Plot the two curves and determine the current equilibrium levels of the interest rate (i) and the total amount of private borrowing (in zees) and saving.

Figure 32-3

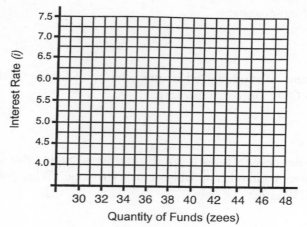

(b) Zed's government introduces, at the beginning of the year, some public spending programs that will cost 12z. This program will be financed entirely by issuing 12z of long-term government bonds and selling them in the financial funds market. Hence, the new demand for funds is D = 72 – 5i, which is the sum of private and public borrowing. No taxes are planned. Suppose that the spending program has no effect on either real GDP or the price level. If the private-sector supply curve for funds remains stable, determine the new equilibrium levels for i and total borrowing either by plotting the new demand curve or by solving algebraically.

(c) At the new equilibrium, what is the level of private-sector borrowing? How does this compare with private-sector borrowing before the increase in government borrowing? What has happened to the level of national saving? Can savers in Zed be characterized as "Ricardian" consumers?

(d) How much investment (borrowing) has been crowded out?

(e) At the beginning of the year, what is the deficit-to-GDP ratio? What is the debt-to-GDP ratio? If no debt is redeemed at the end of the year, what debt service payments will the government of Zed owe? What is its total deficit at the end of the year?

4. *The Mathematics of the Change in the Debt-to-GDP Ratio*
Suppose that an economy has a real interest of 4 percent, a growth rate of real GDP of 2 percent, a debt-to-GDP ratio of 50 percent and a primary budget deficit-to-GDP ratio of 1 percent.
(a) Calculate the change in the debt-to-GDP ratio. What does this value imply about government borrowing?

(b) Calculate the value of the primary budget deficit-to-GDP ratio that would be required to keep the debt-to-GDP ratio constant.

(c) Assuming a zero inflation rate, what annual budget deficit-to-GDP ratio is required to have a constant debt-to-GDP ratio of 50 percent?

(d) Recalculate your answers to parts (a), (b), and (c), assuming that the economy had a debt-to-GDP ratio of 60 percent; all other variables remain the same. What policy issues arise because of the higher debt-to-GDP ratio?

5. Can an annually balanced budget be a short-run destabilizing force in the economy? The proof to this proposition involves showing that private-sector shocks have a greater multiplier effect with a balanced budget requirement than without it. Consider the following behavioural equations for the economy of Soo.

$C = 50 + 0.8(Y - T)$ $I = 100$
$G = g$ $(X - IM) = 10 - 0.04Y$
$T = 0.2Y$ Potential $Y(Y^*) = 800$

(a) If $g = 160$, what is the current equilibrium level of Soo's real national income? What is the current budget balance for Soo's government? What is the current value of the output gap?

(b) Now assume that Soo's exports fall by 2 such that the new net export function is $8 - 0.04Y$. Assume also that the price level, the exchange rate, and the interest rate in Soo are unaffected by this change. Determine the new equilibrium levels of Y and the government's budget position. What is the value of the (simple) multiplier? What is the value of the output gap?

(c) Suppose that the conservative forces in Soo's government had been successful in implementing an annually balanced budget requirement before exports fell. Hence, in each year g must equal $0.2Y$ (spending equals taxation revenue). Substitute $g = 0.2Y$ into the equation for G and prove that the equilibrium level of Y is 800.

(d) As before, exports fall by 2 such that the net export equation becomes $8 - 0.04Y$. Using the fact that $g = 0.2Y$, solve for the equilibrium level of Y. What is the value of g at the new equilibrium level of Y? What is the multiplier value now? What is the value of the output gap? How does this value compare with that of having no annually balanced budget requirement? Why are they different?

ANSWERS

Multiple-Choice Questions

1.	(a)	**2.**	(d)	**3.**	(c)	**4.**	(d)	**5.**	(a)
6.	(b)	**7.**	(a)	**8.**	(b)	**9.**	(e)	**10.**	(b)
11.	(b)	**12.**	(e)	**13.**	(d)	**14.**	(a)	**15.**	(c)
16.	(c)	**17.**	(c)	**18.**	(d)				

Exercises

1. (a) 10 (= .10 x 100).

(b) 25 (= government spending on goods and services plus transfer payments).

(c) A primary budget deficit of –5 (a surplus of 5). This value is obtained by subtracting 30 from 25. An overall budget deficit of 5 (= a primary deficit (surplus) of – 5 plus debt service payments of 10).

(d) The overall budgetary deficit of 5 must be financed by borrowing.

(e) 50 percent (= 100 ÷ 200 × 100%). 52.5 percent (= 105 ÷ 200 × 100%).

(f) 2.5 percent (= 5 ÷ 200 × 100%).

2. (a) $150 billion; –10 (recessionary gap); 0; 20 percent; $90 billion (60 percent of $150 billion); $30 billion (the intercept term); $2 billion surplus (= 30 – 0.2 × 160).

(b) $160 billion; 0; 5 percent (8 ÷ 160); 20 percent; $96 billion (60 percent of $160 billion); $40 billion (the intercept term); cyclically adjusted deficit of $8 billion (40 – 32).

(c) Although the tax rate has not changed, government expenditures have fallen by $10 billion from 1997 to 1998. This change in fiscal policy is best seen by noting that the government plans a cyclically adjusted surplus in 1998 (and reducing outstanding debt), while it ran a cyclically adjusted deficit in 1997. Also note that the change in fiscal policy stance is at a time when real national income is falling; i.e., fiscal policy is procyclical.

(d) The government appears to want to stabilize the debt-to-GDP ratio. Notice that the government ran a budget deficit in 1994 when the economy was at its potential level of output. With the downturn in the economy in 1998, tax revenues will be lost. If the government had continued its expenditures at $40 billion in 1998, the deficit would have grown and the government would have had to increase the debt-to-GDP ratio. Future tax liabilities will be higher and possibly some of the crowding-out effects discussed in the text may cause declines in investment and exports.

3. (a) i = 5 percent and total private saving borrowing (investment) = 35 zees.

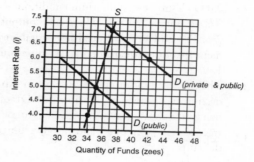

Figure 32-4

(b) i = 7 percent and total private saving (= borrowing) is 37 zees.
$72 – 5i = 30 + i$; i = 7 percent.

(c) With the original demand curve for funds, private-sector borrowing at an interest rate of 7 percent would have been 25. We know that total borrowing at 7 percent is 37, 12 of which is government borrowing. National saving is equal to private saving at 7 percent minus the budgetary deficit, or 37 – 12 = 25. Notice that private savings increased by 2 with the increase in the interest rate. Since private saving did not increase by the value of the budget deficit, national saving fell, with the result that savers in this economy cannot be characterized as "Ricardian" consumers.

(d) 10 (= 35 – 25).

(e) The deficit-to-GDP and debt-to-GDP ratios are both 1.2 percent. Since the interest rate is 7 percent, debt service payments are 0.84 zees. The total deficit is therefore 12.84 zees.

4. (a) The change in the debt-to-GDP ratio is given by the formula $\Delta d = x + (r – g) \times d$. In this case, the change in the debt-to-GDP ratio is 2 percent [= 0.01 + (0.04 – 0.02) × 0.50]. Since this value is positive, government borrowing increased.

(b) To obtain $\Delta d = 0$, a primary surplus of 0.01 (a primary deficit of –0.01) is required to offset the growth in real debt service payments of 0.01.)

(c) The formula is given by deficit/GDP = $(\pi + g) \times$ (debt/GDP). Since π = 0, then the deficit/GDP ratio is 1 percent (= 0.02 × .50).

(d) The change in the debt-to-GDP ratio is 2.2 percent. The primary surplus required to keep $\Delta d = 0$ is 0.012. The new deficit/GDP ratio is 1.2 percent. One policy implication is that program spending must be reduced more than before because of a higher debt-to-GDP ratio. Hence, the flexibility in conducting counter-cyclical fiscal policy has been diminished.

5. (a) $AE = 50 + 0.8(Y - 0.2Y) + 100 + 160 + 10 - 0.04Y$. Using the equilibrium condition $Y = AE$, we obtain $Y = 800$. There is no output gap. The budget is balanced since total government spending equals total taxation revenue of 160.

(b) The new equilibrium GDP is 795. An export decline of 2 generated a decline in GDP of 5; hence, the multiplier is 2.5. There is an output (recessionary) gap of –5 and the government deficit is 1.0.

(c) The expression for aggregate expenditure is now $50 + 0.8(Y - 0.2Y) + 100 + 0.2Y(= g) + 10 - 0.04Y$. As before, $Y = 800$.

(d) With the decline in net exports of 2, the new equilibrium GDP is 790. Since total taxation revenue is 158, g must also be 158. The multiplier value is 5, since a decline in net exports of 2 created a reduction of 10 in GDP. The output gap is now –10, which is greater than in part (b), which required no balanced budget. The multiplier with an annually balanced budget requirement is larger because the recessionary gap automatically reduces tax revenue, which must be matched by an equal reduction in government spending. Thus, as the text suggests, an annually balanced budget serves as a *built-in destabilizer*.

CHAPTER 33

ECONOMIC GROWTH

CHAPTER OVERVIEW

This chapter considers economic theories of how and why economies grow. Factors that affect the rate of economic growth include the quantity of labour and capital; the stock and quality of human capital; technological change; the structure of the economy; and legal, social, and economic institutions. The importance of ideas, knowledge, and new technology is the focus of recent theories of economic growth.

The chapter discusses the costs and benefits of economic growth. One of the potential costs of economic growth is that current consumption might be diverted to capital formation. The distinction between economic growth and living standards (measured by *per capita* output) is discussed.

Neoclassical growth theory stresses diminishing returns to investment and constant returns to scale. New growth theories emphasize the possibility of increasing returns to investment because of fixed costs and knowledge. The chapter concludes by discussing the limits to economic growth.

LEARNING OBJECTIVES

After reading this chapter, you should be able to:

■ distinguish between, on the one hand, once-and-for-all increases in real GDP caused by increases in aggregate demand and reductions in structural unemployment, and on the other hand, economic growth, which increases potential GDP due to changes in factor supplies or in the productivity of factors;

■ explain both the long-run and short-run effects of investment and saving on real national income;

■ recognize the cumulative nature of growth;

■ describe the income-raising potential of economic growth relative to that achieved either by removing inefficiencies or by redistributing the existing national income;

■ cite the factors that affect economic growth;

■ understand the differences between *neoclassical* and new theories of economic growth;

■ compare the costs, including the loss of current consumption, with the benefits of economic growth;

■ understand the repercussions of economic growth on resource depletion and the environment.

MULTIPLE-CHOICE QUESTIONS

1. Economic growth is best defined as
   (a) a rise in real national income as unemployment is reduced.
   (b) fluctuations of GDP around its potential level.
   (c) a rise in potential national income due to increases in factor supplies or in the productivity of factors.
   (d) increases in current real GDP as structural unemployment decreases.
   (e) a reduction in the inequality of income distribution.

2. In terms of aggregate demand and aggregate supply, economic growth refers to
   (a) rightward shifts of the *LRAS* curve.
   (b) rightward shifts of the *AD* curve.
   (c) leftward shifts of the *SRAS* curve.
   (d) simultaneous rightward shifts of the *AD* curve and the *SRAS* curve.
   (e) the elimination of a recessionary gap.

3. Theories of economic growth stress
   (a) ways of reducing income inequalities.
   (b) the elimination of short-term inefficiencies.
   (c) the process of increasing potential GDP over time.
   (d) the need to increase consumption and decrease saving over time.
   (e) the need for countries to become self-sufficient in food production.

4. In the long run, all else equal, an increase in saving in a country is likely to
   (a) cause the aggregate demand curve to shift to the left.
   (b) cause real national income to fall because of inadequate aggregate demand.
   (c) increase economic growth because more investment expenditure can be financed from these funds.
   (d) reduce structural unemployment and therefore increase potential GDP.
   (e) increase the reliance on foreign capital to finance investment.

5. According to the "rule of 72," a growth in population of 2 percent per year means that population will double in approximately
   (a) 2 years.   (b) 144 years.
   (c) 72 years.   (d) 260 years.
   (e) 36 years.

6. Suppose that two countries have the same per capita output. Country A has an annual economic growth rate of 6 percent, while country B grows at 3 percent per year. According to the rule of 72, country A will have a per capita output four times as large as country B's in
   (a) 12 years.   (b) 36 years.
   (c) 24 years.   (d) 48 years.
   (e) 72 years.

7. Ken and Bill begin the same job with a first-year salary of $18,000. If Ken's salary grows at 3 percent each year and Bill's grows at 2 percent per year, then after 8 years
   (a) Ken's yearly salary will be about $1,710 more than Bill's.
   (b) Ken's yearly salary will be about $21,100.
   (c) Ken's yearly salary will be about $1,440 more than Bill's.
   (d) Ken's yearly salary will be about $22,320.
   (e) Both (c) and (d).

8. Which of the following would normally *not* be considered a beneficial result of economic growth?
   (a) Higher living standards.
   (b) Greater inequality of income distribution.
   (c) Ease in achieving some types of income redistribution.
   (d) Technological changes that produce substitutes for dwindling resource stocks.
   (e) A higher quality of life.

9. A contemporary view of the relationships among economic growth, economic efficiency, and income redistribution is that
   (a) all three are interrelated.
   (b) the income-raising potential of economic growth exceeds that of the other two.
   (c) achieving one of them may have unfavourable effects on the others.
   (d) All of the above.
   (e) None of the above.

10. In neoclassical theories of growth that assume unchanging technology, capital accumulation
    (a) causes the capital-output ratio to fall over time.
    (b) generates a constant rate of growth in GDP per capita.
    (c) increases output per worker subject to the law of diminishing returns.
    (d) has no effect on GDP in the short run or the long run.
    (e) has no effect on the standard of living in the long run.

Questions 11 through 14 refer to the following data for an economy with a constant technology:

Labour	Capital	Output
10.0	10	10.0
10.0	15	11.8
10.0	20	13.2
15.0	15	15.0
22.5	15	19.1

11. The marginal product of capital (extra output per extra unit of capital input, other inputs unchanged)
    (a) is 1.8 when capital rises from 10 to 15.
    (b) is 0.14 when capital rises from 15 to 20.
    (c) rises when progressively more capital is used.
    (d) demonstrates the principle of increasing returns to scale.
    (e) is 0.36 when capital rises from 10 to 15.

12. The marginal product of labour (extra output per extra unit of labour input, other inputs unchanged)
    (a) is 0.547 (approximately) when labour rises from 15 to 22.5.

    (b) is 4.1 when labour rises from 15 to 22.5.
    (c) is 1.8 when labour rises from 10 to 15.
    (d) cannot be estimated in this table.
    (e) demonstrates the principle of increasing returns to scale.

13. This economy operates under constant returns to scale because
    (a) increasing capital inputs has a constant positive effect on output.
    (b) increasing labour and capital inputs by 50 percent increases output by 50 percent.
    (c) increasing labour inputs has a constant positive effect on output.
    (d) both marginal productivities are positive and constant.
    (e) of the law of diminishing returns.

14. When labour (workers) increases from 15.0 to 22.5 and capital remains at 15,
    (a) living standards per worker increase because marginal productivity is positive.
    (b) output per worker stays constant because capital is constant.
    (c) living standards per worker decrease even though marginal productivity is positive.
    (d) the average productivity of labour (workers) is 0.547 approximately.
    (e) living standards per worker increase because average productivity of labour increases.

15. Which of the following is *not* a feature of the increasing returns theory of economic growth?
    (a) Firms that first develop new investment opportunities receive low initial rates of return because of high fixed costs.
    (b) Investors who follow "pioneer" investors face higher investment costs and therefore decreasing rates of return.
    (c) Once a technological breakthrough has been made, new investors garner high rates of return since this technology is usually available to them.
    (d) New products, usually readily accepted by customers, lead to significant early returns for pioneering firms.
    (e) Both (b) and (d).

16. The neoclassical assumption of constant returns to scale means that
    (a) economic growth occurs with increased GDP per capita.
    (b) GDP per capita increases with economic growth.
    (c) living standards must decrease with economic growth.
    (d) living standards must decrease if technological change is labour augmenting.
    (e) None of the above.

17. Which one of the following is least likely to increase the potential for economic growth?
    (a) Population growth accompanied by a constant capital stock.
    (b) Improvements in health that reduce absenteeism and illness among labour force participants.
    (c) Increases in the capacity to develop and market new innovations in products and production processes.
    (d) Improvement in labour productivity generated by on-the-job training programs and/or a better-educated labour force.
    (e) Government policies that provide tax advantages to R&D.

18. According to the Brundtland Commission, sustainable development
    (a) is development that meets the needs of the present without compromising the ability of future generations to meet their own needs.
    (b) means that the environment imposes no limits on sustained economic growth.
    (c) entails governments ignoring the detrimental effects of growth on the environment, thereby encouraging the private sector to expand capital as rapidly as possible.
    (d) requires advanced countries to limit their donations of financial capital to third-world countries in order to guarantee sustainable development.
    (e) entails governments encouraging farmers in advanced countries to overproduce.

19. Which of the following is least likely to be an appropriate government policy for sustaining an advanced industrial economy's competitive advantage?
    (a) Revise government policy that has inhibited competition.
    (b) Change the tax system in order to promote consumption and to discourage saving.
    (c) Phase out traditional subsidization policies supporting industries that cannot compete in the long run.
    (d) Provide tax advantages to R&D activities that have the greatest potential of increasing the competitiveness of many industries.
    (e) Ensure that a portion of government expenditure is directed to improving social infrastructure such as transportation and communication networks.

20. An increase in economic growth
    (a) will usually require a reduction in the proportion of current national income consumed.
    (b) will require an economy to decrease its savings ratio.
    (c) will be aided by high real interest rates.
    (d) can be accomplished only by accumulating more and more capital.
    (e) will require less rather than more competitiveness in world markets.

21. For the economy as a whole, the primary opportunity cost of economic growth is
    (a) the reduction in GDP per capita in future time periods.
    (b) the widespread environmental deterioration that inevitably results from economic growth.
    (c) the loss of current consumption opportunities.
    (d) increased unemployment in the short run.
    (e) a greater inequality of income within a country that inevitably results from economic growth.

22. Which of the following is *not* a feature of the recent theories of economic growth?
  (a) Technological change is an exogenous variable.
  (b) The diffusion of technology is endogenous.
  (c) Investment often confers externalities that increase economic growth.
  (d) Innovation is encouraged by a strongly competitive environment and discouraged by monopoly practices.
  (e) Managing innovation better than one's competitors is one of the most important objectives of modern firms.

EXERCISES

1. Suppose that an economy's current GDP is 100. Economists have estimated that the country's potential national income could grow by either 1 percent, 2 percent, or 6 percent, depending on its policies with respect to promoting savings and investment, providing eduction, allowing free international trade, and protecting the environment. You are asked to determine the economic implications of the alternative growth scenarios.

(a) Fill in the following table. Use the compound growth formula, $Y(1 + r)^n$, where Y is current GDP, r is the rate of growth over a given time period, and n is the number of compounding periods.

Estimated GDP at Various Growth Rates			
Year	1 percent	2 percent	6 percent
0	100	100	100
1	_____	_____	_____
10	_____	_____	_____
12	_____	_____	_____
36	_____	_____	_____
72	_____	_____	_____
100	_____	_____	_____

(b) What is the effect on GDP of a doubling of the annual growth rate from 1 percent to 2 percent after 1 year? After 10 years? After 100 years?

(c) What is the effect on GDP of a trebling of the annual growth rate from 2 percent to 6 percent after 1 year? After 10 years? After 100 years?

(d) Use your calculations to illustrate the "rule of 72" by filling in the following blanks. Refer to Mathematical Note #1 at the back of the textbook.
  At 1 percent annual growth, GDP doubles after about _____ years; at 2 percent annual growth, GDP doubles after about _____ years; at 6 percent annual growth, GDP doubles after about _____ years.

(e) What additional information would you need to determine how living standards would change in the three scenarios?

2. Assume that the productivity of labour increases by 2.5 percent a year, the labour force increases by 1.75 percent a year, hours worked per member of the work force decline by 0.25 percent a year, and population increases by 1 percent a year.

(a) Predict the annual increase in real national income.

(b) Predict the annual increase in per capita real national income.

(c) Predict the number of years to double real national income.

(d) Predict the number of years to double per capita real national income.

3. Discuss how each of the following factors would affect standards of living as measured by real GDP per capita, now and twenty years from now. As an intermediate step, explain how output and consumption are affected in each time frame. Assume other things remain constant and that there is full employment of resources.
(a) An increase in the birthrate.

(b) A decrease in current national saving.

(c) A technological innovation reducing input requirements.

(d) An increase in current expenditures for technical education financed by increased taxes.

(e) A decrease in the working life span of the labour force.

(f) An increase in labour force participation rate.

4. This exercise focuses on the opportunity costs of growth. Suppose that the national income of an economy was 100 in year 0, consumption expenditure was 85, and investment expenditure was 15. The growth of real national income on an annual basis is expected to be 2 percent. The current government urges the citizens of this nation to pursue policies to increase the growth rate to 4 percent on an annual basis. Its economic forecasters suggest that by reducing consumption to 70 (increasing saving by 15) and by increasing investment expenditure to a level of 30, (1) consumption expenditure 7 years hence will be equal to that level of consumption without these policies (with the economy growing at 2 percent), and (2) the aggregate level of consumption in 20 years would be *double* the level associated with a 2 percent growth rate.

Annual Level of Consumption			
Year	2 percent growth	4 percent growth	Cumulative (loss) or gain
0	85.0	70.0	(15.0)
1	86.7	72.9	(28.8)
2	88.5	75.8	(41.5)
3	90.3	78.9	(52.9)
4	92.1	82.1	(62.9)
7	97.8	92.6	(83.3)
8	99.7	96.4	(86.6)
9	101.8	100.3	(88.1)
10	103.8	104.4	(87.5)
17	119.4	138.2	(14.9)
18	121.8	143.8	7.1
20	126.8	155.8	61.5
30	154.9	232.4	
40	189.2	346.7	
50	231.1	517.2	

Your task is to confirm the accuracy of the government's economic forecasts by answering the following questions.

(a) What is the loss in consumption in year 4 because of the government's growth policy? What is the cumulative loss after four years?

(b) In what year will the level of consumption with a 4 percent growth rate equal the level of consumption with a 2 percent growth rate? Compare your answer with the government's assertion.

(c) In what year does this economy recoup all of the cumulative losses in forgone consumption?

(d) Is the government's assertion that this society will double its consumption level in 20 years correct?

• • • • • • • • • • • • • • •

ANSWERS

Multiple-Choice Questions

1. (c) **2.** (a) **3.** (c) **4.** (c) **5.** (e)
6. (d) **7.** (a) **8.** (b) **9.** (d) **10.** (c)
11. (e) **12.** (a) **13.** (b) **14.** (c) **15.** (b)
16. (b) **17.** (a) **18.** (a) **19.** (b) **20.** (a)
21. (c) **22.** (a)

Exercises

1. (a)

Year	1%	2%	6%
1	101.0	102.0	106.0
10	110.5	121.9	179.1
12	112.7	126.8	201.2
36	143.1	204.0	814.7
72	204.7	416.1	6,637.8
100	270.5	724.5	33,930.2

(b) After 1 year, GDP is about 1 percent more; after 10 years, GDP is 11.4 more or about 10 percent more; after 100 years, GDP is 168 percent greater (454 more).

(c) After 1 year, GDP is 4 percent more; after 10 years, GDP is about 47 percent more (57.2 more); after 100 years, GDP is almost 46 times more.

(d) 72; 36; 12.

(e) Most importantly, we would need population information because, if we are interested in improved living standards, we are concerned with increasing GDP per person. If we are concerned with a broader definition of economic welfare, factors such as health and environmental standards mights also be considered. The actual distribution of income, rather than its average value per person, may also interest us.

2. (a) 4 percent (2.5 + 1.75 − 0.25).
    (b) 3 percent (4 percent − 1 percent).
    (c) 18 = 72/4 (rule of 72).
    (d) 24 = 72/3 (rule of 72).

3. (a) A higher birth rate results in more consumption and less saving now. In twenty years the work force will be larger, but without growth in the capital stock, output per capita will be lower due to the declining marginal productivity of labour.

    (b) A decrease in the saving rate raises current consumption but reduces the future standard of living because there will be less investment in physical and human capital.

    (c) A technological innovation that reduces input requirements raises current output, unless the use of resources to develop that innovation causes a larger current reduction in the output of other goods.

(d) An increase in taxes is likely to reduce current consumption, and as workers leave the labour force to receive more training, total production declines. Once the trained workers re-enter the labour force, the productive capacity of the economy is greater and the future standard of living increases.

(e) A decrease in the economically productive life span of workers reduces labour inputs and therefore current output. With more dependants (retirees) in the population, saving falls. The effect on the current standard of living may be small, but the future negative impact will be larger.

(f) An increase in the labour force participation rate increases labour inputs and output per person in the population. Successive increases in the participation rate will have a progressively smaller effect without an increase in the capital stock.

4. (a) The loss in consumption is 10 (92.1 − 82.1); 62.9 is the cumulative loss.

    (b) According to the schedule, consumption (C) at 4 percent growth will equal C at 2 percent growth sometime in years 9 and 10. This is substantially longer than suggested by the government.

    (c) Sometime between the seventeenth and eighteenth years. Note that we have treated all gains and losses the same, regardless of the year in which they occur.

    (d) No; it is much later. According to the schedule, C at 4 percent growth is double C at 2 percent growth in approximately 45 years.

(Note: All calculations assume annual compounding.)

CHAPTER 34

GROWTH IN THE DEVELOPING COUNTRIES

CHAPTER OVERVIEW

About one-quarter of the world's population still exists at a level of bare subsistence, and nearly three-quarters are poor by Canadian standards. Although some poorer societies have grown rapidly, the gap between the very richest and very poorest remains large and is not decreasing.

Impediments to economic development include excessive population growth; resource limitations; inefficient use of resources; inadequate infrastructure; excessive government intervention; lack of property rights; and institutional and cultural patterns that make economic growth difficult.

The older model for development policies included heavy tariff barriers; hostility to foreign direct investment; controls and subsidization of local activities; and exchange rates pegged at excessively low values. The so-called "Washington consensus" describes the conditions that are necessary for a poorer country to get itself on a path of sustained development.

LEARNING OBJECTIVES

After studying the material in this chapter, you should be able to:

- comprehend the uneven pattern of development in the world;
- recognize how population growth, inadequate human resources, limited infrastructure, and inefficiently used resources pose barriers to economic development;
- explain the post-war consensus in favour of inward-looking, highly interventionist government policies to promote development and indicate how it has evolved to a more outward-looking approach;
- identify the role for international trade and foreign direct investment in this out-looking strategy;
- summarize the set of government policies advocated by the major international development agencies;
- explain how technical change and its diffusion is the focus of a new debate over the role of government in development.

MULTIPLE-CHOICE QUESTIONS

1. Increases in real GDP in developing countries do not necessarily lead to economic advancement if
    (a) growth in productivity is greater than real GDP growth.
    (b) population growth exceeds real GDP growth.
    (c) market-oriented processes replace command-economy decision making.
    (d) foreign capital is the major source of the expansion in real GDP.
    (e) None of the above.

2. Which one of the following would *not* be among the barriers to economic development of particular countries?
    (a) Rapid population growth.
    (b) Inefficient use of resources.
    (c) International trade.
    (d) Inadequate human resources.
    (e) Inadequate services such as communications and transportation.

3. Which of the following is the best example of *allocative inefficiency*?
    (a) Some productive processes use too much labour relative to capital.
    (b) Some productive processes use too much capital relative to labour.
    (c) Firms do not seek to maximize their profits.
    (d) Owners of factors of production do not seek to maximize their material welfare.
    (e) Society is at the "wrong" point on its production possibility boundary.

4. Which of the following was *not* a feature of the *older view* of development policies?
    (a) Import substitution.
    (b) Fixed exchange rates and exchange controls.
    (c) Governments were receptive to foreign investment.
    (d) Investment policies were focused on government-owned industries.
    (e) Heavy subsidization of private local firms.

5. Outward-looking growth strategies became more accepted in the 1980s as a result of the
    (a) successful performance of countries such as Taiwan, Korea, Hong Kong, and Singapore.
    (b) successful performance of countries such as Poland, Cuba, and the former Soviet republics.
    (c) ability of the Indian government to promote rapid growth in exports.
    (d) inability of multinational corporations to make high profits selling in protected host-country markets.
    (e) None of the above.

6. Which of the following is *not* a feature of the newer view of economic development?
    (a) Abandon both the heavy subsidization and the pervasive regulations of economic activity.
    (b) Acceptance of the beneficial role played by competition and trade-oriented development.
    (c) Foreign investors are subject to significantly different regulations than those that are in force for locally owned firms.
    (d) Upgrading social infrastructure.
    (e) Strong enforcement of property rights and contracts.

7. One of the important implications of modern growth theory, as it applies to developing countries is
    (a) some industries must be subsidized as long as they cannot compete with global companies.
    (b) the costs of foreign direct investment (*FDI*) usually outweigh the benefits for most traditionally based economies.
    (c) adopting someone else's technology, for the most part, is a costless task.
    (d) the new technologies brought by transnational companies must be diffused into the local economy.
    (e) population growth will continue to be the most important source of economic growth.

8. The 1980s consensus position regarding the appropriate policies for developing countries to pursue includes all but which of the following items?
   (a) Limiting government budget deficits in order to avoid the need for inflationary finance or higher interest rates.
   (b) Relying on market-determined exchange rates.
   (c) Applying protection to infant industries in selected cases for a limited period of time.
   (d) Education, health, and infrastructure investment are desirable forms of public expenditure.
   (e) Ignoring the consequences of growth on the distribution of income

9. The vicious circle of poverty
   (a) refers to insufficient domestic savings generated at low levels of income to raise the capital stock.
   (b) applies to countries that borrow from abroad and spend the proceeds on consumer goods.
   (c) results from the failure of policies in developing countries to hold population growth to zero percent.
   (d) describes a situation in which savings out of domestic income are invested abroad, lowering the domestic rate of capital accumulation.
   (e) implies that a widening of income-distribution inequality is an inevitable aspect of economic development.

10. Which of the following is a potential cost of economic development?
    (a) Some traditional ways of doing things may have to be altered.
    (b) Current consumption may have to be sacrificed in order to generate economic development.
    (c) The inequality of income distribution may increase in the absence of redistributive policies.
    (d) Governments may have to increase their expenditures to improve economic infrastructures.
    (e) All of the above.

11. Financial institutions are important in the development process because they
    (a) accept short-run savings deposits to make long-term investment loans.
    (b) can more effectively invest surplus funds outside of the country.
    (c) generate profits that can be used to finance development.
    (d) All of the above.
    (e) None of the above.

12. Highly planned government intervention is most likely successful in
    (a) promoting entrepreneurial activity.
    (b) encouraging risk-taking and adapting to changing consumption desires.
    (c) providing basic infrastructure to facilitate economic development.
    (d) identifying market niches for profitable productive activity.
    (e) Both (c) and (d).

13. A country can obtain capital for economic development from
    (a) domestic savings.
    (b) loans or investment from abroad.
    (c) contributions from foreigners.
    (d) foreign exchange receipts from net exports.
    (e) Any or all of the above sources.

14. Opponents of strong efforts to control population growth
    (a) must base their arguments on religious, not economic, reasoning.
    (b) are pessimistic over the prospects for strong growth in productivity, and, therefore, favour a growing labour force.
    (c) believe population growth will fall automatically as industrialization and urbanization occur.
    (d) believe growth in the capital stock is a much more significant economic variable than growth in population.
    (e) are also opponents of market-oriented economies for developing countries.

EXERCISES

1. Although development economists no longer consider domestic investment to be the single most important determinant of a country's development prospects, it remains an important factor to evaluate. The World Bank data for investment and saving as a share of GDP for a sample of developing countries are included in the table below.

Country	GDP growth rate 1980-89	Gross domestic investment		Gross national saving		Current account balance	
		1973-80	1980-89	1973-80	1980-89	1973-80	1980-89
Brazil	3.0	24.0	21.5	19.3	19.7	−4.6	−1.8
Mexico	0.7	24.2	23.1	20.2	21.3	−4.0	−1.8
Columbia	3.5	18.8	20.4	19.0	17.4	0.2	−3.0
Kenya	4.1	26.0	25.4	16.3	18.0	−9.7	−7.4
Nigeria	−0.4	22.8	13.8	24.4	12.4	1.6	−1.4
Indonesia	5.3	24.5	30.4	24.6	27.6	0.1	−2.8
Korea	9.7	31.2	31.2	25.9	29.6	−5.3	1.6
India	5.3	21.3	23.9	21.0	21.5	−0.3	−2.4

   (a) Which of these countries devoted the largest share of GDP to gross private investment during the 1970s and how did that situation change in the 1980s?

   (b) Which countries were able to generate a higher rate of national saving? Did major oil producers (Mexico, Nigeria, Indonesia), have relatively larger saving due to their windfall in the 1970s? Is there evidence from the 1980s that countries that faced a debt crises (Mexico, Brazil) and outside pressure to raise public saving actually accomplished this goal?

   (c) Countries with a large current account deficit often have been able to obtain foreign financing to allow investment to exceed saving. In what cases does the ability to obtain foreign funds appear to have led to faster subsequent growth?

2. Suppose there are two countries, A and B, both of which are less developed in terms of advanced country standards. Both countries have x units of working labour and y units of land, but very little capital. Country A has a population of 8 and country B has a population of 10. Assume that either country produces and consumes only wheat and peanuts. The production possibilities (in bushels) are given in the schedules below.

Country A		Country B	
Wheat	Peanuts	Wheat	Peanuts
100	0	200	0
90	10	180	18
80	19	160	35
70	27	140	51
60	34	120	66
50	40	100	80
40	45	80	93
30	49	60	105
20	52	40	116
10	54	20	126
0	55	0	135

(a) With successive increases in wheat production, what happens to the rate of peanut production in country A? In country B? What can be said about the change in opportunity costs?

(b) Suppose that production and consumption in country A are 16 bushels of peanuts and 80 bushels of wheat and in country B are 160 bushels of wheat and 35 bushels of peanuts. Does inefficiency in the use of resources exist in either country? What type?

(c) Assume production as in (b). If wheat is worth $2 (U.S.) per bushel and peanuts are worth $0.50 per bushel, what is the value of national income in each country (in U.S. dollars)? What is the per capita level of national income in each country?

(d) Assuming production as in (b), give possible reasons why country B is using its resources more efficiently than country A.

3. Briefly explain the advantages and drawbacks of the following development policies.
   (a) A policy of developing a strong agriculture-based economy.

   (b) Specialization in producing a single commodity.

   (c) Development of domestic industries that produce substitutes for imported products.

   (d) Encouraging foreign direct investment to finance economic development.

ANSWERS

Multiple-Choice Questions

1. (b)	**2.** (c)	**3.** (e)	**4.** (c)	**5.** (a)
6. (c)	**7.** (d)	**8.** (e)	**9.** (a)	**10.** (e)
11. (d)	**12.** (c)	**13.** (e)	**14.** (c)	

Exercises

1. (a) Korea, followed by Kenya, Indonesia, Mexico and Brazil, devoted the largest share of GDP to investment in the 1970s. In the 1980s Korea, Indonesia, and Kenya still lead this category, while Brazil and Mexico (who were severely indebted nationals in the 1980s) cut back investments.

    (b) In the 1970s high saving occurs in Korea, Indonesia, and Nigeria. The latter two countries appear to have saved part of their oil revenue windfall. In the 1980s national saving did rise in Brazil and Mexico—countries facing IMF-World Bank pressure to reduce their government budget deficits.

    (c) In the 1970s large current account deficits were reported by Kenya, Korea, Brazil, and Mexico. Korea's reliance on foreign funding led to successful economic growth. The record for the other three countries is more mixed.

2. (a) Opportunity costs are increasing in both countries. For example, in country A, to obtain an increase of 10 bushels of wheat from 20 to 30, the loss in production in peanuts is 3 bushels. However, to increase wheat from 30 bushels to 40 bushels, a loss of 4 is required. For country B, an increase of wheat from 20 to 40 bushels requires a loss of 10 bushels of peanuts. An increase of wheat from 40 to 60 bushels requires a loss of 11 bushels of peanuts.

    (b) A combination of 80 wheat and 16 peanuts represents a point inside the production possibility boundary in country A. It is technically possible for country A to produce 80 wheat and 19 peanuts. Thus, country A is incurring productive inefficiency. Country B is operating on its production possibility boundary, but there may be allocative inefficiency, depending upon how domestic opportunity costs compare with those set by world prices.

    (c) National income in country A is $\$2 \times 80$ plus $\$0.5 \times 16$, which equals $\$168$. National income in country B is $\$2 \times 160$ plus $\$0.5 \times 35$, which equals $\$337.50$. Per capita national income in country A is $\$168$ divided by 8, which equals $\$21$. Per capita national income in country B is $\$337.50$ divided by 10, which equals $\$33.75$.

    (d) Country B has avoided productive inefficiency. Although country A and country B have the same amount of land and labour, these resources are being employed more productively in country B than in country A. The causes may be differences in social and cultural attitudes, market organization, or in labour skills and productivity, or the quality of land and other natural resources.

3. (a) Advantages: It meets the fundamental needs of its population and may allow a surplus for export; technical training requirements are low; the congestion of urban areas is avoided. Disadvantages: Agricultural commodities have faced worsening terms of trade in the past because price and income elasticities in world markets are low; countries able to expand output in areas where they account for a small share of world production (and thus face a nearly horizontal demand curve) will benefit most. Moreover, the government should be confident that agricultural producers will be able to compete globally.

    (b) Advantages: Stresses specialization in commodities with the greatest comparative advantage and possibly leads to the highest immediate growth and standard of living. Disadvantages: Subjects country to short-term fluctuations in demand and supply and long-term secular risk of resource exhaustion or technological obsolescence.

    (c) Advantages: Easy to start by establishing a tariff, giving subsidies to import-competing industries, or import licensing; may lead to diversification and less reliance on foreign supplies for domestic consumption. Disadvantages: Greater risks of long-term inefficiencies relative to global competition; long-term growth jeopardized. Also, consumers pay higher prices unless protection generates scale efficiencies.

    (d) Advantages: Lessens the pressure for domestic saving to finance economic growth. State of the art technology is available immediately. Provides the opportunity for the diffusion of technology and managerial techniques over sectors of the economy. Increases employment and may result in more efficient labour use. Disadvantages: Foreign technology and managerial techniques may not be easily adaptable to domestic economy. Once resources have been exhausted, foreign companies may pull out. Some have argued that "branch-plant" economy may breed inefficiencies particularly if companies do not invest in R & D and demand tariff protection in the host economy.

PART ELEVEN

INTERNATIONAL ECONOMICS

CHAPTER 35

•••••••••••••••

THE GAINS FROM INTERNATIONAL TRADE

•••••••••••••••

CHAPTER OVERVIEW

This chapter explains how international trade makes possible a higher average standard of living for a country. A country benefits from buying goods abroad at a lower cost; this avoids diversion of resources from more efficient domestic industries. A country is said to have *absolute advantage* in the production of a particular commodity when it can produce more of the good with a given amount of resources than can other countries. A country has a *comparative advantage* in producing a particular good when it has a lower opportunity cost in production than other countries. The gains from trade do not depend upon absolute advantage, but rather upon comparative advantage. Even if a country has an absolute advantage in the production of all goods, both trading partners can share in the gains from trade.

Comparative advantage can be attributed to differences in exogenous considerations such as factor endowments and climate. Today, there is widespread acceptance by economists that comparative advantage may also be acquired. This has led to attempts by governments to influence comparative advantage; this intervention has not always been successful.

International trade encourages countries to specialize in the products where they have a comparative advantage as opposed to the costly product diversification associated with self-sufficiency. The gains from trade are likely to be even greater when countries can achieve economies of scale, or benefit from learning-by-doing.

The division of the gains from trade between two countries depends upon the terms of trade which refers to the ratio of the price of exported goods to the price of imported goods. This determines the quantity of imported goods that can be obtained per unit of exported good.

•••••••••••••••

LEARNING OBJECTIVES

After studying this chapter, you should be able to:

- recognize that international trade among countries involves basically the same principles of exchange that apply to trade among individuals;

- realize that although gains from trade occur even when production is fixed, further gains arise when nations increase output of goods in which they have a comparative advantage;

- understand that comparative advantage arises from differences in the opportunity costs of producing particular goods;

- acknowledge that comparative advantage may be determined by natural resource endowments and climate but may also be determined dynamically by changing human skills and experience in production;

- explain that the terms of trade, defined as the ratio of export prices to import prices, indicate how the gains from trade are divided between buyers and sellers.

MULTIPLE-CHOICE QUESTIONS

1. Country X has an absolute advantage over country Y in the production of widgets if
   (a) fewer resources are required in X to produce a given quantity of widgets than in Y.
   (b) a given amount of resources in X produces more widgets than the same amount of resources in Y.
   (c) relative to Y, more widgets can be produced in X with fewer resources.
   (d) All of the above.
   (e) None of the above.

2. If, given the same amount of inputs, Canadian farmers produce 1 tonne of rice per hectare while Japanese farmers produce a 1/2 tonne of rice per hectare, we can be certain that
   (a) Canada should export rice to Japan.
   (b) Canada has a comparative advantage in rice production.
   (c) Canada has an absolute advantage in rice production.
   (d) Japanese rice farmers must be paid twice as much as Canadian farmers.
   (e) Both (a) and (b) are correct.

3. Comparative advantage is said to exist whenever
   (a) one country can produce a given level of output with fewer resources compared to another country.
   (b) a given amount of resources produces more output in one country compared to another.
   (c) one country has an absolute advantage over another country in the production of all goods.
   (d) different countries have different opportunity costs in production.
   (e) two countries are of different sizes.

4. If there are two countries, A and B, and two goods, X and Y, and if A has a comparative advantage in the production of X, it necessarily follows that
   (a) A has an absolute advantage in the production of X.
   (b) B has an absolute advantage in the production of X.
   (c) A has a comparative disadvantage in the production of Y.
   (d) B has an absolute advantage in the production of Y.
   (e) B has a comparative disadvantage in the production of Y.

5. In a two-country and two-good model, gains from trade would not exist if
   (a) one country had an absolute advantage in the production of both goods.
   (b) a given amount of resources produced more of both goods in one country.
   (c) one country was endowed with far more resources than the other.
   (d) the countries had the same opportunity costs in the production of both goods.
   (e) only one country had a comparative advantage in the production of one good.

6. Which of the following statements is not true about opportunity cost?
   (a) Equal opportunity costs for pairs of commodities between two countries lead to gains from trade.
   (b) Opportunity costs depend on relative production costs.
   (c) Differences in opportunity costs across countries can enhance total output of both goods through trade and specialization.
   (d) Comparative advantage can be expressed in terms of opportunity costs.
   (e) Opportunity cost can be read as the slope of a tangent to a country's production possibility curve.

7. If production of each unit of wool in country A implies that beef production must be decreased by four units, while in country B each additional unit of beef decreases wool output by four units, the gains from trade
   (a) are maximized if country A specializes in wool production and country B in beef.
   (b) are maximized if country A specializes in beef production and country B in wool.
   (c) are maximized if country A allocates 80 percent of its resources to wool and the remainder to beef, while country B does the opposite.
   (d) are maximized if country A allocates 20 percent of its resources to wool and the remainder to beef, while country B does the opposite.
   (e) cannot be realized because opportunity costs in the two countries are the same.

8. Gains from specialization can arise when
   (a) countries have different opportunity costs in production.
   (b) there are economies of scale in production.
   (c) experience gained via specialization lowers cost through learning by doing.
   (d) comparative advantage is either nature-given or acquired.
   (e) All of the above.

9. Free trade within the European Community led to
   (a) each member country specializing in specific products (e.g., furniture, cars, etc.).
   (b) a large increase in product differentiation, with countries tending to specialize in subproduct lines (e.g., office furniture, household furniture, etc.).
   (c) no perceptible alteration in production patterns.
   (d) less trade among EC members.
   (e) less product diversity.

10. Economies of scale and learning by doing are different because
    (a) one refers to an increase in variable costs and the other to a decrease.
    (b) economies of scale refer to a movement along the average cost curve, whereas learning by doing shifts the average cost curve.

(c) economies of scale affect variable costs, but learning by doing affects only fixed costs.
(d) learning by doing affects profits, but not costs.
(e) economies of scale affect costs, whereas learning by doing affects revenue.

11. The gains from specialization and trade depend on the pattern of _____ advantage, not _____ advantage.
    (a) absolute, comparative.
    (b) monetary, nonmonetary.
    (c) absolute, reciprocal.
    (d) comparative, absolute.
    (e) size, cost.

12. The terms of trade
    (a) refer to the quantity of imported goods that can be obtained for each unit of an exported good.
    (b) are measured by the ratio of the price of exports to the price of imports.
    (c) determine the division of the gains from trade.
    (d) All of the above.
    (e) None of the above.

13. A rise in export prices as compared to import prices is considered a favourable change in the terms of trade since
    (a) one can export more per unit of imported goods.
    (b) employment in export industries will increase.
    (c) one can acquire more imports per unit of exports.
    (d) total exports will increase.
    (e) All of the above.

14. By trading in international markets, countries
    (a) can consume beyond their production possibility boundary.
    (b) will always produce the same commodity bundle as before trade.
    (c) can produce outside of their production possibility boundary.
    (d) must choose one of the intercepts on the production possibility boundary, indicating complete specialization.
    (e) always produce and consume the same bundle of commodities.

Questions 15 to 18 refer to the data in the following table.

	One unit of resource can produce	
Country	Lumber (bd m)	Aluminum (kg)
Australia	4	9
Canada	9	3
Brazil	3	2

15. Considering just Australia and Canada,
(a) Australia has an absolute advantage in lumber.
(b) Australia has an absolute advantage in aluminum.
(c) There are no possible gains from trade.
(d) Canada should specialize in aluminum production.
(e) Australia has a comparative advantage in lumber.

16. Considering just Canada and Brazil,
(a) Brazil has an absolute advantage in lumber.
(b) Brazil has a comparative advantage in aluminum.
(c) Canada has an absolute advantage in only one commodity.
(d) There are no possible gains from trade.
(e) None of the above.

17. In Australia, the opportunity cost of 1 board metre (bd m) of lumber is
(a) 2.25 kg of aluminum.
(b) 0.44 kg of aluminum.
(c) 0.36 kg of aluminum.
(d) 3.60 kg of aluminum.
(e) 3.00 kg of aluminum.

18. In Canada, the opportunity cost of 1 kilogram of aluminum is
(a) 0.33 bd m of lumber.
(b) 2.70 bd m of lumber.
(c) 3.0 bdm of lumber.
(d) 3.33 bd m of lumber.
(e) 1.50 bd m of lumber.

19. According to the Hecksher-Ohlin theory,
(a) resource-rich countries benefit the most from trade.
(b) different opportunity costs across countries can be explained by differences in factor endowments.
(c) different opportunity costs across countries can be explained by differences in production functions.
(d) low-wage countries gain the most from trade.
(e) countries with similar opportunity costs can gain the most from trade.

20. For a country with one important export commodity such as coffee or oil,
(a) a rise in the commodity's price will improve the country's terms of trade.
(b) a fall in the commodity's price is a favourable change in its terms of trade.
(c) its terms of trade will improve only if it is able to increase the quantity of exports.
(d) its terms of trade will improve only if world demand for its exports is inelastic.
(e) its terms of trade improve only if the price of imports decrease.

21. The concept of dynamic comparative advantage is best characterized by
(a) the importance of factor endowments in determining trade patterns.
(b) changes in a country's terms of trade due to depletion of natural resources.
(c) acquiring new areas of specialization through investment in human capital.
(d) changes in a country's variable costs due to economies of scale.
(e) Both (a) and (b) are correct.

EXERCISES

1. For each of the situations described determine the opportunity costs of producing each good in each country, and indicate in which commodity each country should specialize its production and trade.

   (a)

One unit of resources can produce:			The opportunity costs are:		
	Radios	*Cameras*		*1 Radio*	*1 Camera*
Japan	2	4	Japan	_____	_____
Korea	3	1	Korea	_____	_____

   Japan should specialize in the production of _____.
   Korea should specialize in the production of _____.

   (b)

One unit of resources can produce:			The opportunity costs are:		
	Radios	*Cameras*		*1 Radio*	*1 Camera*
Japan	2	4	Japan	_____	_____
Korea	1	3	Korea	_____	_____

   Japan should specialize in the production of _____.
   Korea should specialize in the production of _____.

   (c)

One unit of resources can produce:			The opportunity costs are:		
	Radios	*Cameras*		*1 Radio*	*1 Camera*
Japan	2	4	Japan	_____	_____
Korea	1	2	Korea	_____	_____

   Japan should specialize in the production of _____.
   Korea should specialize in the production of _____.

   (d) Which case represents reciprocal absolute advantage?
   (e) Which case demonstrates that absolute advantage is not a sufficient condition for trade to occur? Explain.

   (f) Which case suggests why a nation as technologically advanced as Japan can gain from trading with other countries with lower wages? Explain.

2. Countries *A* and *B* each currently produce both watches and dairy products. Assume that country *A* gives up the opportunity to produce 100 litres of dairy products for each watch it makes, and *B* could produce one watch at a cost of 200 litres of dairy products.
   (a) The opportunity cost of making watches (in terms of dairy products) is lower in country _____.
   (b) The opportunity cost of making dairy products (in terms of watches) is lower in country _____.
   (c) Country *B* should specialize in _____ and let country *A* produce _____.
   (d) The terms of trade (the price of one product in terms of the other) would be somewhere between _____ and _____ litres of dairy products for one watch.

3. The following table provides data on the index of merchandise export prices and the index of merchandise import prices during the 1980s in Canada.

Year	Index of export prices	Index of import prices	Terms of trade
1980	100.6	98.6	_____
1982	103.3	102.3	_____
1984	157.1	135.6	_____
1986	176.6	157.9	_____
1988	205.4	200.7	_____

(a) Using the definition of the terms of trade that involves indexes, complete the table by calculating the terms of trade to one decimal place.

(b) What does an increase in the terms of trade signify?

(c) Would you classify the change in the terms of trade during the period 1982 to 1984 as favourable to Canada? Explain.

4. The following table provides data on the productivity of a single unit of resource in producing wheat and microchips in both Canada and Japan.

	One unit of resources produces	
	Wheat (t)	**Microchips**
Canada	50	20
Japan	2	12

(a) Which country has an absolute advantage in the production of wheat? Of microchips?

(b) What is the opportunity cost of producing a tonne of wheat in Canada? In Japan?

(c) Which country has a comparative advantage in the production of wheat? Of microchips?

(d) Suppose that Canada is endowed with 2 units of this all-purpose resource while Japan is endowed with 10 units. Draw each country's production possibility boundary on the following grids.

Figure 35-1

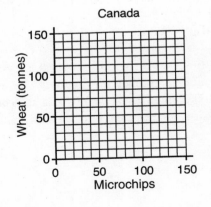

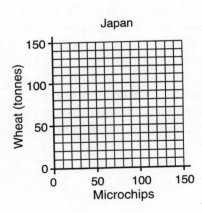

(e) Suppose that prior to trade, each country allocated half of its resource endowment to production of each good. Indicate the production and consumption points of each country in the graphs (for simplicity, assume that these are the only two countries in the world).

(f) What is world output of each good?

(g) Indicate the production points of each country after trade, and determine world production levels.

(h) Suppose that the terms of trade are one microchip for one tonne of wheat and that Canada consumes as much wheat after trade as it did before trade. Indicate the post-trade consumption points of each country and each country's imports and exports.

(i) If the terms of trade changed to two microchips for one tonne of wheat, which country would benefit? Explain.

*5. The graph in Figure 35-2 depicts a country's production possibility curve between wool and lumber. Prior to trade, the country is producing and consuming at point R, which involves 10 units of wool and 10 units of lumber. Due to large increases in construction activity in this economy, the country now decides that it wishes to consume 14 units of lumber.

Figure 35-2

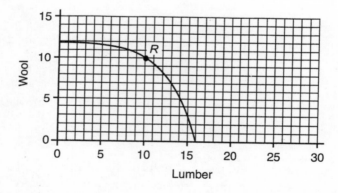

(a) How much wool must this country give up to obtain the additional four units of lumber in a no-trade environment. Explain.

(b) Suppose that the terms of trade in international markets are one unit of wool for two units of lumber. Assuming that production remains at R, how much wool would the country have to give up to obtain the additional four units of lumber if it engages in international trade? Explain.

ANSWERS

Multiple-Choice Questions

1. (d)	**2.** (c)	**3.** (d)	**4.** (c)	**5.** (d)
6. (a)	**7.** (b)	**8.** (e)	**9.** (b)	**10.** (b)
11. (d)	**12.** (d)	**13.** (c)	**14.** (a)	**15.** (b)
16. (b)	**17.** (a)	**18.** (c)	**19.** (b)	**20.** (a)
21. (c)				

Exercises

1. (a) Japan: 1 radio costs 2 cameras; 1 camera costs 1/2 radio.
        Korea: 1 radio costs 1/3 camera; 1 camera costs 3 radios.
        Japan should produce cameras. Korea should produce radios.
    (b) Japan: 1 radio costs 2 cameras; 1 camera costs 1/2 radio.
        Korea: 1 radio costs 3 cameras; 1 camera costs 1/3 radio.
        Japan should produce radios. Korea should produce cameras.
    (c) Japan: 1 radio costs 2 cameras; 1 camera costs 1/2 radio.
        Korea: 1 radio costs 2 cameras; 1 camera costs 1/2 radio.
        Japan should produce both and Korea should produce both. There would be no gains from trade.
    (d) Case (a) represents reciprocal absolute advantage; Japan has an absolute advantage in cameras, and Korea has an absolute advantage in radios.
    (e) Case (c) shows that even though Japan has an absolute advantage in producing both goods, no trade will occur because relative prices (or opportunity costs of production) are identical to those in Korea.
    (f) Case (b) shows that even though Japanese workers are more productive in both industries (and therefore can expect to earn more than Korean workers), mutually beneficial trade can still occur if each country exports the good for which it has a comparative advantage.

2. (a) *A.*
    (b) *B.*
    (c) dairy products, watches.
    (d) 100, 200.

3. (a) 102.0, 101.0, 115.9, 111.8, 102.3.
    (b) An increase in the terms of trade means that fewer exports are required to pay for a given amount of imports.
    (c) The terms of trade changed from 101.0 to 115.6; this was a favorable change in our terms of trade. It cost us fewer exports to buy the same imports, or for the same exports we received more imports.

4. (a) Canada has an absolute advantage in both goods.
    (b) 0.4, 6.0.
    (c) Canada, Japan.
    (d) **Figure 35-3**

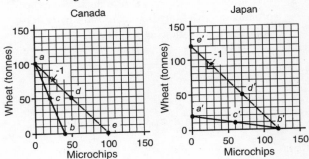

Canada's production possibility boundary is denoted *ab*, and Japan's is *a′b′*.

    (e) Canada would be producing and consuming 50 tonnes of wheat and 20 microchips (point *c* in the diagram), and Japan would be producing and consuming 10 tonnes of wheat and 60 microchips (point *c′*).
    (f) Assuming that these are the only countries making up the world, total output of wheat is 60 tonnes and world production of microchips is 80 units.
    (g) Each country specializes in the commodity in which it has a comparative advantage. Thus, Canada specializes completely in wheat production (see point *a*), and Japan specializes completely in microchip production (see point *b′*). World output is now 100 tonnes of wheat and 120 microchips.
    (h) Terms of trade equal to one tonne of wheat for one microchip mean that Canada can trade from its production point *a* to any point on its consumption possibility curve *ae* which has a slope of −1, representing the terms of trade. Similarly, Japan can trade from point *b′* to any point on its consumption possibility curve *b′e′*. Since it was assumed that Canada consumes the same amount of wheat both before and after trade, its consumption bundle is represented by point *d*, which contains 50 units of each good. Therefore, Canada is exporting 50

tonnes of wheat in return for imports of 50 microchips. Japan, having exported 50 microchips to Canada, has 70 remaining for its own consumption. When this is combined with its 50 tonnes of wheat imports, Japan consumes at point d'.

(i) The terms of trade lines in the graphs would become flatter with a slope of −1/2. Thus, Canada's consumption possibilities would increase (the dashed line rotates outward on point a), while Japan's decrease (the dashed line rotates inward on point b'). Thus, Canada would get a larger share of the gains from trade.

*5. Five units. This requires a movement along the production possibility boundary from point R to point A on the following graph.

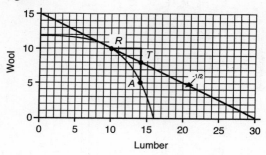

Figure 35-4

(b) Two units. The terms of trade line has a slope of −1/2 and is tangent to the production possibility curve at R. Thus, the economy can export two units of wool in return for imports of four units of lumber, this is represented by a movement from point R to point T on the graph.

CHAPTER 36
· · · · · · · · · · · · · · ·
TRADE POLICY

· · · · · · · · · · · · · ·
CHAPTER OVERVIEW

This chapter examines the means by which a government may intervene in markets to restrict international trade and the resulting consequences. Protectionist trade policy usually takes one of two forms: tariffs that serve to raise import prices, and nontariff barriers, such as quotas or voluntary export restrictions, that serve to reduce import quantities.

Free trade maximizes world output of all products and living standards. Arguments for protection may rest on objectives other than maximizing living standards, such as reduction in fluctuations in national income, national defence, or economic diversification. Protection may also be advanced by a large country as a means of gaining a favourable improvement in the terms of trade and thereby increasing national income. Several fallacious but widely employed arguments for protection are also discussed.

Since its inception in 1947, the General Agreement on Trade and Tariffs (GATT) has served to substantially reduce tariffs through a series of multilateral negotiations. The most recent set of negotiations, the Uruguay Round, concluded in agreement in several important areas that will serve to promote more liberal trade. It also saw the replacement of the GATT with the World Trade Organization (WTO).

Recently, there has been a sharp increase in the number and extent of regional trade-liberalizing agreements such as free trade areas and common markets. The North American Free Trade Agreement (NAFTA) created the world's largest and most successful free trade area, and the European Union is the world's largest and most successful common market. These regional agreements bring about efficiency gains through trade creation, but may also lead to efficiency losses from trade diversion.

· · · · · · · · · · · · · ·
LEARNING OBJECTIVES

After studying this chapter, you should be able to:

- ■ cite the benefits and costs of expanding international trade;
- ■ understand how tariffs and quotas influence patterns of output and trade and affect a nation's standard of living;
- ■ recognize fallacious arguments for protection;
- ■ understand trade policy remedies and procedures available in major trading countries;
- ■ grasp issues under consideration in multilateral, regional, and bilateral trade negotiations;
- ■ discuss the important highlights of the NAFTA and the early evidence of its impact on the Canadian economy.

MULTIPLE-CHOICE QUESTIONS

1. Which of the following statements is *not* true of free trade?
   (a) Free trade leads to a maximization of world output.
   (b) Free trade maximizes world living standards.
   (c) Free trade always makes each individual better off.
   (d) Free trade can increase the average income in a country.
   (e) Free trade encourages countries to specialize in production.

2. Which of the following trade practices is *not* specifically designed as a device to promote protectionism?
   (a) Tariffs.
   (b) Voluntary export restrictions.
   (c) Countervailing duties.
   (d) Import quotas.
   (e) Costly customs procedures.

3. A central difference in the effects of a tariff and a voluntary export restriction (VER) — set at the same quantity as under the tariff — is that
   (a) the VER yields a higher price for consumers than the tariff.
   (b) the tariff pushes the consumer price beyond the price associated with the VER.
   (c) government tariff revenue becomes suppliers' revenue with a VER.
   (d) as the quantity sold decreases under the VER, the revenue of producers decreases.
   (e) Both (a) and (c) are correct.

4. The infant industry argument for tariffs is
   (a) only appropriate for industries where there are no economies of scale.
   (b) an example of dynamic comparative advantage.
   (c) theoretically valid if a new producer can sufficiently reduce average costs as output increases.
   (d) a proposal to earmark tariff revenues to finance day-care facilities.
   (e) most applicable in developing countries because of their relative abundance of labour.

5. Which of the following national objectives is a valid argument for some degree of protectionism?
   (a) Concentration of national resources in a few specialized products.
   (b) Increases in average incomes.
   (c) Diversification of a small economy in order to reduce the risk associated with cyclical fluctuations in price.
   (d) Ability of domestic firms to operate at minimum efficient scale.
   (e) Maximization of the national standard of living.

6. Protection against low-wage foreign labour is a fallacious protectionist argument because
   (a) free trade benefits everyone.
   (b) the gains from trade depend on comparative, not absolute, advantage.
   (c) when the foreign country increases its exports to us, their wages will rise.
   (d) the terms of trade will equalize for low- and high-wage countries.
   (e) low-wage labourers are necessarily less productive.

7. A large country, accounting for a significant share of world demand for an imported product, can increase its national income by
   (a) encouraging domestic production.
   (b) restricting domestic demand for the product, thereby decreasing its price and improving the terms of trade.
   (c) imposing import quotas on the product.
   (d) subsidizing imports of the good and thereby monopolize world consumption.
   (e) negotiating voluntary export restrictions.

8. If the objective of a government is to maximize national income, which of the following is the least valid reason for using tariff protection?
   (a) To protect against unfair subsidization of foreign firms by their governments.
   (b) To protect against unfair low wages paid to foreign labour.
   (c) To protect newly developing industries.
   (d) To protect against dumping of foreign-produced goods.
   (e) To alter the terms of trade.

9. Countervailing duties are attempts to maintain a "level playing ground" by
   (a) retaliating against foreign tariffs.
   (b) raising or lowering tariffs multilaterally.
   (c) establishing a common tariff wall around a customs union.
   (d) assessing tariffs that will offset foreign government subsidies.
   (e) subsidizing exports.

10. Strategic trade policy
   (a) involves government assistance for key growth industries by protecting domestic markets and/or providing subsidies.
   (b) involves erecting higher tariff and nontariff barriers across the board to protect domestic industry.
   (c) means that the government negotiates special trade agreements with its important defence partners.
   (d) is designed to encourage the migration of certain industries to other countries to better exploit domestic comparative advantage.
   (e) attempts to encourage investment for domestic production in those markets that a country currently imports.

11. Which of the following is *not* a fallacious protectionist argument?
   (a) Buy Canadian, and both the money and the goods stay at home.
   (b) Trade cannot be mutually advantageous if one of the trading partners is much larger than the other.
   (c) Too many imports lower Canadian living standards as our money is shipped abroad.
   (d) A foreign firm, temporarily selling in Canada at a much lower price than in its own country, threatens the Canadian industry's existence.
   (e) A high-wage country such as Canada cannot effectively compete with a low-wage country such as Mexico.

12. The problem with restricting imports as a means of reducing domestic unemployment is that
   (a) it merely redistributes unemployment from import-competing industries to our export industries when trading partners retaliate.

(b) Canadians would rather do without than have to buy Canadian-produced goods.
(c) our import-competing industries are not labour intensive.
(d) our import-competing industries are always fully employed.
(e) Both (c) and (d) are correct.

13. Which of the following statements about non-tariff barriers to trade (NTBs) is *incorrect*?
   (a) The use of NTBs has been declining worldwide for the last 50 years.
   (b) The misuse of antidumping and countervailing duties unilaterally constitutes an increasingly important NTB.
   (c) Voluntary export restraints, negotiated agreements, and quotas are examples of NTBs.
   (d) Most NTBs are ostensibly levied for trade relief purposes but end up being protectionist.
   (e) Environmental and labour standards can be used as disguised NTBs.

14. Which of the following motivations for dumping can be of permanent benefit to the buying country?
   (a) Predatory pricing.
   (b) Cyclical stabilization of sales.
   (c) Enabling foreign producers to achieve lower average costs and therefore price.
   (d) Altering the terms of trade.
   (e) All of the above.

15. Suppose the nominal tariff rate applied to finished widgets is 20 percent, and that widgets cost $100 to produce in Canada, but this includes $40 of raw materials that were imported duty free. The effective rate of tariff protection is
   (a) 33.3 percent.
   (b) 20.0 percent.
   (c) 40.0 percent.
   (d) 10.0 percent.
   (e) 50.0 percent.

16. Which of the following is an example of trade diversion?
    (a) A government promotes diversification of a country's industries.
    (b) Liberalized trade encourages industries to specialize in subproduct lines.
    (c) The NAFTA encourages more trade between low- and high-wage countries.
    (d) The NAFTA encourages Canada to switch imports from low-wage nonmember countries to Mexico.
    (e) Publicized trade disputes divert attention from the gains from trade.

17. Which of the following is *not* true of the EU's Common Agricultural Policy (CAP)?
    (a) The CAP has led to agricultural surpluses in the EU.
    (b) The CAP has turned the EU from a net importer of agricultural products into a net exporter.
    (c) The CAP is the general reason why the EU opposed trade liberalization in agricultural products during the Uruguay Round.
    (d) The CAP benefits agricultural producers in less-developed countries.
    (e) Quotas that support the CAP are being replaced with tariff equivalents.

18. A common market includes *all but which* of the following?
    (a) Tariff-free trade among members.
    (b) A common trade policy with the rest of the world.
    (c) Rules of origin.
    (d) Free movement of labour.
    (e) Free movement of capital.

19. The countries in a free-trade area
    (a) impose no tariffs on each other's goods.
    (b) each have an independent tariff structure with the rest of the world.
    (c) do not permit the free movement of labour across their borders.
    (d) do not have a common monetary policy.
    (e) All of the above.

20. Which of the following was *not* one of the features of the Canada–United States Free Trade Agreement (FTA)?
    (a) Elimination of all tariffs within 10 years.

    (b) Elimination of countervailing duties between the two countries.
    (c) Exemption of cultural industries.
    (d) Continuance of quotas to support provincial supply management schemes.
    (e) Provision for national treatment for most service industries.

21. The principle of national treatment that is embedded in the NAFTA means that Canada could, for example, introduce any product standards it likes, so long as
    (a) they apply only to Canadian-produced goods.
    (b) the standards are no more stringent than those existing in either Mexico or the United States.
    (c) they apply equally to Canadian-, Mexican- and American-produced goods sold in Canada.
    (d) they apply only to Canadian exports.
    (e) they apply only to Canadian imports.

22. A major effect of a tariff is to
    (a) redistribute income from consumers to domestic producers and the government.
    (b) allow consumers to benefit at the expense of domestic producers.
    (c) discourage domestic production.
    (d) encourage consumers to buy more of the good.
    (e) reduce government revenues.

23. Which of the following was *not* an outcome of the Uruguay Round of GATT negotiations?
    (a) Major trade liberalization in agriculture.
    (b) Repacement of the GATT with the World Trade Organization (WTO).
    (c) A new dispute settlement mechanism..
    (d) Developing countries are now obliged to liberalize trade.
    (e) Phasing out of the Multifiber Agreement.

24. A free-trade agreement
    (a) must include rules of origin.
    (b) eliminates the need for customs controls on the movement of goods.
    (c) allows for free cross-border movement of labour.
    (d) erects a common tariff wall against non-member countries.
    (e) Both (a) and (d) are correct.

25. Which of the following is *not* a feature of the NAFTA?
  (a) A common regime for antidumping and countervailing duties.
  (b) The principle of national treatment.
  (c) Stronger protection of intellectual property.
  (d) Accession clause whereby other countries may join.
  (e) Reduction in the barriers to trade in both goods and services among member countries.

• • • • • • • • • • • • •

EXERCISES

1. (a) The three graphs in Figure 36-1 illustrate the demand and supply of an imported commodity Z in a free trade environment. Revise these graphs according to the protectionist policy outlined below each panel, and indicate the new price as P^* and the new quantity as Q^*.

Figure 36-1

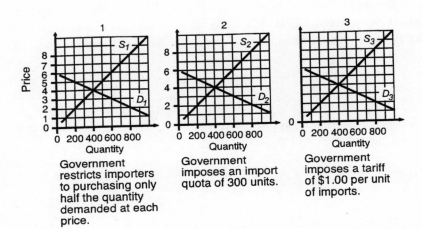

Government restricts importers to purchasing only half the quantity demanded at each price.

Government imposes an import quota of 300 units.

Government imposes a tariff of $1.00 per unit of imports.

(b) If the demand for Z were highly inelastic, which policy would the government likely *not* choose if it wanted to maximize its restriction on the amount of the import purchased? Why?

(c) Which policy would the government likely choose if it were concerned that protectionist policies might be inflationary? Why?

2. Consider the market for canned tuna (assume all canned tuna is homogeneous). The foreign supply curve (S_f) is horizontal (as drawn in Figure 36-2), which implies that Canada accounts for a relatively small share of the world market and any change in Canadian purchases does not affect world prices. The domestic demand and supply curves are denoted D_C and S_C, respectively.

Figure 36-2

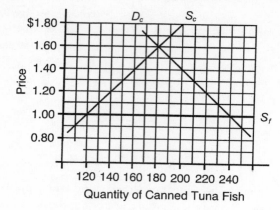

(a) Under free trade, what is the quantity of tuna consumed in Canada, the quantity supplied by Canadian producers, and the quantity supplied by foreign producers?

(b) If a 20 percent tariff is imposed, by how many cents does the foreign supply curve shift upward? Draw the new foreign supply curve, and calculate the consequent changes in domestic consumption, domestic production, and imports. Why is the change in imports greater than the change in domestic production?

(c) If the government wants to ensure that domestic production rises to 160, how large a quota for imported tuna should it allow? Explain.

3. The graph in Figure 36-3 depicts the demand and supply curves for an imported good in a market where Canada does not have any domestic production. D_C represents demand in Canada, and S_f represents foreign supply.

Figure 36-3

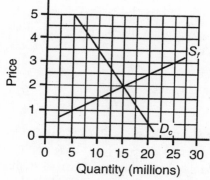

(a) What are equilibrium price and quantity and the total revenue of foreign firms?

(b)   Suppose that the government imposes a specific tariff on this commodity equal to $2 per unit. What are the resulting equilibrium price Canadian consumers pay and the quantity they import? Illustrate this on the graph.

(c)   What are the revenues of foreign firms and the Canadian government?

(d)   Instead of the tariff, suppose that the Canadian government imposed an import quota on this good equal to 10 million units. What is the new supply curve that Canadian consumers effectively face?

(e)   What would be the resulting market price and revenue of both foreign firms and the government under the quota scheme?

*4.   The graph in Figure 36-4 illustrates the domestic supply of steel (S_D), the foreign supply of steel (S_F), and the domestic demand (D).

(a)   Draw the total supply curve for steel and establish the overall price (P_0).

Figure 36-4

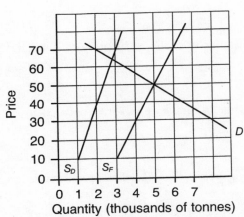

(b)   What is the level of Canadian consumption, and how much of this is due to imports and how much to domestic production?

(c)   The domestic government now levies a tariff of $20 per tonne on steel from foreign suppliers. Using a broken line, draw the after-tariff supply curve for foreigners and the new total supply curve. Label the new price and quantity P_1 and Q_1, respectively.

(d)   What effect has the tariff had on imports and domestic production?

*5. This exercise addresses the efficiency gain from free trade by measuring the impact on consumer and producer surplus of moving from a no-trade situation to free trade for an imported good and then an exported good (the same analysis can be applied to the removal or reduction of tariffs). In what follows, assume that Canadian demand is a small part of world demand so that the world price, P_W, is independent of both Canadian demand, D_C, and supply, S_C. Thus, foreign supply is perfectly elastic at P_W. In the no-trade situation, the equilibrium price and quantity are P_E and Q_E.

(a) In Figure 36-5, P_W is less than P_E, so trade will result in imports of this good.

Figure 36-5

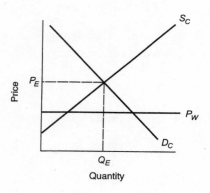

Once trade is permitted,
(i)   label domestic consumption D_D.
(ii)   label domestic production S_D.
(iii) What is the change in consumer surplus in Canada?

(iv)   What is the change in producer surplus of Canadian firms?

(v)   Is the net change in total surplus for Canada positive or negative?

(b) In Figure 36-6, P_W is greater than P_E, so trade will result in exports of this commodity.

Figure 36-6

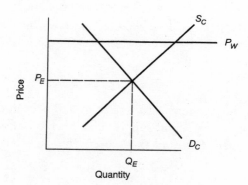

Once trade is permitted,
(i)   label domestic consumption D_D.
(ii)   label domestic production S_D.

(iii)   What is the change in consumer surplus in Canada?

(iv)   What is the change in producer surplus of Canadian firms?

(v)   Is the net change in total surplus for Canada positive or negative?

• • • • • • • • • • • • • • •

ANSWERS

Multiple-Choice Questions

1. (c)	**2.** (c)	**3.** (c)	**4.** (c)	**5.** (c)
6. (b)	**7.** (b)	**8.** (b)	**9.** (d)	**10.** (a)
11. (d)	**12.** (a)	**13.** (a)	**14.** (c)	**15.** (a)
16. (d)	**17.** (d)	**18.** (c)	**19.** (e)	**20.** (b)
21. (c)	**22.** (a)	**23.** (a)	**24.** (a)	**25.** (a)

Exercises

1.   (a)   **Figure 36-7**

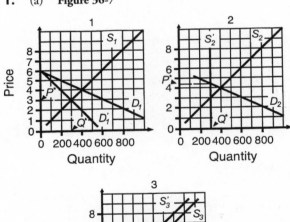

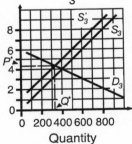

(b)   It would not choose the tariff policy. Price would rise by almost the full amount of the tariff, and there would be little change in equilibrium quantity.

(c)   Policy (1): A restriction on demand not only reduces imports but also lowers the price.

2.   (a)   Canadian production is 120, Canadian consumption is 240, and imports are 120.

(b)   The foreign supply curve shifts upward by 20 cents. Domestic production rises by 20, domestic consumption falls by 20, and imports fall by 40. Imports fall by more than domestic production rises due to the decline in total quantity demanded.

(c)   At a price of $1.40, domestic production rises to 160, and domestic consumption falls to 200. The government can allow imports of 40 if this is to be an equilibrium position.

3.   (a) $2, 15 million units, and $30 million, respectively.

(b) $3.50 and 10 million units, respectively.

Figure 36-8

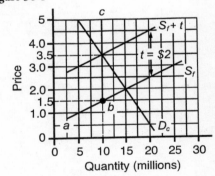

(c)   Canadian consumers pay $3.50 per unit, of which $2 goes to the government. Therefore, government tariff revenue is $20 million and that of foreign firms is $15 million.

(d)   The new effective supply curve is labeled *abc* on the graph.

(e)   The price per unit is $3.50, revenue of foreign firms equals $35 million, and, since there is no tariff, government revenue is zero.

*4. (a) and (c) **Figure 36-9**

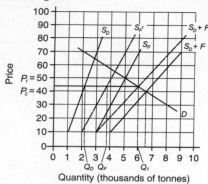

Figure 36-9

(b) Approximately 6,500 tonnes are consumed, of which 4,500 are imported and 2,000 are produced domestically.

(d) The tariff forces a reduction in the quantity supplied by foreign producers (i.e., imports) to Q_F and an increase in the quantity supplied by domestic producers to Q_D.

*5. (a) (i) and (ii)

Figure 36-10

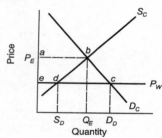

Figure 36-10

(iii) Canadian consumer surplus increases by area *abce*.

(iv) Canadian producer surplus decreases by area *abde*.

(v) Positive. The increase in consumer surplus outweighs the loss in producer surplus; Canada receives a net gain in efficiency equal to area *bcd*.

(b) (i) and (ii)

Figure 36-11

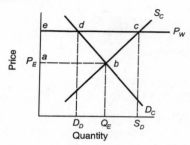

Figure 36-11

(iii) Canadian consumer surplus decreases by area *abde*.

(iv) Canadian producer surplus increases by area *abce*.

(v) Positive. The increase in producer surplus outweighs the loss in consumers surplus; Canada receives a net gain in efficiency equal to area *bcd*.

CHAPTER 37

EXCHANGE RATES AND THE BALANCE OF PAYMENTS

CHAPTER OVERVIEW

This chapter discusses the accounting framework for the balance-of-payments accounts and how various international transactions determine the value of the exchange rate.

The balance of payments is divided into three major accounts: the current account (trade in goods, services, and net factor income payments); the capital account (trade in assets); and the official financing account (central bank foreign exchange transactions). A credit entry results from the sale of a good, asset, or foreign exchange to a foreigner; it represents extra demand for a country's currency or an extra supply of a foreign currency. A debit entry results from the purchase of a good, asset, or foreign exchange from a foreigner; it represents extra supply of a country's currency or an extra demand for foreign currency.

Under flexible exchange rates, important determinants of the price of foreign exchange are relative inflation rates, relative interest rates, and expectations. The equilibrium exchange rate is determined by demand and supply conditions in the exchange market. At the equilibrium exchange rate, the sum of the current and capital accounts should be zero with no changes in the official financing account.

Under fixed exchange rates, the central bank may take steps to set an exchange rate that differs from the equilibrium value. A pegged rate that is set above the equilibrium value implies that the sum of the current and capital accounts will be positive (a surplus). To maintain the pegged rate, the central bank increases its holdings of the foreign currency.

LEARNING OBJECTIVES

After studying this chapter, you should be able to:

- ■ understand that the exchange rate is the reciprocal of the external value of the domestic currency; if the exchange rate appreciates, the external value of the domestic currency depreciates;
- ■ explain the variety of international transactions that determine the demand for and supply of foreign currency;
- ■ explain the economic factors that will cause changes in the equilibrium level of the exchange rate;
- ■ categorize various international payments and receipts as either current or capital account transactions;
- ■ understand what is meant by the official financing account and how central bank actions affect this account;
- ■ understand that, although the sum of the three accounts must be zero (an overall balance of payments), neither the current nor the capital accounts by themselves or added together need be balanced;
- ■ explain that an overall balance-of-payments deficit or surplus refers to the sum of the current and capital accounts, without reference to the official financing account;
- ■ learn how the official financing account is used to fix the value of the exchange rate.

MULTIPLE-CHOICE QUESTIONS

1. The exchange rate is
(a) the ratio of exports to imports.
(b) the amount of home currency that must be given up in order to obtain one unit of foreign currency.
(c) the rate at which one country exchanges gold with another.
(d) the volume of foreign goods that can be obtained for one unit of domestic currency.
(e) always equal to the external value of a currency.

Questions 2 through 5 refer to the following exchange rates in Canadian dollars for two years:

Currency	1989	1990
Swedish krona	$0.184	$0.197
French franc	$0.186	$0.215
U.S. dollar	$1.184	$1.167
Japanese yen	$0.0086	$0.0081
British pound	$1.942	$2.082

2. Which of the following was *not* true in 1989? The external value of the Canadian dollar was
(a) 5.435 krona.
(b) 5.376 French francs.
(c) 1.184 U.S. dollars.
(d) 116.279 yen.
(e) 0.515 pounds.

3. Which of the following was *not* true in 1990? The external value of the Canadian dollar was
(a) 5.076 krona.
(b) 4.651 French francs.
(c) 0.857 U.S. dollars.
(d) 123.457 yen.
(e) 0.080 pounds.

4. Which of the following statements concerning exchange rate movements between 1989 and 1990 is *not* true?
(a) The Swedish krona appreciated.
(b) The British pound depreciated.
(c) The external value of the Canadian dollar with respect to the yen appreciated.
(d) The U.S. dollar depreciated.
(e) The external value of the Canadian dollar with respect to the French franc depreciated.

5. Suppose that a week's skiing vacation (meals, ski tows, accommodations, but excluding travel) costs $1,000 (U.S.) in the United States, 8,000 francs in France and 11,000 krona in Sweden during this two-year period. Which of the following statements is *not* correct?
(a) A Canadian paid $1,184 (Canadian) in 1989 for a skiing vacation in the United States.
(b) A Canadian supplied $1,720 (Canadian) and demanded 8,000 francs in 1990 for a skiing vacation in France.
(c) The Canadian dollar price of a skiing vacation in the United States increased between 1989 and 1990.
(d) The Canadian dollar price of a skiing vacation in France increased between 1989 and 1990.
(e) A Canadian supplied $2,024 (Canadian) in 1989 to get 11,000 krona for a skiing vacation in Sweden.

6. In the exchange market between Canadian dollars and Mexican pesos, a demander of dollars is also a
(a) supplier of dollars.
(b) supplier of pesos.
(c) demander of pesos.
(d) Canadian exporter.
(e) Canadian who is buying assets in Mexico.

7. In the exchange market between U.S. dollars and pounds, the supplier of pounds is also a
(a) buyer of U.S. dollars.
(b) supplier of U.S. dollars.
(c) demander of pounds.
(d) U.S. exporter.
(e) U.S. company that buys a British firm.

8. If the domestic price level increases (and foreign prices remain constant),
   (a) the demand curve for foreign currency will shift to the right assuming that the demand for foreign products is inelastic.
   (b) the demand curve for foreign currency will shift to the left assuming that the demand for foreign products is elastic.
   (c) the supply curve of foreign currency will shift to the right assuming that the foreign demand for domestic products is inelastic.
   (d) the supply curve of foreign currency will shift to the left assuming that the foreign demand for domestic products is elastic.
   (e) Both (a) and (c) are correct.

9. The supply curve of foreign currency will be positively sloped if
   (a) the foreign price elasticity of demand for a country's exports is less than one.
   (b) the foreign price elasticity of demand for a country's exports is greater than one.
   (c) a country's demand for imported goods is price elastic.
   (d) a country's demand for imported goods is price inelastic.
   (e) the external value of the domestic currency increases.

Questions 10 through 16 refer to Figure 37-1. The two countries are Canada (the home country) and Japan. The currency of Japan is the yen.

Figure 37-1

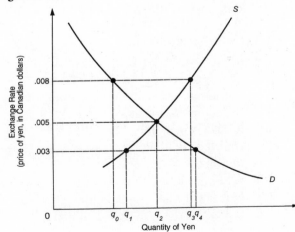

10. A movement down the vertical scale means that
    (a) the Canadian dollar is depreciating.
    (b) the yen is depreciating.
    (c) the external value of the Canadian dollar is fixed.
    (d) the exchange rate is appreciating.
    (e) None of the above.

11. If the current exchange rate is 0.005,
    (a) 200 Canadian dollars trade for one yen.
    (b) 0.005 yen trades for one Canadian dollar.
    (c) one yen trades for 0.005 Canadian dollars.
    (d) the quantity demanded of yen is less than the quantity supplied.
    (e) the quantity supplied of yen is less than the quantity demanded.

12. At an exchange rate of 0.008,
    (a) there is an excess demand of yen.
    (b) there is an excess supply of yen.
    (c) there is an excess supply of Canadian dollars.
    (d) 0.008 yen trades for one Canadian dollar.
    (e) the external value of the Canadian dollar is 12.5 yen.

13. At an exchange rate of 0.003,
    (a) the quantity demanded for yen is q_4 and the quantity supplied is q_1.
    (b) the external value of the Canadian dollar is 333.33 yen.
    (c) there is an excess demand for Canadian dollars of $q_4 - q_1$.
    (d) the exchange rate has reached an equilibrium level.
    (e) Both (a) and (b).

14. Assuming that the initial exchange rate is 0.008, market forces are likely to cause the
    (a) Canadian dollar price of yen to rise.
    (b) external value of the Canadian dollar to fall.
    (c) yen to depreciate to 0.005.
    (d) external value of the Canadian dollar to rise to 333.33 yen.
    (e) quantity demanded of Canadian dollars to increase and the quantity supplied of dollars to decrease.

15. As the exchange rate changes from 0.008 to 0.005,
    (a) the quantity demanded of yen increases with the decline in the prices of Japanese goods in Canadian dollars.
    (b) Japanese imports from Canada increase.
    (c) the quantity demanded of Canadian dollars increases because Canadian exports rise.
    (d) the prices of Canadian goods imported into Japan decrease.
    (e) the Canadian price of traded goods increases.

16. Ignoring international capital flows, the supply curve of yen is upward sloping because
    (a) as the dollar price of yen increases, the total dollar value of Canadian exports to Japan rises.
    (b) as the dollar price of yen decreases, the total dollar value of Canadian exports to Japan falls.
    (c) as the external value of the Canadian dollar rises, the total dollar value of Canadian exports to Japan falls.
    (d) as the external value of the Canadian dollar falls, the total dollar value of Canadian exports to Japan rises.
    (e) All of the above.

17. A lower inflation rate in Canada than in Great Britain, other things being equal, is predicted to cause
    (a) the Canadian dollar price of sterling to rise.
    (b) the sterling price of dollars to fall.
    (c) the demand curve for sterling and the supply curve of sterling to shift to the right, assuming that Canadian and British goods are price elastic.
    (d) a depreciation of the pound.
    (e) an increase in British net exports.

18. A desire by Canadians to invest more in France than before, other things being equal, will cause
    (a) the dollar price of francs to appreciate.
    (b) the demand curve for francs to shift to the right.
    (c) the supply curve of francs to shift to the right.

    (d) both the demand and supply curves of francs to shift to the left.
    (e) Both (a) and (b).

19. If short-term interest rates in Canada increase relative to short-term U.S. interest rates, other things being equal, then
    (a) capital flows from the United States to Canada are likely to increase and the external value of the Canadian dollar is likely to rise.
    (b) the supply curve of U.S. dollars will shift to the left.
    (c) the demand curve for U.S. dollars will shift to the right.
    (d) the external value of the Canadian dollar will fall.
    (e) capital flows from Canada to the United States will increase, thereby causing the exchange rate to appreciate.

20. Which of the following is *not* likely to cause an appreciation of the external value of the Canadian dollar?
    (a) An increase in interest rates in Canada relative to rates elsewhere.
    (b) A lower inflation rate in Canada relative to foreign rates, assuming all internationally traded goods are price elastic.
    (c) Lower earnings expectations on Canadian assets relative to those elsewhere.
    (d) Expectations of a future appreciation of the Canadian dollar.
    (e) A higher propensity to buy Canadian produced goods in international markets.

21. If the Bank of Canada wishes to prevent a depreciation of the external value of the dollar in the foreign exchange market, it could
    (a) transfer government deposits from itself to the commercial banks.
    (b) lower the bank rate.
    (c) add to its holdings of foreign exchange in its *official reserves account*.
    (d) sell bonds in the open market.
    (e) None of the above would prevent the depreciation of the Canadian dollar.

22. Consider the purchasing power parity (PPP) hypothesis in its simplest form and how it applies to the price of a McDonald's Big Mac in two border cities: Windsor, Ontario; and Detroit, Michigan. If the world price of the Big Mac is $1.40 (U.S.), then
    (a) the price of the same burger in Windsor should be $1.40 (Canadian) regardless of the PPP exchange rate.
    (b) the price of a same burger in Windsor should be $1.68 (Canadian) if the PPP exchange rate is 1.20 Canadian dollars per U.S. dollar.
    (c) the Canadian dollar price of the burger in Windsor will be $1.17 if the external value of the dollar is $0.833 (U.S.).
    (d) there will be an incentive for Windsor residents to buy their Big Macs in Detroit if the external value of the dollar is below its PPP value of $0.833 (U.S.).
    (e) None of the above.

23. According the purchasing power parity (PPP) hypothesis, if domestic inflation in country A exceeds that in country B by 10 percent, the external value of B's currency (in terms of A's currency) should
    (a) increase by about 10 percent.
    (b) not change, since any trade deficit will be offset by a capital inflow.
    (c) not change, since the theory applies only to fixed or pegged exchange rate systems.
    (d) decrease by about 10 percent.
    (e) not change, since inflation rates are calculated on the basis of domestically produced goods and services.

24. Which of the following would tend to increase the external value of a currency above its PPP rate?
    (a) The country's central bank buys bonds in the open market.
    (b) The country's central bank ensures that domestic interest rates are always less than foreign interest rates.
    (c) Speculators sell this currency in large volumes.

(d) The country's central bank transfers government deposits from itself to the commercial banks.
(e) None of the above.

25. If, at existing values of relative price levels and the exchange rate, a currency has a higher purchasing power in its own country, then
    (a) the external value of the currency is overvalued.
    (b) the exchange rate is undervalued.
    (c) purchasing power parity has been achieved.
    (d) the external value of the currency is undervalued.
    (e) Both (a) and (b).

26. Suppose that the PPP external value of country A's currency is $1.40 (U.S) while its actual rate falls to $1.25 (U.S.). The actual rate would adjust to the PPP value if
    (a) country A's inflation rate rose relative to the U.S. inflation rate.
    (b) speculators bought country A's currency with the expectation that the actual rate would adjust back to its PPP value.
    (c) speculators believed that the actual rate would continue to fall.
    (d) country A experienced large short-term capital outflows.
    (e) the central bank of country A purchased bonds in the open market.

27. Suppose that Canadian interest rates are 2 percent higher than U.S. interest rates in the short run. We would expect
    (a) the supply curve for U.S. dollars to shift to the right in the short run.
    (b) the Canadian dollar price of the U.S. dollar to fall in the short run.
    (c) large capital inflows into Canada in the short run.
    (d) the Canadian exchange rate to rise in the long run in order to offset the interest rate differential.
    (e) Any or all of the above.

Questions 28 through 35 refer to the balance-of-payment items for a particular country. Before attempting these questions, you should be familiar with the components of the capital and current accounts discussed in the text. All foreign currency purchases have been converted into millions of the domestic currency (dollars) at a given exchange rate value.

(1)	Long-term capital imports	785
(2)	Merchandise exports	17,785
(3)	Exports of traded services	1,170
(4)	Short-term capital imports	932
(5)	Addition to official reserves	7
(6)	Merchandise imports	15,556
(7)	Long-term capital exports	814
(8)	Short-term capital exports	1,158
(9)	Investment income receipts	545
(10)	Investment income payments	1,613
(11)	Net transfer payments	721
(12)	Imports of traded services	1,348

28. The balance on merchandise trade is
(a) a credit (favourable) balance of $33,341.
(b) a credit balance of $2,229.
(c) a debit (unfavourable) balance of $2,229.
(d) an unfavourable balance of $33,341.
(e) a credit balance of $1,330.

29. Which of the following is *not* a credit item in the balance of payments accounts?
(a) Item 2.   (b) Item 4.
(c) Item 9.   (d) Item 7.
(e) Item 1.

30. The value of the current account balance is a
(a) credit (favourable) balance of $262.
(b) deficit (unfavourable) balance of $262.
(c) surplus of $1,508.
(d) favourable balance of $380.
(e) None of the above.

31. Which of the following is *not* a capital account item?
(a) Item 8.   (b) Item 4.
(c) Item 1.   (d) Item 7.
(e) Item 9.

32. The value of the capital account balance, excluding official reserves, is
(a) a deficit of $255.
(b) a surplus of $255.

(c) an unfavourable balance (deficit) of $262.
(d) a surplus of $777.
(e) None of the above.

33. The sum of the current and capital accounts, ignoring the official financing account, indicates that the balance of payments at the current exchange rate is in
(a) a surplus position of $7.
(b) a deficit position of $517.
(c) a deficit position of $7.
(d) a surplus position of $517.
(e) an equilibrium position.

34. If there had been no central bank intervention in the foreign exchange market (the situation described in question 33), then
(a) the external value of this country's currency would ultimately appreciate.
(b) the exchange rate would ultimately depreciate.
(c) at the current exchange rate there is an excess supply of foreign currency or an excess demand for the country's currency.
(d) the country's balance of payments ultimately would be in equilibrium at a lower exchange rate.
(e) All of the above.

35. Given your answers to questions 33 and 34, what central bank intervention in the exchange market would be necessary in order to prevent the exchange rate from changing from its current value?
(a) The central bank would have to buy up the excess supply of the domestic currency of $7 (million) by reducing its official reserves.
(b) The central bank would have to supply the excess demand for the domestic currency of $7 (million) and add to its official reserves.
(c) By increasing the domestic interest rate, the central bank could eliminate the surplus balance of $7 (million).
(d) By selling bonds to foreigners, the central bank would finance the deficit in the balance of payments of $7 (million).
(e) The central bank would have to buy up the excess supply of the domestic currency of $517 (million) by reducing its official reserves.

EXERCISES

1. Suppose that the exchange rate between Canadian dollars and German marks is established in a free exchange market without any intervention by the Bank of Canada. For each of the following events, indicate whether the exchange rate (in this case the Canadian dollar price of marks) will tend to appreciate, depreciate, or remain unchanged. Explain your answer briefly and indicate whether the event is likely to affect the demand curve for marks (denoted by D_M), the supply curve of marks (denoted as S_M), or both. Assume that all internationally traded goods are price elastic.

   (a) Attendance of German rodeo fans at the Calgary Stampede doubles.

   (b) The rate of inflation in Canada increases relative to the German inflation rate.

   (c) Short-term interest rates rise in Germany relative to those in Canada.

   (d) Prolonged German economic expansion causes Canadian exports to Germany to increase from previous levels.

   (e) Germans buy several farms in southwestern Ontario.

   (f) Speculators anticipate a depreciation of the mark relative to the Canadian dollar.

   (g) The Bank of Canada reduces its holdings of German marks in its official reserve account.

2. Figure 37-2 represents the hypothetical market for Canadian imports of Japanese cameras, with prices given in Canadian dollars.

Figure 37-2

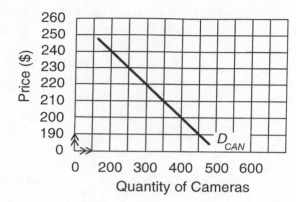

(a) The Canadian demand for imported Japanese cameras is shown in the diagram. The Japanese supply schedule is given below, with prices shown in yen (the Japanese currency). If Japanese producers quote yen prices to their Canadian buyers, determine what the supply schedule must be in terms of Canadian dollars if the external value of the Canadian dollar is 150 yen per dollar. Put your answers in column (i).

Quantity	Price in yen	Price in dollars (i)	Price in dollars (ii)
200	27,000	_____	_____
300	28,500	_____	_____
400	30,000	_____	_____
500	31,500	_____	_____
600	33,000	_____	_____

(b) In the diagram, plot the supply curve you derived in column (i), and determine the equilibrium price and quantity of imported cameras.

(c) If the Canadian dollar depreciates to 129.5 yen, enter the values for the new supply curve in column (ii) in the table above (round to the nearest dollar). Determine the new equilibrium price and quantity of imported cameras.

(d) By how much has Canadian spending on imports changed as a result of the dollar's depreciation?

(e) What does your answer to (d) indicate about the price elasticity of demand for imported Japanese cameras? Will the supply curve of yen be positively sloped?

3. You are given the demand for and supply of U.S. dollars at alternative prices in terms of Canadian dollars. Assume that the U.S. dollar changes without intervention from any central bank. The curves labelled D_0 and S_0 on Figure 37-3 represent the initial case. The other curves represent changes in economic conditions between the two countries. Use them to answer (b) to (d).

Figure 37-3

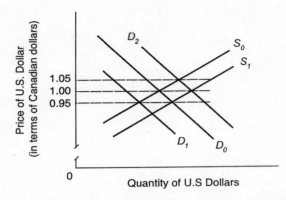

(a) Determine the equilibrium Canadian dollar price of the U.S. dollar, assuming that D_0 and S_0 apply.

(b) Suppose that there is a sizeable increase in short-term capital flows from Canada to the United States, other things being equal. Which curves would shift and why? What will happen to the exchange rate (the Canadian dollar price of the U.S. dollar)?

(c) Which curve or curves would shift if Canadians were to import significantly less from the United States? What will happen to the Canadian dollar price of the U.S. dollar?

(d) Suppose that Canadian exports to the United States were to increase significantly, other things being equal. Predict the effect on the price of the U.S. dollar.

4. Suppose that current real interest rates on one-year assets in Canada and the United States were the same (3 percent) and that one Canadian dollar traded for one U.S. dollar. Assume that this exchange rate is the PPP level for both countries. The Federal Reserve (the central bank of the United States) now increases U.S. interest rates to 5 percent, but the Bank of Canada does not follow the U.S. move and doesn't intervene in the foreign exchange market. Winnipeg Mutual Fund Corporation buys $10 million (U.S.) of one-year U.S. Government bonds at the current exchange rate.

(a) Describe the transactions in the foreign exchange market involved in this purchase of U.S. securities and indicate how Canada's balance-of-payments accounts are affected.

(b) If the Winnipeg company sells the U.S. securities at their maturity date (one year from now), what assumption must be made so that it receives a 5 percent rate of return on its original Canadian dollar investment?

(c) If many Canadian companies followed this firm's lead, what would happen to the external value of the Canadian dollar? To the exchange rate (the Canadian dollar price of the U.S. dollar)? What happens to their rate of return as the exchange rate changes from its PPP level?

(d) One year from now, when U.S. securities mature and Canadians repatriate their funds, what will happen to the exchange rate? To the external value of the Canadian dollar?

(e) Investors will expect the deviation of the exchange rate from its PPP level in part (c) to reverse itself. What exchange rate change is required to exactly offset the interest differential between the two countries?

5. The purchasing power parity hypothesis predicts that over the long run, exchange rates will reflect relative rates of domestic inflation. Test this hypothesis for the period 1967-1982 for the following five countries.

	United States	Canada	United Kingdom	West Germany	Japan
1982 CPI (1967=100)	290.0	304.0	517.8	196.5	304.2
Exchange rate (U.S. cents)					
1967	—	92.69	275.0	25.08	0.2763
1982	—	80.18	175.2	41.48	0.3981

What are the predicted PPP 1982 exchange rates? Compare these values with actual values. (*Hint:* Use the formula (U.S. CPI/foreign CPI) (1967 exchange rate).)

*6. A country has a demand curve for foreign currency given by $D = 6 - 2e$ and a supply curve given by $S = 0.5 + 3e$, where e is the price of the foreign currency in terms of the domestic currency and quantities are in millions.
(a) If its policy had allowed the exchange rate to be determined freely on the exchange market, what would the equilibrium levels of e and the quantity of foreign currency have been?

(b) Suppose that this equilibrium value also represents the PPP value. Now the country's central bank increases domestic interest rates relative to those in other countries with the result that the new demand curve is $D = 5.8 - 2e$ and the new supply curve is $S = 0.8 + 3e$. Explain why both the demand and supply curves for foreign currency changed, and predict the new short-term equilibrium exchange rate value. How does this value compare with the PPP value?

(c) If the country's PPP value is not likely to change in the future, what is likely to happen to the value of e? Explain.

7. **Maintaining a Fixed Exchange Rate**
Figure 37-4 represents the market for pounds sterling. The horizontal axis denotes millions of pounds, and the vertical axis is the Canadian dollar price of pounds.

Figure 37-4

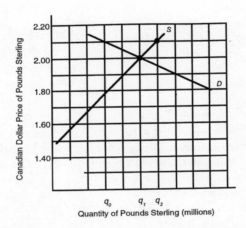

(a) If the exchange rate were flexible, what would be the equilibrium dollar price of sterling?

(b) If the Bank of Canada wants to maintain a fixed value of $2.10, what foreign exchange transactions must it conduct at the current market conditions depicted by the demand and supply curves? What will happen to the Bank of Canada's holdings of international currency reserves?

(c) What would happen in the foreign exchange market if the Bank of England pursued a target of 0.48 pounds per Canadian dollar?

ANSWERS
Multiple-Choice Questions

1.	(b)	**2.**	(c)	**3.**	(e)	**4.**	(b)	**5.**	(c)
6.	(b)	**7.**	(a)	**8.**	(d)	**9.**	(b)	**10.**	(b)
11.	(c)	**12.**	(b)	**13.**	(e)	**14.**	(c)	**15.**	(a)
16.	(e)	**17.**	(d)	**18.**	(e)	**19.**	(a)	**20.**	(c)
21.	(d)	**22.**	(b)	**23.**	(a)	**24.**	(e)	**25.**	(d)
26.	(b)	**27.**	(e)	**28.**	(b)	**29.**	(d)	**30.**	(a)
31.	(e)	**32.**	(a)	**33.**	(a)	**34.**	(e)	**35.**	(b)

Exercises

1. (a) When more Germans visit Calgary, this is a German import of a service. Hence, S_M will shift to the right, with the result that the mark should depreciate.

    (b) A greater inflation rate in Canada will cause Canadian exports to Germany to fall and imports from Germany to increase. D_M will shift to the right, and S_M will shift to the left. Both are likely to cause the Canadian dollar price of the mark to appreciate (the Canadian dollar depreciates).

    (c) Germany is likely to experience more capital inflows from Canada, and less international capital will flow from Germany to Canada. Hence, both the demand and supply curves for marks are affected such that the mark will appreciate.

    (d) S_M will shift to the right, and hence the mark will depreciate.

    (e) These transactions constitute capital outflows from Germany. The supply curve for marks will shift to the right, and hence the mark will depreciate.

    (f) The mark will depreciate. Both the demand and supply curves for marks will be affected.

    (g) S_M will shift to the right and the mark should depreciate.

2. (a) Column (i) entries are $180, $190, $200, $210, and $220.

    (b) The equilibrium price is $200, and 400 cameras are sold.

    (c) Column (ii) entries are $208, $220, $232, $243, and $255. The new equilibrium price is $220, and 300 cameras are sold.

    (d) Spending on imports falls from $80,000 to $66,000.

    (e) Because total spending fell when the price increased, demand must be elastic. More pre-cisely, the point elasticity at the initial equilibrium is –2.5 [= (–100/20) × (200/400)]. Since the Canadian demand for imports is elastic, the supply curve for foreign currency (yen) is positively sloped.

3. (a) One Canadian dollar trades for one U.S. dollar.

    (b) The demand curve for U.S. dollars will shift to the right (such as that labelled D_2). The U.S. dollar will appreciate and will equal $1.05 Canadian.

    (c) The demand curve for U.S. dollars will shift to the left (such as that labelled D_1). The U.S. dollar will depreciate to a price of $0.95 Canadian.

    (d) The supply curve for U.S. dollars will shift to the right (such as that labelled S_1). The U.S. dollar will depreciate to a price of $0.95 Canadian.

4. (a) Winnipeg Mutual Fund Corporation will supply Canadian dollars and demand $1 million U.S.. This transaction will appear as a Canadian capital export of $1 million and as a capital import in the U.S. balance of payment accounts.

    (b) The exchange rate must stay constant at 1 Canadian dollar per U.S. dollar. Otherwise, the rate of return will be affected.

    (c) As more companies attempt to take advantage of the higher U.S. interest rate, more capital outflows from Canada will occur. The U.S. dollar will appreciate and the Canadian dollar will depreciate. Hence, their Canadian dollar outlays will increase in order to buy U.S. securities, and their rate of return will fall.

    (d) When the securities mature, Canadians will sell U.S. dollars and buy Canadian dollars. Hence, the U.S. dollar will depreciate and the Canadian dollar will appreciate.

    (e) An appreciation of the Canadian dollar by about 2 percent over the year will offset the 2 percent interest differential. Specifically, Canadian investors will receive $10.5 million U.S. in a year. If the exchange rate is about 98 Canadian cents per U.S. dollar, they will receive $10.3 million Canadian. The U.S. dollar has depreciated by 2 percent and the Canadian dollar has appreciated from parity to $1.02 U.S. (or a 2 percent appreciation). Thus, the rate of return is 3 percent in both countries after factoring in the change in the exchange rate.

5. Canada: 88.4; United Kingdom: 154.0; West Germany: 37.0; Japan: 0.2634. The depreciation of the Canadian dollar and the pound sterling and the appreciation of the mark are correctly (but not accurately) predicted.

*6. (a) Quantity demanded equals quantity supplied at $e = 1.1$; equilibrium quantity is 3.8 million.

(b) An increase in the domestic interest rate will cause less capital outflows and more capital inflows. Less capital outflows decrease the demand for foreign currency and more inflows increase the supply of foreign currency. The new equilibrium exchange rate will be 1.0. Relative to the PPP value, foreign currency is undervalued while the domestic currency is overvalued.

(c) Assuming that no additional interest rate differentials are created, we would expect the price of foreign currency to appreciate (domestic currency depreciates). This might occur through the activity of speculators who gamble that the undervalued foreign currency will rise to its PPP value in the future. Thus, by selling domestic currency and buying foreign currency, speculators may cause the foreign currency to reach its PPP value.

7. (a) $2.00 where $D = S$.

(b) At a fixed price of $2.10, there is an excess supply of pounds (and an excess demand for dollars). Thus the Bank must sell dollars and buy $q_2 - q_0$ pounds in the exchange market. The Bank's holdings of sterling (which may be held for reserves) will increase.

(c) Probably confusion, increased speculation, and destabilized exchange markets. The Bank of England's target of 0.48 pounds translates into a dollar price of pounds of $2.08, which is different from the Bank of Canada's target of $2.10.

CHAPTER **38**
......
MACROECONOMIC POLICY IN AN OPEN ECONOMY

......
CHAPTER OVERVIEW

The first section of this chapter focuses on the relationships among the balance of trade, aggregate demand, and national income and on the role of the exchange rates. These relationships depend on the exchange rate regime (flexible versus fixed) and on the degree to which international capital is mobile. Various multipliers are derived for fixed and flexible exchange rate models, assuming that there is no international capital mobility.

The issue of the role of international capital mobility is discussed. The capital account balance must be included in the analysis of open-economy macroeconomics. Capital flows depend on interest rate differentials among countries. Hence, the capital account is influenced by both fiscal and monetary policies since both influence domestic interest rates.

Under a flexible exchange rate, monetary policy is effective in influencing national income if international capital is mobile. However, fiscal policy is generally less effective in changing national income in an open economy that has a flexible exchange rate than it would be in a closed economy.

......
LEARNING OBJECTIVES

After studying this chapter, you should be able to:

- demonstrate how the simple multiplier in a closed economy must be modified in an open economy without international capital flows with a fixed exchange rate;
- understand how the open-economy multiplier analysis (with no international capital flows) is modified when the central bank allows exchange rates to fluctuate freely;
- explain the effects of fiscal and monetary policies on the capital account;
- discuss why the effectiveness of fiscal policy under flexible exchange rates is reduced when international capital is mobile because of a crowding out of net exports;
- understand why monetary policy is most effective under flexible exchange rates and mobile international capital;
- understand the link between the government's budget deficit and the current account deficit.

MULTIPLE-CHOICE QUESTIONS

Questions 1 through 3 assume an open economy with a *fixed exchange rate*, a constant price level, and no international capital flows.

1. The open-economy (simple) investment multiplier
   (a) is larger than the simple closed-economy investment multiplier.
   (b) indicates that the induced nature of imports causes greater fluctuations than would occur in a closed economy.
   (c) is smaller than the closed-economy multiplier because the change in income is mitigated by a change in net exports.
   (d) incorporates the change in net exports when national income changes shift the net export function.
   (e) is equal to the closed-economy investment multiplier.

2. A country that pursues expansionary fiscal policy
   (a) will face a deteriorating trade balance.
   (b) will find that the simple government expenditure multiplier is exactly the same as it would be in a closed economy.
   (c) will find that the simple multiplier is larger than it would be in a closed economy.
   (d) will face a growing surplus in the trade balance.
   (e) Both (c) and (d).

3. When exports increase,
   (a) the *AD* curve shifts to the right.
   (b) real national income will increase by $1/[1 - b(1 - t) + m]$ times the change in autonomous exports.
   (c) the net export function will shift upward.
   (d) a balance-of-trade surplus will result even though import expenditures are increased with the increase in national income.
   (e) All of the above.

Questions 4 through 7 refer to the following information and Figure 38-1 for a particular economy.

The marginal propensity to spend if the economy were *closed* is 0.6. If the economy were *open* and operated on a *fixed exchange rate* system, the marginal propensity to spend would be 0.5; hence, the marginal propensity to import is 0.1. Potential GDP is 400, the price level is constant at $P = 1$, and there are no international capital flows. Point *a* refers to the initial situation.

Figure 38-1

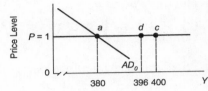

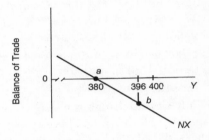

4. At the initial situation (point *a*),
   (a) there is a negative output gap of 20.
   (b) net exports are zero.
   (c) the closed-economy multiplier is 2.5.
   (d) the fixed-exchange-rate open-economy multiplier is 2.0.
   (e) Any or all of the above.

5. Which of the following statements is *not* true? If the economy were *closed*, then
   (a) to eliminate the recessionary gap, government expenditure would have to increase by 8.
   (b) an increase in government expenditure of 8 would shift the *AD* curve to the right so that the new aggregate demand curve intersected the constant price line at point *c*.
   (c) an increase in government expenditure of 10 would increase GDP beyond its potential level.
   (d) with an increase in *G* of 8, the economy would reach its potential GDP level.
   (e) an increase in *G* of 10 would be required to eliminate the current GDP gap.

6. Which of the following statements is *not* true? If the economy were *open* and government expenditures increased by 8,
  (a) the output gap would be reduced but not totally eliminated.
  (b) the new equilibrium level of national income would be 396.
  (c) a trade deficit (depicted at point *b*) would be created.
  (d) the *AD* curve would shift rightward from point *a* to point *d.*
  (e) the net export curve would shift as real national income rose by 16.

7. Assuming an initial situation at point *a* and an *open* economy, an increase in exports of 10 will
  (a) shift the net export function upward by 10 at every level of national income.
  (b) eliminate the output gap.
  (c) create a permanent trade surplus of 8 at an income level of 400.
  (d) shift the *AD* curve from point *a* to point *c.*
  (e) Any or all of the above.

Questions 8 through 10 assume an open economy with *flexible exchange rates*, constant prices, and no international capital flows.

8. The open-economy investment multiplier under flexible exchange rates is
  (a) the same as the open-economy investment multiplier with a fixed exchange rate.
  (b) equal to the *closed-economy* investment multiplier because the exchange rate must appreciate to counteract the trade deficit that is created by an increase in investment expenditure.
  (c) equal to the *closed-economy* investment multiplier because the exchange rate must depreciate to counteract the trade surplus that is created by an increase in investment expenditure.
  (d) less than the open-economy investment multiplier with a fixed exchange rate because exchange rate changes offset some of the change in investment expenditure.
  (e) less than the closed-economy investment multiplier.

9. A country that pursues an expansionary fiscal policy
  (a) will not affect its balance of payments after all exchange rate changes have occurred.
  (b) will create a permanently larger deficit in its balance of trade.
  (c) cannot influence real national income because the government-expenditure multiplier value is zero.
  (d) will create a permanently larger surplus in its balance of trade as the exchange rates depreciates.
  (e) will shift the *AD* curve to the right, but not as much as would have happened for a closed-economy model.

10. When exports increase,
  (a) the *AD* curve will shift upward initially.
  (b) an excess supply of foreign currency is created, and hence the exchange rate depreciates.
  (c) as the exchange rate depreciates, the net export curve will shift downward.
  (d) the net export curve will shift downward until GDP reaches its former value.
  (e) Any or all of the above.

Questions 11 through 13 assume an open economy, with *flexible exchange rates*, constant prices, and no international capital flows. The hypothetical closed-economy multiplier is 2.5 and the fixed-exchange-rate multiplier is 2.0. The initial situation is portrayed at point *a* in Figure 38-2. Potential GDP is 400 and the marginal propensity to import is 0.1.

Figure 38-2

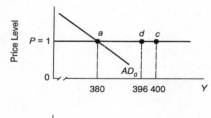

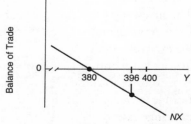

11. If government expenditure increased by 8 and the exchange rate did not change momentarily, then
    (a) the new equilibrium level would be 396.
    (b) a balance-of-payments deficit would be 1.6.
    (c) the economy's recessionary gap would not be eliminated totally.
    (d) the *AD* curve would shift rightward to point *d*.
    (e) Any or all of the above.

12. The scenario described in question 11 is only temporary because
    (a) the trade deficit causes the exchange rate to depreciate.
    (b) the trade deficit causes the external value of the domestic currency to appreciate.
    (c) the exchange rate will appreciate, causing the net export function to shift downward, and the *AD* curve will return to point *a*.
    (d) as the exchange rate depreciates, the net export function shifts upward.
    (e) None of the above.

13. Assuming an initial situation at point *a*, if exports increase by 10, then
    (a) the *AD* curve will shift to point *c* and the new, permanent level of national income is 400.
    (b) real national income will return eventually to 380 as the exchange rate depreciation reduces net exports.
    (c) a permanent trade surplus of 8 will be created.
    (d) national income will remain at 396.
    (e) Both (c) and (d).

14. Comparing the two models (questions 4 through 7 versus 11 through 13), which of the following statements is correct?
    (a) The export multiplier is zero with flexible exchange rates.
    (b) The investment multiplier is higher for a fixed exchange rate system than for flexible exchange rates.
    (c) To close any output gap, government expenditures must be increased more for flexible exchange rates than for a fixed exchange rate system.

    (d) An increase in investment expenditures will cause an appreciation of the external value of the domestic currency if exchange rates are allowed to move.
    (e) None of the above.

Questions 15 through 20 assume an open economy, with flexible exchange rates, constant prices, and *mobile* international capital.

15. Which of the following actions by the Bank of Canada would generate a capital inflow?
    (a) The Bank sells bonds on the open market.
    (b) The Bank buys bonds on the open market.
    (c) The Bank transfer government deposits from itself to the commercial banks.
    (d) Consistent with a policy designed to increase the reserves of the banks, the Bank lowers the bank rate.
    (e) Both (b) and (c).

16. With a constant supply of money, an expansion in government expenditure is likely to
    (a) increase domestic interest rates.
    (b) increase international capital inflows.
    (c) decrease international capital outflows.
    (d) cause an exchange rate depreciation.
    (e) All of the above.

17. The *crowding out* effect of increased government expenditure in an open economy refers to
    (a) a reduction in net exports caused by an appreciation of the exchange rate.
    (b) an increase in net exports caused by a depreciation of the exchange rate.
    (c) more takeovers of domestic companies as capital imports increase.
    (d) a reduction in net exports caused by a depreciation of the exchange rate.
    (e) more takeovers of foreign companies as capital exports increase.

18. A reduction in the Canadian government expenditures, all else equal, is likely to
    (a) reduce capital inflows.
    (b) create a greater deficit on the current account.
    (c) increase Canadian interest rates.
    (d) decrease national saving in Canada.
    (e) None of the above are correct.

19. The effectiveness of expansionary monetary policy will be enhanced because
    (a) reductions in interest rates reduce capital inflows, and hence the exchange rate depreciates.
    (b) reductions in interest rates reduce capital inflows, and hence the exchange rate appreciates.
    (c) reductions in interest rates reduce capital inflows, and hence the external value of the domestic currency appreciates.
    (d) reductions in interest rates lead eventually to decreased net exports.
    (e) Both (a) and (d).

20. The effectiveness of contractionary fiscal policy is mitigated because
    (a) reductions in interest rates reduce capital inflows, and hence the exchange rate appreciates.

    (b) reductions in interest rates reduce net capital inflows, and hence the external value of the domestic currency appreciates.
    (c) reductions in interest rates reduce net capital inflows, and hence the exchange rate depreciates.
    (d) reductions in interest rates lead eventually to less net exports.
    (e) Both (a) and (d).

21. A country that has national saving in excess of domestic investment must have a
    (a) capital account deficit.
    (b) current account surplus.
    (c) current account deficit.
    (d) capital account surplus.
    (e) Both (a) and (b) are correct.

EXERCISES

1. An open economy exchanges goods but not international capital with other countries. Its marginal propensity to consume out of disposable income is 0.8, the tax rate is 0.2, the marginal propensity to import is 0.14, and the price level remains constant.
   (a) Fill in the blanks below.
       The government expenditure multiplier with a fixed exchange rate is _____ .
       The government expenditure multiplier with flexible exchange rates is _____ .
       The export multiplier with a fixed exchange rate is _____ .
       The export multiplier with flexible exchange rates is _____ .
   (b) Indicate the potential effects of a government expenditure decrease on both the current and capital accounts. Do this for both the fixed and flexible exchange rate cases.

2. This problem considers how the simple multiplier is affected in an open economy with flexible exchange rates. Assume that the price level and interest rates are constant, capital is immobile internationally, and potential GDP is 1,325. The following equations describe aggregate demand for output, where e is the exchange rate.

   $C = 400 + 0.6Y$
   $I = 100$
   $G = 20$
   $X = 80 + 20e$
   $IM = 0.1Y - 30e$

(a) Explain why the coefficient for e is positive in the export equation and negative in the import equation.

(b) Derive the aggregate expenditure function as a function of income and the exchange rate. What is the marginal propensity to spend?

(c) If e equals 1, what is the equilibrium level of income? What is the trade balance at this level of income?

(d) Suppose the government attempts to eliminate the recessionary gap by increasing its purchases by 10. If the exchange rate is fixed at its former value, solve for the new level of income and the new trade balance.

(e) You found that the increase in government expenditure of 10 led to a trade deficit. If the exchange rate were flexible, explain why it appreciates. Suppose that the new value of e consistent with balanced trade is 1.05. Assuming that G increases by 10, solve for the new equilibrium values of income, exports, and imports using the new exchange rate value.

(f) In (d) you found that an increase in government expenditures of 10 led to an increase in equilibrium income of 20, while in (e) you found that the same increase in government spending led to an increase in income of 25. Explain why this difference exists. Also, compare the value of the multiplier you found for the economy in (e) to the value you would obtain if no foreign trade occurred in this economy.

*3. This problem extends the analysis of exercise 2 to consider how the simple multiplier from an autonomous change in net exports is altered under flexible exchange rates. Again, assume that the price level and interest rates are constant, that capital is immobile internationally, and that the aggregate demand function you derived in 2(a) holds initially ($e = 1$).

(a) Suppose that instead of the government increasing its purchases of goods, there is a major shift in worldwide preferences for this country's products. The export function becomes $X = 90 + 20e$. If e remains constant, solve for the new equilibrium level of income and the trade balance.

(b) In part (a) you found that a trade surplus emerges. Under flexible exchange rates, what will be the direction of change in the value of the exchange rate? Explain.

(c) The text explains that the export multiplier with flexible exchange rates and immobile international capital is zero and that the trade account must balance. What value of e is consistent with this conclusion?

(d) Confirm your answer to part (c) by substituting the new value of e into the aggregate expenditure function and solve for the new equilibrium values of national income and the trade balance.

4. This exercise focuses on the implications of monetary policy with a fixed exchange system. Country T has a recessionary gap of 20; its potential real GDP is 820, and its current real GDP is 800. T's interest rate of 6 percent is equal to world interest rates. The central bank of T is committed to maintaining the external value of its currency at some pegged value. For the purpose of this exercise, assume stable prices in T and all countries. Moreover, assume that the investment multiplier is 2.0.

The central bank has reliable information about T's net export and capital account functions. Specifically, they are given by the following equations:

$$(X - IM) = 22 - 0.02Y$$
$$K = -30 + 4i$$

where $X - IM$ is the trade balance, Y is real GDP, K is the capital account balance, and i is the interest rate in percentage terms.

The government, which is under great pressure to solve the recessionary gap problem, considers using expansionary monetary policy to deal with the problem. You, as the governor of the central bank, are asked to present your comments and recommendations to the cabinet. To ensure that your cabinet briefing is complete, you ask the central bank's economists to give you information about the current state of the economy and the effects of expansionary monetary policy on T's real national income and the balance of payments. The following are the major points they make. You must respond to each of them in terms of whether you agree or disagree. Ask for any clarifications that need to be made.

(a) They point out that T's current trade balance is a surplus of 6. What is your response?

(b) They tell you that T's current capital account is in a deficit position of 6 and that combined with the trade balance, T has an external balance. What is your response?

(c) Previous research indicates that a money supply increase of 8 will decrease T's interest rate by 1 (percent), which in turn will increase domestic investment spending by 10. Using these numbers, they suggest that the recessionary gap could be eliminated if appropriate open-market operations increased the money supply by 8. What is your response? You ask for a clarification of the type of open-market operation they have in mind and why this policy will reduce T's interest rate.

(d) Assuming that the interest rate and GDP goals are achieved, they point out that T will have a balance-of-payments deficit of 4.4. What is your response?

(e) Your officials warn you that the central bank exchange will have to undertake certain exchange market actions in order to protect the external value of the domestic currency. The cabinet must be made aware of this situation.

*5. A country that operates under a flexible exchange rate regime has a recessionary gap situation. The initial conditions in the economy are an interest rate of i_0, a balance in both the trade account and the capital account, and an exchange rate of e_0. The government increases its expenditure in order to eliminate the recessionary gap without increasing the domestic price level. As shown in the diagrams in Figure 38-3, the effects of the economy are as follows: (1) the demand curve for money shifts to the right such that the interest rate increases to i_1; (2) although capital outflows are assumed to be unaffected, capital flows into this economy from other nations will increase; and (3) the exchange rate depreciates to e_1.

Figure 38-3

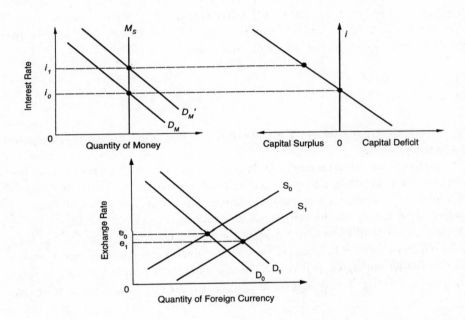

(a) Explain why the government's fiscal policy caused the demand curve for money to shift and the interest rate to increase.

(b) Why is the curve relating the interest rate and the capital account balance downward sloping?

(c) Why is a capital account surplus generated by the government's action?

(d) Why did the supply curve for foreign currency in international markets shift to the right? Why did the demand curve for foreign currency shift to the right?

(e)   At an exchange rate of e_0, with the demand and supply curves in the exchange market labelled D_1 and S_1, what situation exists for this country's balance of payments? What will happen to the exchange rate?

(f)   Outline some of the effects of the fiscal policy on the country's net export curve.

● ● ● ● ● ● ● ● ● ● ● ● ● ●

ANSWERS
Multiple-Choice Questions

1. (c)	**2.** (a)	**3.** (e)	**4.** (e)	**5.** (e)
6. (e)	**7.** (e)	**8.** (b)	**9.** (a)	**10.** (e)
11. (e)	**12.** (c)	**13.** (b)	**14.** (a)	**15.** (a)
16. (e)	**17.** (d)	**18.** (a)	**19.** (b)	**20.** (a)
21. (e)				

Exercises

1. (a) $1/[1 - b(1 - t) + m] = 1/[1 - 0.8(1 - 0.2) + 0.14] = 2.0$.
$1/[1 - b] = 1/[1 - .8] = 5.0$.
2.0.
0.0.

(b)   A government expenditure decrease will decrease national income. Imports will fall, thereby generating a trade balance surplus. Lower government expenditures will reduce the demand for money. With a constant money supply, the interest rate will fall. Since capital outflows are increased and capital inflows are reduced, the capital account will be in a deficit position. The overall effect on the balance of payments is uncertain. If the policy change causes an overall balance-of-payments deficit (the capital account deficit is greater than the trade balance surplus), the exchange rate will appreciate if exchange rates are allowed to change. Hence, national income will increase as net exports increase with the appreciation of the exchange rate. The contractionary fiscal policy is offset by the change in the exchange rate. If the exchange rate is fixed, the central bank will have to intervene in the exchange market, by using the official reserves account, in order to maintain the pegged value of the exchange rate.

2. (a)   An appreciation of the exchange rate will stimulate more exports and should decrease imports by increasing the domestic price of imports.

(b) $AE = 400 + 0.6Y + 100 + 20 + 80 + 20e - (0.1Y - 30e)$.
$AE = 600 + 0.5Y + 50e$.
The marginal propensity to spend is 0.5.

(c)   Equilibrium national income is found by equating Y to AE. In this case, $650 + 0.5Y = Y$ or Y is equal to 1,300. The trade balance is zero at $Y = 1,300$ and $e = 1$.

(d) $Y = 1,320$ and a trade balance deficit of 2.0.

(e)   Since imports have changed, the demand for foreign currency increases; hence, the exchange rate will appreciate. With the increase in government expenditure of 10 and the new exchange rate, the AE curve becomes $400 + 0.6Y + 100 + 30 + 80 + 20(1.05) - 0.1Y + 30(1.05)$ or $0.5Y + 662.5$. Equating aggregate expenditure to national income, we obtain 1,325 for the new equilibrium level of national income. Exports and imports are both equal to 101.

(f)   An increase in government expenditure caused a trade deficit. In the flexible exchange rate case, the exchange rate appreciated, causing exports to rise and imports to fall. Hence, net exports increased by 2.5 (0.05×50). This led to an additional increase in real national income of 5 (2.0×2.5). The multipliers for the closed-economy case and for the flexible exchange rate case are the same.

*3. (a)   National income rises to 1,320. There is a trade balance surplus of 8 (exports increased by 10 and 2 additional units of imports were induced when national income rose from 1,300 to 1,320).

(b)   The trade surplus at an exchange rate of 1 causes an excess supply of foreign currency and an excess demand for domestic currency. The exchange rate must depreciate and the external value of the domestic currency must appreciate.

(c)   The exchange rate value is 0.8. First, notice that the export function is $90 + 20e$. Second, if the statement is correct, national income equilibrium is 1,300. Hence, the import function is $0.1(1,300) - 30e$. Third, the balance of trade must be zero. Hence, equate the export function with the import function, and solve for the exchange rate: $e = 0.8$.

(d) The AE function becomes $610 + 0.5Y + 50$ (0.80). Equating this expression with Y, we obtain an equilibrium value of 1,300. Hence, the export multiplier is zero. Moreover, we already know that the trade balance is zero.

4. (a) You agree. Substituting $Y = 800$ into the net export equation, it is clear that there is a surplus on the trade balance of 6.

(b) You agree. Since the current rate of interest is 6 (percent), the capital account is in a deficit position of 6. This result is obtained from the capital account balance equation. The sum of the trade and capital accounts is zero, which represents an equilibrium in the balance of payments.

(c) You agree. An increase in the money supply of 8 increases investment expenditure by 10. Since the expenditure multiplier is 2, real national income will increase from 800 to 820. They should tell you that the central bank must purchase bonds on the open market. By doing so, the price of bonds is bid up and the bond yield falls. Moreover, the interest rate should fall as domestic banks expand deposits and loans.

(d) After some analysis, you should agree. After GDP and the interest rate have changed, there will be a trade surplus of 5.6 and a capital account deficit of 10. Hence, there will be a 4.4 deficit in the balance of payments.

(e) You agree. A balance-of-payments deficit creates an excess supply of the domestic currency and an excess demand for foreign currency on foreign exchange markets. To maintain a fixed exchange rate, T's central bank will have to buy its currency and sell off its reserves. You know as governor that these adjustments to

the official reserves will tend to decrease the domestic money supply, which offsets the planned initial monetary expansion. Good luck explaining to the cabinet the likelihood of monetary policy successfully solving a recessionary gap when the central bank is committed to a pegged exchange rate!

*5. (a) An expansionary fiscal policy increases real national income, which in turn increases the transactions demand for money. This causes the demand curve for money to shift to the right. Excess demand for money is created, and hence decision makers will sell bonds in order to obtain the additional money. This will lower the price of bonds and increase the interest rate.

(b) For high interest rates (relative to foreign rates), capital inflows should be large and capital outflows small, thereby creating a capital account surplus. For low interest rates, capital inflows will be small and capital outflows will be large, thus creating a deficit on the capital account.

(c) Since the interest rate has risen, more capital will flow into this country from other nations, thus creating a capital account surplus.

(d) Increased real national income will induce more imports (a movement along the net export function) and shift the demand curve for foreign currency to the right. Since capital outflows are assumed to be unaffected, increased capital flows will cause the supply curve for foreign currency to shift to the right.

(e) Excess supply of foreign currency exists (excess demand for domestic currency). The exchange rate will depreciate (the external value of the domestic currency will appreciate).

(f) The increase in real national income causes a movement down the net export function; the appreciation of the domestic currency causes the net export function to shift downward (or to the left). This second effect is the crowding-out effect.